Golden Entrepreneuring

Also by James B. Arkebauer

THE MCGRAW-HILL GUIDE TO WRITING A HIGH-IMPACT BUSINESS PLAN

ULTRAPRENEURING: TAKING A VENTURE FROM START-UP TO HARVEST IN THREE YEARS OR LESS

Golden Entrepreneuring

The Mature Person's Guide to Starting a Successful Business

James B. Arkebauer

McGraw-Hill, Inc.
New York San Francisco Washington, D.C. Auckland Bogotá
Caracas Lisbon London Madrid Mexico City Milan
Montreal New Delhi San Juan Singapore
Sydney Tokyo Toronto

Library of Congress Cataloging-in-Publication Data

Arkebauer, James B., date.
    Golden entrepreneuring : the mature person's guide to starting a successful business / James B. Arkebauer.
       p.   cm.
    Includes index.
    ISBN 0-07-003025-1
    1. Success in business.   2. Entrepreneurship.   3. Aged—Employment.   I. Title.
HF5386.A73   1995
658.4'21—dc20   95-6653
                                                                                 CIP

Copyright © 1995 by James B. Arkebauer. All rights reserved. Printed in the United States of America. Except as permitted under the United States Copyright Act of 1976, no part of this publication may be reproduced or distributed in any form or by any means, or stored in a data base or retrieval system, without the prior written permission of the publisher.

1 2 3 4 5 6 7 8 9 0   DOC/DOC   9 0 0 9 8 7 6 5

ISBN 0-07-003025-1

The sponsoring editor for this book was David J. Conti, the editing supervisor was Stephen M. Smith, and the production supervisor was Donald F. Schmidt. It was set in Palatino by Victoria Khavkina of McGraw-Hill's Professional Book Group composition unit.

Printed and bound by R. R. Donnelley & Sons Company.

McGraw-Hill books are available at special quantity discounts to use as premiums and sales promotions, or for use in corporate training programs. For more information, please write to the Director of Special Sales, McGraw-Hill, Inc., 11 West 19th Street, New York, NY 10011. Or contact your local bookstore.

 This book is printed on recycled, acid-free paper containing a minimum of 50% recycled de-inked fiber.

This book is dedicated to Pamela Kim, Shelly Kay, Jeffrey Bernard, Timothy Michael, and Bradley James

Contents

Acknowledgments   xvii

Introduction   1

The Number One Advantage   2
   From Fifty to the Grave   2
An Overview of the Parts and Chapters   3
   Complex Problems and Great Challenges   3
   Getting Started   4
   Getting Going   4
   Getting Financed   4
   Operations to Exit   4

Part 1. Getting Started

1. Complex Problems and Great Opportunities   9

Changes and Trends   10
   Changes   10
   Trends   13
   Confirmed and Accepted Changes and Trends   14
Coming Full Circle   18
Do You Have What It Takes to Be an Entrepreneur?   20
The Challenges Ahead   21

2. A Most Fortuitous Occasion?   24

What It Takes to Be an Entrepreneur   25
Hardy, Ambitious Goal Achievers   25
Characteristics—The Basics   26
    Achievement   26
    Action Orientation   26
    Commitment   27
    Communication   27
    Energy   28
    Goal Setting   28
    Growth Orientation   28
    Honesty   29
    Innovation   29
    Intelligence   30
    Leadership   31
    Risk Tolerance   32
    Self-Confidence   32
Success Qualities   33
    Hard Work   33
    Enthusiasm   33
    Creativity   33
    Flexibility   34
    Empathy   34
    Knowledge   34
Differentiating Factors   34
An Age-Old Debate   35
    Risk Is Back   35
    There Are Four Generations of Risk Takers   35
    Seniorpreneurs Build a Mixed Team   36
Passion   37
Successful Senior Entrepreneurs   17
    Roy Carver—Bandag Tires   38
    Marion Isbell—Ramada Inns   38
    Lowell Paxson and Roy Speer—Home Shopping
      Network, Inc.   39
    Anthony Rossi—Tropicana Juice   39
    Carl Sontheimer—Cuisinart, Inc.   40
    William Gore—Gore-tex   40
    John Hanson—Winnebago Motor Homes   41
It Takes All Kinds   41
Senior Assets   42
    Commitment   42
    Confidence   43
    Freedom   43
    Insider's Knowledge   43
    Objectivity   43
    Reputation   43
    Resiliency   43

Resourcefulness 44
Seniors Are Better Qualified for Entrepreneurship 44
Why Seniors Are Taking to Entrepreneuring 45

3. The Problems (as They Are Perceived)—and Advantages—in Senior Entrepreneuring 46

The Beginnings of a National Challenge 46
The Perception Is Changing 47
Old Perceptions Die Hard 48
Problems Turned to Myths 48
  Set in Their Ways, Inflexible, Unable to Change 48
  Being Opinionated 49
  The Generation Gap 50
  Adopting to Technology 51
Advantages of Age 52
  Prudence 52
  Delayed Gratification 53
  Patience and Persistence 53
  Money Smarts 53
  Contacts 54
  Customer Service 54
  Success Wisdom 54
  Work Ethic 55
Conclusions 55

4. Senior Entrepreneurial Opportunities Abound 56

Small Is Back 57
Make Time to See the World through Different Eyes 59
  The Revolution Is Coming in Double Time 60
Seniorpreneuring—The Basic Challenges 61
  Opportunity Testing Marketing Guides 61
Senior High-Tech Qualifiers 63
  Two Approaches 63
Partnering Strategically 65
  Acquisitions Make Them Larger 66
  Seniorpreneurs Can Do It Faster and Cheaper 67
Using a Senior Advantage in Making the Opportunity
  Decision 68
Basic Questions Checklist 69
  Basic Feasibility 69
  Competitive Advantages 69
  Buyer Decisions 69
  Marketing 69
  People 70
  Control 70

Finance   70
   Benefits from This Checklist   71
Taking Aim at the Future   71
Reviewing the Opportunity   72

5. Should You Start, Buy, or Franchise?   74

Starting a Business   75
   Pioneering Can Be Tough   75
   Seek Longer-Term Opportunities   75
   Find a Gap   76
   Don't Guarantee   76
   Think Diversity   76
   And Contemplate These Points   76
Buying a Business   77
   Four Golden Rules for Buying a Business   77
   Six Advantages of Buying   77
Where to Find a Business to Buy   77
   Where to Start the Search   78
   How to Find Out Information on an Industry   78
   How to Get a Deal Flow Going   79
Due Diligence   83
   Due Diligence Checklist   83
   Marketing Checklist   85
Valuations—The Discussion Goes On   86
   The Scientific Approach   87
   Fashioning the Art   91
Negotiation   92
   Negotiation Is an Art   92
   Qualify Yourself Quickly   93
   Don't Discuss Price or Terms   93
   Getting into the Nitty-Gritty   94
   Getting the Deal Done   94
Franchising   96
   New Franchise "Watch Points"   96
   Some Basics   96
   Ideal Characteristics of a Franchise   98
   Seniorpreneurs Love Their Job   100

Part 2. Getting Going

6. Building the Inside Seniorpreneurial Team   103

One or More Seniorpreneurs?   104
   Staff   104
   Hire the Well-Qualified   104
Seniorpreneurial Management Types   105
Getting Intimate with the Management Team
   Requirements   106

Administrative and General Management   106
Operations Management   107
Financial Management   107
Marketing Management   107
Engineering and R&D Management   108
Personnel Management   108
Legal Management   108
Five Basic Management Functions   109
Seniorpreneurial Hiring   109
  The Search Process   109
  Seniorpreneurial Interviewing Techniques   111
  Interview Guide   113
Your Board of Directors   115
  The Difference between Good Boards and Bad Boards   115
  Determine the Outsider's Role   116
  An Informed Board Is a Helpful Board   116
  What to Expect from a Board of Directors   117
  Makeup of the Board   119
  Committees of the Board   119
  The Board of Advisers   120

7. Assembling the Outside Seniorpreneurial Team   121

Consultants and Advisers   121
What Consultants Are Really For   122
  Consultants Can Come from Anywhere   122
  Hire When Ready!   123
  Consultants Are Not Always Necessary   123
  How Much Should You Pay?   124
  Some Advice on Advisers   124
Accountants   125
  Compilations, Reviews, and Audits   125
  Be Prepared   126
  Seniorpreneurial Considerations with Regard to Audit Accountants   126
Attorneys   129
  The Difference between Large and Small Legal Firms   129
  Getting Along   130
  Specific Questions to Ask Prospective Attorneys   130
  What Lawyers Are Selling, and How They Charge   131
  The Multiple Counsel Approach   132
Conclusion   133

8. Planning the Seniorpreneurial Venture   134

The Primary Purposes of Your Business Plan   135
Incorporate the Nine Guiding Principles into Your Plan   136
  Make It Easy to Read   136
  Be Sure Your Approach Is Market-Driven   136

Qualify the Competition 136
Present Your Distribution Plan 136
Exploit Your Company's Uniqueness 137
Emphasize Management Strength 137
Present Attractive Projections 137
Zero In on Possible Funding Sources 137
Close with a Bang 137
The Next Step: Obtain Critical Reviews 137
Outline for a Business Plan 138
Cover Sheet 138
Table of Contents 139
Executive Summary 139
History 139
Product or Service 139
Market Description and Analysis 140
Marketing Strategy 140
Operations Plan 141
Research and Development 141
Schedule 141
Management 141
Risks and Problems 142
Use of Proceeds 142
Finances 142
Appendix 143
Your Plan Is a Lot of Work 143
The Seniorpreneurial Difference 143
Groom a Management Team 144
Purchase "Key Person" Insurance 144
Consider the Effects of Change 144
Seniorpreneurial Structuring and Valuations 145
Choosing the Right Structure: Legal and Tax Advantages 145
Several Points of Caution 146
Looking Forward to Limited-Liability Companies 146
Previewing Valuations 147
Previewing Ratios 147
Expense Ratios 148
Profitability Ratios 148
Utilization Ratios 149
Liquidity Ratios 149
Debt Ratios 149
Coverage Ratios 150
Investor Equity Valuation 150
Creating a Special Executive Summary 153
Making the Transition from Business Plan to Operating Plan 154
Seniorpreneurial Plans Take Your Best Effort 154

Contents   **xiii**

Part 3. Getting Financed

9. Securing Seniorpreneurial Debt Financing   **157**

There Are Several Types of Financing   157
Your Two Basic Choices for Financing: Debt and
   Equity   158
   Advantages of Self-Funding   159
   External Funding Is More Complicated   159
Seniorpreneurs Use Combinations   159
So Debt or Equity?   160
   Understanding the Stages of Seniorpreneurial
   Development   161
     Seed or Concept Stage   161
     Start-up Stage   162
     First Stage   162
     Second Stage   163
     Third Stage (also Mezzanine Stage)   163
     Harvest Stage   163
   Identifying Debt Financing: Forms and Sources   164
     Understanding the Forms of Debt Financing   164
     You May Have to Sweeten the Deal   167
   Subordinated Debt: An Alternative   167
   Understanding the Sources of Debt Financing   168
     Commercial Banks   168
     Commercial Finance Companies   169
     Factors   169
     Leasing Companies   170
     Savings and Loan Associations   171
     Small Business Administration   171
     Small Business Investment Companies (SBICs)   172
     Minority Enterprise Small Business Investment Companies
        (MESBICs)   172
     Industrial Revenue Bonds   172
     Life Insurance Companies and Pension Funds   173
     Government Sources   173
     Small Business Innovation Research Grants (SBIRs)   173
     Other Grants   174
     Leveraged Buyouts (LBOs)   174
     Credit Enhancement   174
     Trade Credit   175

10. Securing Seniorpreneurial Equity Financing   **176**

Seed-Stage Financing   176
You're Looking for Angels   177
   What's an Angel Look Like?   177

How to Find Your Angel   178
The Best Ways to Approach Angels   179
Preparing the Scene   180

Understanding Traditional Professional Venture Capital   180
A Brief History   181
Venture Capital in General   181
Traditional Venture Capital   182
There are Three Categories to Consider   183
Corporate Venture Capital   184
How to Find a Venture Capital Firm   187
How to Qualify a Venture Capitalist   187
How to Get in the Door   188
How to Present to Venture Capitalists   188
What to Ask a Venture Capitalist   190
What to Expect from the Meeting   191
What Will Happen Next?   191
The Commitment Letter: Its Five Sections   191
Due Diligence: A Complete Checkup   192
The Marriage   193
The Ongoing Relationship   194
Traditional Venture Capital Funds   194

The Preferred Investment Vehicles   194
The Selling of Securities   195
Regulation D   195
There Are Six Basic Rules   196
Rule 504   196
Alternate Exemptions   198
Regulation A Offerings   198
Small Company Offering Registration (SCOR)   199
A Final Exemption Note   199
Seniorpreneurs Use Both   199

Part 4. Operations to Exit

11. Making It Happen Seniorpreneurial Style   203

The Secrets Are Several   203
Breaking Out the Planning Process   204
Getting Clear on the Difference between Administrative and Operational Planning   205
Operational Planning: Making Your Dreams Come True   205
It's Demanding Mental Work   206
The Seven Criteria of a Good Operational Plan   207
Why People Fail to Plan   207
Why Plans Fail   208

Seniorpreneurial Street Smarts in Action   209
Management by Objective   209

Contents

   Alternatives 210
   Expand Carefully from a Profit Mindset 210
   Gain Eyes, Arms, Ears, and Legs 211
   Lead People; Manage Things 211
   Leadership 212
   You Can't Fight Reality 212
   What You Got When You Got What You Didn't
    Expect 213
   Management Must Manage 213
   Monitor and Respond 214
   Success and Unsuccess 214
   Marketing Variables 215
   Outside Pressures 217
   Inside Pressures 217
   Cashflow: It's Your Lifeblood 219
   Inventory: You Have to Control It 219
   Accounts Receivable: Control Them Also 220
   Here Are Some Cashflow Pointers 220
  The Strategy for Now 222
   Three Approaches 222
   Street Smarts in Action 223

12. Selling Out or Succession 224

  Pricing and Terms 224
   Pricing 225
   Terms 229
   Other Considerations 231
  Senior Harvest Choices 232
   Absentee Ownership 233
   Management Buyouts 233
   Outright Sales 235
   Employee Stock Option Plans (ESOPs) 236
   Mergers and Acquisitions 237
   Going Public 238
  So What's a Senior to Do? 241

Epilogue 243

  Seniorpreneuring Contact 244

  Index 245

Acknowledgments

As a senior entrepreneur, I recognize the value of teamwork, which was applied to the genesis of this book. I had a "think-tank" team that helped me explore this book's subject in depth. The members of this team included Jon Fitzgerald, Tom Higgins, Mike Hudson, Chuck Kaufmann, and Seeleg Lester. And for over a year, an almost daily dialogue was carried on with my associate Kent Wooldridge regarding various aspects of our seniors projects. Thank you, gentlemen. I also thank Maita Lester for providing yet another sounding board and offering effective critiques.

Initial inspiration for this book was provided by the founder of the Senior Entrepreneur's Foundation, Mort Levand. He is truly a senior entrepreneurial legend in his own time. If you would like more information on the Senior Entrepreneur's Foundation or would like to discuss your Seniorpreneurial venture, you are welcome to contact me at:

James B. Arkebauer
P.O. Box 24210
Denver, CO 80222

This is my third book with McGraw-Hill and second with Editorial Director David Conti. An author would be hard-pressed to work with a better team.

This book is dedicated to my children, each of whom is an entrepreneur. From them I have learned. To them, I wish Golden Entrepreneuring success.

James B. Arkebauer

Introduction

This book explains how senior entrepreneurs conceive and execute a strategy of starting or buying, and then operating, a successful business managed and operated by seniors.

Our country has a new crisis forming that it is barely even aware of. Ironically, this same crisis presents many new opportunities. Millions of healthy, ambitious, energetic senior citizens (50 years of age and older)—or soon to be seniors (baby boomers)—are seeking a way to maintain gainful employment and lifestyle, while continuing to feel good about themselves and their contribution to their families and society. The crisis is that many of these seniors have been or are facing corporate downsizing or forced early retirement and then must turn around and face discreet hiring turndowns because of age.

The author has had a 5-year association with an organization known as the Senior Entrepreneur's Foundation (SEF). Its mission statement reads, in part:

> SEF is a nonprofit foundation formed to assist seniors (over 50) in educating, promoting, and securing self-employment opportunities. This is accomplished through a variety of activities specifically designed to enhance the efforts of emerging businesses through education, networking and to connect with service professionals and funding sources.

My involvement with SEF has made me intimately aware of this crisis and opportunity.

Today's larger companies have an over-abundance of baby boomer middle management workers from which to choose. At the same time, these companies are very concerned with their much increased health care cost. Their solutions are to carefully discriminate in the hiring of those in middle management who are over 50, while also encouraging early retirement by offering healthy bonuses.

This results in hundreds of thousands of people over 50 who are looking for alternatives for employment. The term *Seniorpreneuring* has not gotten much play yet. But it's going to come on like gang busters.

These same seniors, young and old alike, have talent, ambition, experience, networking skills, and money. They are recognizing that there's no longer any job security in working for large corporations. They're willing and financially capable of trusting their own abilities to strike out on their own. They see the home office trend right in their own neighborhoods. They recognize that the lone ranger, gun slinging entrepreneur is part of the past, that this solo person is being replaced by entrepreneurial teams. They have cultivated and established a network of peers to draw upon for team members.

In short, they're ready, willing, and able to consider stepping out on their own. To establish a team, focus on an enterprise, and become Golden Entrepreneurs.

This book is their guidebook to becoming successful senior entrepreneurs.

The Number One Advantage

"We get too soon old and too late smart"—*Old German saying*

The number one advantage that Golden Entrepreneurs (senior entrepreneurs over age 50) have is their *street smarts*—the intelligence that seasoning provides. This helps them recognize that entrepreneurs need to be both thought-oriented and action-oriented. This "experience" knowledge helps them understand that times are changing and our business economy is more service and knowledge oriented and that this requires an emphasis on work smarts alongside of work harder. Golden Entrepreneurs have it all. *Not* too soon old and just right smart.

From Fifty to the Grave

Golden Entrepreneurs encompass those entrepreneurs from age 50 to the grave. They represent the movers and shakers of the last half of this century and are our leaders into the next. They have conceived, guided, and in many cases, driven the business world and its major accomplishments since World War II. They are going to continue to shape business events, more so than past generations of seniors, for numerous reasons.

The differences between today and the immediate post World War II generations of seniors are many and varied. Today, those who qualify for senior entrepreneurship have had at least one career change, where their fathers most likely retired from one career and, often, one company. Todays senior women work while their mothers' workplace was at home. Seniors today are college educated, commonly with advanced degrees, while many of their parents barely graduated from high school. Their parents read about world events in the newspapers, while today, we witness them as they happen on live television. While their parents read books about far-away places in Europe or the Far Eastern countries, today's seniors visit them for both business and pleasure. While their parents may have spoken some of the language from the "old country," they themselves may speak two or three foreign tongues. While their parents gracefully accepted, even looked forward to retirement, today's seniors' mindset is different. They haven't spent their worklife under a lot of manufacturing economy, physically induced labor. Their bodies aren't as worn out and they have the benefit of a much improved healthcare system which continues to push past aging norms. And there are more differences.

America is waking up to a growing awareness of mature entrepreneurs, and it's a double-edged sword. Senior entrepreneurs have more money than most people suspect and they're willing to spend it. On the other hand, their increasing longevity is allowing them to be productive business people, way past what their parents considered the norm. While our current business environment continues to "downsize" and encourage early retirement, our acceptable employable base of seniors is increasing. The American Association of Retired Persons (AARP) has a membership of 33 million, of which 47 percent are between the ages of 50 and 64. And this is just as the first of the 76 million baby boomers reach the 50-year-old membership age. These baby boomers, just by their sheer numbers, set the standards for many areas of our society. Their continuing productivity, awareness of their problems, their solutions for solving them, backed by very adequate financing, will make their collective impact on entrepreneurship awesome.

And that's what this book is about, how senior entrepreneurs will open the eyes of our general population to the evolving management techniques and the latest efficiencies that technology offers. Work smarter is, or should be, their credo, backed by their experience and "work harder" work ethic.

An Overview of the Parts and Chapters

Complex Problems and Great Challenges

The practice of senior entrepreneuring is not established. We're in the very early stages of determining the problems and challenges that this phenomenon will present. Consequently, Seniorpreneurs will be on a fast learning curve. This book presents the pros and cons we can currently identify, recognizing that as senior entrepreneurs exercise their skills, more and probably complex societal interactions will come forth.

Getting Started

In Chapter 1, you'll be exposed to the major changes and trends that validate the movement to Seniorpreneuring. We'll also explore the undercurrents of these and the challenges of the near-term future. Chapter 2 unfolds the characteristics of an entrepreneur, relates the stories of some successful senior entrepreneurs, and discusses the distinct assets that seniors bring to entrepreneurship.

In Chapter 3, some common myths of being a senior are brought forth and then dispelled by noting the advantages of age. Chapter 4 expands on more senior entrepreneuring opportunities and provides you with some checklists to use to when you are qualifying an entrepreneurial prospect. Chapter 5 will help you sort through the decision-making process of starting a new company, buying an existing operation, or buying a franchise business.

Getting Going

When an opportunity is qualified, the next step is to assemble both the inside and outside members of a management team. Chapters 6 and 7 explore these important areas, show how to best identify, qualify, and bring together the management team members. This is followed by Chapter 8, which provides a discussion and an outline for putting together a business plan that will successfully guide a senior-led enterprise.

Getting Financed

All companies have two primary financing choices: debt and equity. Chapter 9 explores the debt side, including a detailed discussion of debt financing sources. Chapter 10 shows how to identify and approach equity funders along with some uncommon ways to raise equity capital.

Operations to Exit

After identifying the opportunity, assembling the team, and obtaining financing, the Seniorpreneur's challenge is to make the operations effectively bring about the results desired by the owners. Chapter 11 shows you how, with discussions about planning, management by objectives, and a group of helpful management assistance tips.

At some point in time, every person and every company needs to move on. Chapter 12 examines the process of cashing in on the Seniorpreneurial opportunity. This includes such topics as pricing and terms, and the senior harvest choices.

To review, the Golden Entrepreneuring concept is to explore the advantages and disadvantages of seniors as entrepreneurs, and advance the process of selecting proper senior business opportunities. It requires the assembly of a senior-dominated management team, development of a well-thought-out business plan, and identifying adequate financing. The goal is to create an operating company that offers seniors a variety of choices from which they can derive both financial benefit and a rewarding lifestyle. This book provides a road guide that allows seniors to create and meet personally challenging situations in which they can learn how to stretch their abilities and continue to grow while they answer the entrepreneurial call.

PART 1
Getting Started

1
Complex Problems and Great Opportunities

Bear with me for a few pages while I set out several theories that are central to the balance of this book. The need is to establish some common ground that should help us further explore Golden Entrepreneuring together.

In the next several decades, our existing seniors, bolstered by tens of millions of former outspoken, protesting, baby boomers, will force a realignment of our present concept of our business world and how we work. Our increasingly healthy lifestyles prompt longer and more productive lives. Our actual work is becoming less physically demanding through the use of new technologies, especially in manufacturing. This workplace realignment will also come about because of corporate downsizing and the elimination of multilayers of middle management.

With increased life expectancy changes, seniors need to work. Because we want to, because it gives us fulfillment, control over our lives, a useful place in society, and we need the money. We desire the ability to maintain a reasonable standard of living, and to further pursue our American dreams.

Society and the business environment is adapting. Midlife career changes are more acceptable, regular job skill retraining is common, lifetime learning is replacing once-a-life learning. These themes, these changes and trends, coupled with some complex, evolving situations, indicate that today's seniors contemplating entering entrepreneurship are confronted with many challenges and a great deal of opportunity.

Changes and Trends

Changes

Change can be described as: to cause to be different, to give a completely different form or appearance to, to exchange or replace with another, to lay aside, abandon, switch, alter, correct, modify, transfigure, transform, substitute, vary, and swap.

Most of us hate change, because it requires us to attempt new behaviors we are not comfortable with or don't possess. Almost inevitably, it means we are going to experience a degree of failure. Change can causes problems and problems require solutions. We resist change because it's disturbing, frightening, and sometimes even disastrous. We expect the world to change, in fact we look forward to it, but somehow, we don't think it will effect *us*—our jobs, our businesses.

People lose their jobs or have difficulty making transitions when new technologies bring far-reaching changes to our industries. People have a tough time changing and that's why companies have a hard time changing. It's more than the initial aversion; it's the feeling that we may no longer be competent in the new environment. We've had change all the time. It's not that change is new; it's the pace of change that has gotten quicker. In the business world, we're dealing with dynamics in our organizations that we've never dealt with before. Sometimes we have the challenge to do something in the afternoon differently than how we did it in the morning—a new software program, an improved fax machine. The challenge now is to make sure employees are included and empowered in their respective areas throughout the change process.

Change is a problem, an opportunity, and a responsibility. It's about risk, uncertainty, and innovation. Change *can be* a continual embracing of the best.

A Generation of Changes. As this chapter unfolds, we'll cover a number of areas and societal changes that are affecting us here in the United States as well as the rest of the world. These changes, when viewed from the proper perspective, present many opportunities—opportunities for which seniors are well positioned to take advantage of. Two leading influences of these changes are: downsizing and baby boomers.

Downsizing. It used to be that you got a "job" with the "corporation." By taking your job seriously, you worked your way into a "position," from which, after many faithful years of devoted service, you "retired," if not plush, at least with an adequate pension. As we're all painfully aware, this scenario has changed.

Wholesale elimination of middle management positions in our large corporations is firmly in place. The proverbial corporate steps have shrunk. The overriding necessity of cost reduction will prevent a return to the days of layer upon layer of middle management. Downsized middle management is searching for jobs that don't and won't exist.

The terms "downsizing" and "rightsizing" sound like one-time events. But they're more: they're a deep structural change. Job cutting is the front line result of corporations struggling with a world economy that faces a sustained period of slower growth, low-inflationary expansion and global overcapacity, all of which contribute to an era when companies cannot easily raise prices to expand profit margins.

During the expansionist 1980s, the world's large service companies added almost one-third more employees to their payrolls. Now, instead of adding more employees to keep up with growing demand, they are concentrating on raising employee productivity and using the information technology they have acquired more intelligently. Even if the economy picks up steam, there will be a reluctance to make permanent new hires. The trend is toward overtime or part-time workers, "just-in-time" workers if you will, where high-cost benefits aren't incurred. The trend has been occurring for a decade and now it's a permanent enactment of corporate streamlining which hopefully will make us more fit to be better competitors in the new global economy.

Baby Boomers. The other leading influence in our current generation of change that underlies opportunities for senior entrepreneuring is the baby boomers. Almost one-third of all living Americans—76 million people—were born between 1946 and 1964. We know of them as the "baby boomers," a generational mass that has dominated American culture for four decades. Their concerns, needs, and obsessions have been the dominant force of many entrepreneurial efforts. Witness the following:

We created sugar-coated cereals, Saturday morning cartoon shows, and countless TV toys for boomers as kids. In the mid 1950s—1957, in fact—our local school districts built more elementary schools than in any one year before or since. Then the high school population doubled, and we built more high schools in America in 1967 than in any year before or since.

Boomers created the market for Hula-Hoops, skateboards, Slinkies, and Frisbees, and the list goes on. We've had television shows that have catered to the baby boomers, from *The Mickey Mouse Club, Captain Kangaroo, My Three Sons,* and *Father Knows Best,* to *thirtysomething.* Each of these had commercial sponsors whose products were often created just to serve the boomer audience of the time.

Boomers created the fast-food industry and then went to college. The college student population tripled between 1965 and 1975 from 3.2 million to 9 million. This same group caused the profits from Zig-Zag roll-your-own cigarette papers to rise by 25 percent every year for a decade.

In the 1970s, the boomers' attention turned to concerns over personal identity, lifestyle, and earning a living. What became "in" was *I'm OK, You're OK, Your Erroneous Zones,* and *What Color Is Your Parachute?* Also in was est, Lifespring, Silva Mind Control, and Transcendental Meditation. During the 1980s, the "in" publications were *The Wall Street Journal, Esquire, Money, Forbes,* and *Fortune,* as well as books titled *In Search of Excellence, Megatrends, Iacocca,* and *Trump.*

When a few thousand, even a few hundred thousand, people across the United States share an opinion, read a book, or buy a product, that's interesting, maybe even a trend. But when 76 million people do so, it's a revolution. *When baby boomers arrive at any stage of life, the issues of concern to them become the dominant social, political, and marketplace obsessions of the time.*

As the boomers enter the world of seniors, this generation is destined to be the one force that most profoundly influences our lives. As boomers grow, America grows. What a major Seniorpreneuring opportunity!

Seniorpreneurs Face the Facts on Change. You've heard many variations of the phrase, "The only constant is change." If you aspire to Seniorpreneuring, you better get on the "accepting-change" bandwagon. History is accelerating—events and their communication are being compressed into virtual time and the numbers and complexity are growing exponentially.

Seniors, who are change adaptable and who have and are living through these multiple stages, now have an unprecedented number of opportunities to exercise their knowledge, perspective of change, and insight to capitalize on these changes. While 10 percent of the world population enters the exciting era of applied technology, the remaining 90 percent will be struggling to enter the information age (and in some cases the industrial age). This means that seniors, who have lived through these changes, can help the remaining 90 percent. What an opportunity! While the younger generations are working on the 10 percent and pushing the frontiers of technology further, the Seniorpreneurs can help the 90 percent apply the proven technologies. Just think about the possibilities this brings. It's a super example of a senior benefit. The fact that having been down the road before allows one to travel it the next time faster and with greater comfort.

Trends

While changes usually reflect what has happened in the past, trends attempt to project tomorrow's changes. Trends can be described as: leaning, inclination, propensity, tendency, a fad or craze, a rage or style.

For our purposes, a trend is described as a *definite, predictable direction or sequence of events.* This firm definition allows us to proact versus react after we have confirmed a trend. It means we can anticipate the future and act accordingly as opposed to being taken by surprise and forced to then look for a solution. By seeking out trends, we are allowed to anticipate change. To drive into the future instead of constantly looking into the rear view mirror—a habit which, when overused, causes accidents.

As seniors considering entrepreneuring, we need confirmed trends and not just fads—unless we're specifically looking to entrepreneurially participate in a fad, which is another story. For our purposes, we will consider a fad as something which is unpredictable, short-lived, and without social, economic, and political significance (Hula-Hoops, leisure suits, and Cabbage Patch dolls). Usually they're products that hit the market with the force of a comet, only to disappear in the blink of an eye. Often, a fad idea gets knocked off quickly by a number of companies because it is created to fulfill a short-term demand. Trends, on the other hand, meet real customers needs for an extended period.

Determining Trends. Remembering that trends are *definite, predictable directions or sequences of events,* we can add that they are definite because we confirm them from a number of fields or disciplines. Gerald Celente and Tom Milton in their book *Trend Tracking* (Wiley, 1990) suggest that we get our information, and consequently can define trends, from four worlds: the media world, the political world, the Disney world, and the real world.

The media world is our major news sources such as television, newspapers, radio, and the primary news-oriented magazines. The political world comes to us from such areas as C-SPAN and political free-mailing privileges—which are further distributed by the media world. The Disney world is our entertainment provided by prime-time TV, movies, and popular magazines, all aimed at mass-market audiences. For all entrepreneurs, we accept the fact that the Disney world creates illusions and forms opinions that many people accept at face value. We may not like this fact, but we have to accept it.

The real world encompasses the other three worlds but is substantiated by facts, events, and ideas that affect our lives. The challenge in drawing trend conclusions is careful consideration as to how much of the flow of information from the three dominant sources really affect the facts of detecting the important social, economic, and political events that are forming defined trends.

Although we'll get into some trends in more depth in Chapters 3 and 4, the citing in this chapter of some accepted changes, and the trends they forecast, helps us better understand the growing need for and acceptance of Seniorpreneuring and the opportunities that are offered.

Confirmed and Accepted Changes and Trends

In this section, I want to bring to your attention some major changes and trends that will affect us as Seniorpreneurs. I'm going to cite some examples, and then your challenge is to add your thoughts, to determine how your life experiences coincide with these changes and trends. Entrepreneuring is never easy. I can help you learn, ascertain, and calculate, but you're going to have to discover what works for you. So to continue to form the circle, and as I wrote at the beginning of this chapter, I want to establish some additional common ground for us to explore Golden Entrepreneuring together.

Political. Is the government listening? With all the great things about our country, entrepreneurial freedom being close to the top, we also have a lot of problems: poverty, health care, unemployment, homelessness, divorce, illiteracy, crime, drugs, pollution in many forms, and the list goes on. And what we have from our politicians is their ignoring of these problems. Sure, they give a lot of lip service to these issues, but they really aren't motivated to solve them. They attempt to treat the symptoms instead of getting ahead of the curve and addressing the fundamentals of the problems.

But that's changing. Until the Bush administration, when Dan Quayle was elected Vice President, we didn't have many high-profile leaders who weren't functioning with a World War II mentality. The Clinton administration has further changed this, as both President Clinton and Vice President Al Gore are baby boomers. The baby boomer politicians are filing more posts, clear down to our local city councils. The political change is also partially prompted by the media.

The politicians are not as able to hide behind the doors as before. The press has stalked them out and forced live audiences with real people posing hard questions. We aren't as tolerant of higher Social Security taxes, higher states sales taxes, higher property taxes, and a continual stream of taxes disguised as "fees."

The public is getting involved, helped by the baby boomers longstanding reputation for involvement and media exposure. We're setting priorities and demanding that our political system take action on these priorities. We want and are demanding action on the top concerns of today: jobs, housing, health care, and education. The change in our political system is in place; the trend will continue. Our governmental bodies are turning more and more toward privatization and therein lie many entrepreneurial opportunities.

Family—*The Waltons* Are Gone. It used to be a lot different. There was a father as a breadwinner, mom as a homemaker, and x number of kids. Aunts and uncles, grandparents, and other assorted extended family members lived down the block or across town. The kids came home from all day at school, mom assigned chores and supervised homework. They all sat down for dinner without interruption from a TV set and video games. At least occasionally, they all went out for some mutually enjoyable family-style entertainment.

The trend, with two-income families firmly established, is the recognition that what's been the norm just isn't working. We're attacking it in various ways. We've realized that the breakdown of the traditional family has contributed to many of the social and economic problems we currently face. Formal sex education is firmly in place, especially on an AIDS awareness level. Now the trend is to educate for abstinence. The facts are well established. Single mothers are twice as likely as married mothers to not have graduated from high school. Single-parent families are likely to be living below the poverty level. Children living with single parents are likely to drop out of school. We know we have to stop this self-feeding cycle.

Dual-income families are holding off their production of offspring. They're waiting till they have established a career before having children. Then, they are having fewer children. The parents spend more time with the kids. They have shifted their priorities, and the clear demarcation between breadwinner and homemaker is getting fuzzy as males take a more active role in bringing up the progeny. Daycare facilities are getting more plentiful, many subsidized by employers. Companies are offering flexible work schedules and job sharing as well as extended leaves for both moms and pops (prompted by federal mandates). The home office trend is also helpful.

While it's doubtful that we will return to the Waltons' type of family-value environment, it's clear that many aspects of society are attempting to create a nuclear family that recognizes some of the Walton family values. These values won't be the same, because our society has changed. But they will stem the deterioration that has been so prevalent over the past several decades. This concern for a more cohesive family unit presents opportunities for seniors to be leaders—based on their past experiences—in assisting this change.

Education—What Happened to the Basics? At least "back then," the schools taught the students to read, write, and do arithmetic. The real world (business and making a living) taught them how to think, analyze problems, and find solutions. With the breakdown in the family unit, a lot of the responsibility shifted to schools, who promptly blamed the lack of interest from the family. A vicious circle developed just as the rest of the world rushed into high technology, with its inherent need for basic education derived skills.

Washington didn't help. In the 1980s, there was even an attempt to eliminate the Department of Education. Fortunately that didn't happen, but the result was that spending on education barely kept up with inflation. In 1988, we spent about $330 billion on education (most of it from state and local governments), while defense spending totaled $350 billion. We have a 30 percent dropout rate (50 to 60 percent in urban areas), while our need for basic education to function in a higher tech workplace environment increases. The Department of Education estimates that we have over 72 million Americans who may lack the reading and writing skills they need to find work (27 million over age 17 are illiterate).

Some companies can't find workers with basic education skills and are being forced to "dumb down." Fast-food outlets put pictures of the items on the cash register rather than a digit or word. The National Alliance of Businesses believes that three out of four jobs now require education beyond high school. Even high school dropout auto mechanics are a job of the past. Computers have taken over auto fix-it jobs. There are numerous opportunities being presented that allow seniors to entrepreneurially participate in the growing needs of education and on-the-job training.

Health Care—It's Got to Get Better. We continue to make huge strides in all medical areas, and many of these medical improvements are one of the reasons for this book. But the fact remains that we need to get ahead of the curve. We need to leap forward from our present approach, which is to offer symptomatic relief. We need to permeate our society with preventive and holistic medicine.

Today's seniors have a personally vested interest in improving our health care and its systems. It presents numerous entrepreneurial opportunities on many fronts. Basic research is needed as well as applied research. New products and services are continually being developed. The dissemination of healthcare information and the streamlining of paperwork procedures and facilitating payments are both areas that entrepreneurs can be involved in.

Environment—From the Bad Guys to.... It was a movement born in the 1970s; its name had a lot of negative implications. *Environmentalists* became the "bad guys" in the go-go 1980s, blamed for inflation and unemployment. The 1990s will bring us back to dealing with polluted air, contaminated water, toxic waste, overflowing landfills, acid rain, a damaged ozone layer, and more specific environmental problems worldwide. The trend is established. Humankind will have to address our environment on a serious basis from now on.

The positive impetus that secures this trend is a growing public concern for the environment. This will force federal, state, and local governments, backed by private enterprise and members of the global community, to take action. These calls for action will open many doors for answers from Seniorpreneurs.

Economy—??????? Have you ever looked up the word "economy" in a dictionary? Mine stated, "The careful or thrifty use or management of resources." That can provoke a laugh when you consider our struggles with slow growth rates, low productivity, crumbling infrastructures, enormous debts (governmental, corporate, and personal), huge trade deficits, a growing underclass, and a shrinking middle class—all of which result in a lower standard of living.

Some things in our economy are obvious. We have to get a hold of our borrowing; we have to control deficit spending. We have to increase our exports and change our balance of payments. We have to import productivity tools and export high value-added services and products. Entrepreneurs can help with all these points, create trends, and cause economic change. We can help by spreading the word, showing prudence in our daily business and personal affairs, and creating concepts and systems that economize dollars and maximize people's efforts.

The World. The trend developed before the 1980s, but the change really came into focus during the 1980s. I'm speaking of "globalization." What emerged was a trend away from ideology, as political leaders from around the world shifted their focus from military conflict to economic competition. The most dramatic change was in Eastern Europe as we saw an end to the Cold War. As the Soviet Union moved toward demilitarization, the rest of the world followed. At the same time, the United States was losing its economic dominance of the world, clearing the way for three powerful economic blocs to compete: Western Europe, North America, and the Pacific Rim. By the turn of the century, they will at least to some extent include Eastern Europe, Latin America, and Southeast Asia. This won't regionalize the world; it will advance the trend toward globalization, and a lot faster than most people think. Keep in mind that almost everything today moves a lot faster than it used to.

The United States has strong ties with both Europe and the Pacific Rim. We're the common ground between them and with this lies a major opportunity. While competition has intensified, all countries are becoming more interdependent. All the world has to think globally.

These global markets are the flow across international borders of money, goods, service, jobs, and technology. It usually happens first with money because it's so easy to transport—you only have to move information—and this happens because of the major advances in data processing and communications. We have a integrated world market using a computer network that never sleeps.

You can see it in other markets besides money—automobiles are a good example. The industry no longer thinks only of domestic markets; it thinks and builds cars for the world. The auto industry owns manufacturing plants and has in-depth alliances around the globe. So do a lot of other industries such as beverages, tobacco, branded food products and fast food, as well as entertainment, consumer appliances, and the media. This is a global movement of money, products, services, and most important, jobs. The United States has long been a market unto itself. Now, even with a population of over a quarter-billion, its only 5 percent of a global population of over 5 billion. A lot of the rest of these 4.75 billion people aspire to a higher standard of living, and the United States is their leading role model. They see us every day on their televisions.

The world challenge for Seniorpreneurs is great. If the population continues to grow at the present rate, it will double in about 25 years. It's going to take a lot of resources to feed, clothe, and shelter 5 billion additional people. This will also have an effect on every change and trend we have discussed.

Coming Full Circle

So let's see if we can bring this opening chapter into perspective, especially as regards our subject of Seniorpreneuring. For one, our perspective about work has changed. To some, work now holds less promise, less purpose, less security, and less dignity than it did a generation ago. It used to be, *Work is what I do; it is what I am.*

We have some serious challenges in our workplace. The challenges of dignity and identity are two. If you lose your place in the world of work, do you lose your soul? It's a fundamental question. Around 20 million workers are in low-wage jobs in stores or restaurants. These are jobs with little or no health or pension coverage, with hours the employer can change at will, and often with no assurance that the job will be around next week. Two out of every five jobs in the United States are temporary or part time. The center of our work force has been hollowing out as the top and the bottom have grown. Minimal education has contributed. Automation has contributed. Technology advances have contributed.

We have passed the agricultural and industrial ages of development and are now in a postindustrial era accented by global competitiveness. The age of the solo entrepreneur is past, as we have to compete effectively in a so-called high-performance workplace where management and front-line workers team up to solve problems and improve quality. The era of mass production, in which a few people at the top dictate procedures to a fragmented production line performing routine repetitive tasks, is past. Our challenge is to enhance the competitiveness of American businesses and improve the skills and standard of living for all Americans. We need companies that place as much value on the quality of the work environment—support open communications and flexible scheduling—as they do on salary and advancement. This will create workers who are committed to themselves as well as their employers: workers who work hard and care about the success of their company because they have good relationships with their supervisors and don't have to choose between work and personal responsibilities as well as feel that they have an opportunity to advance.

Today, it no longer takes a lone-ranger type of individual to entrepreneur a company. It takes teamwork, with a group of individuals working together, committed to a common goal with a multiple of objectives that require multidisciplinarian talents. But most important, it takes work smarts that are present only because of experience brought about from a more senior age, with an in-depth reservoir of knowledge and experience.

We may have to break our traditional thinking about seniors into two broadly defined age groups: junior seniors (or young seniors), those aged 50 to 65 or 70; and the balance above the later loosely defined age. It also means we have to readjust our thinking about the standard definition of entrepreneur. We traditionally think of this individual as one with a deep, driving, relentless spirit of determination and practically unlimited physical ability. It is someone who can put in enormous hours, who has incredible physical stamina. However, our current young seniors are the most politically aware, most financially well-off segment of the population. What a time of renewed energy! What a potential force for a new style of entrepreneurialism.

Do You Have What It Takes to Be an Entrepreneur?

As you read about downsizing and baby boomers, and then as you reflect on some of the major changes and trends that are taking place, are you sparking on some potential entrepreneurial ideas and concepts where you can use your senior smarts? Are you searching for some ideas where you can incorporate your knowledge, experience, and entrepreneurial potential?

In the next chapter, we'll explore the characteristics and traits of an entrepreneur. However, this is a good place for you to take a brief self-assessment quiz. Don't worry about right or wrong. However, you might want to really think about some of your answers. Just use a yes or no answer as the questions apply to you.

1. Were either of your parents self-employed?
2. Do you consider yourself a self-starter?
3. Are you basically an optimistic person?
4. Have you ever been fired from a job?
5. Do you consider yourself a social butterfly?
6. Do you get easily bored with repetitive tasks?
7. Are you or were your parents/grandparents immigrants?
8. Do you enjoy leading people?
9. Have you worked in a company with less than 100 employees?
10. Do you mind putting in 60-hour weeks?
11. Were you an average student?
12. Did you start or operate a small business before you were 20?
13. Do you consider yourself a good organizer?
14. Do you like working with people?
15. Do you take a lot of time to make decisions?

16. Do you take on responsibility easily?
17. Are you the oldest child in your family?
18. Did you hold a job while in high school and college?
19. Can people trust what you say?
20. Do you like working for someone else?
21. Do you ask or solicit comments and advice from others?
22. Were you stubborn and independent as a youngster?
23. Are you a good money manager?
24. Is the first thing you need to start a business customers?
25. Do you enjoy having a consistent daily routine?
26. Do you enjoy solving problems?
27. Do you take notes and write down tasks to do?
28. Are you healthy?
29. Do you finish the large majority of your tasks?
30. Do you always have to be in charge?

Numerous studies have shown that the large majority of successful entrepreneurs can answer yes to all the questions except 5, 10, 15, 20, 25, and 30. How did you fare? How do your answers tie into some of the ideas you're generating?

The Challenges Ahead

Your challenge as a Seniorpreneur is to develop concepts and ideas for presently needed or potential services and products. Many of these will be in niche markets or for specialized services and products. Here are some ideas that appear to be well established trends:

Education-driven child care. The two-income family wants its children to have a good start. Private enterprise will be establishing more and more child care facilities that educate as well as provide care. This will start with infants and continue right up to junior high level. There is a great need for "latch-key" kid tutoring.

Automotive industry. How do you capture an entrepreneurial opportunity in such a large industry? Thousands upon thousands of gas stations are closing because they can't justify the cost of replacing the underground tanks. They clean up the environmental problems first and then you can buy or lease the site, most times at very excellent high-traffic points to locate your new enterprise.

Medical management and billing services. The whole medical industry is being revolutionized. The changes are going to keep evolving and the entrepreneurial opportunities to be service providers will continue to evolve. Medical billing and tracking systems are just getting started.

Services for an aging population. This field is as broad as it is wide. It includes many areas that are just beginning to appear: opportunities for in-home care; transportation for shopping, medical services, and recreation; services for assistance in filling out an endless stream of paperwork; financial and property management; outsourcing of daily living needs, and more. Today's seniors are creating new service companies to fit their needs, and then they get to sell them out to the boomers that follow. Not a bad idea!

Environmental services. This is a huge area, from providing air filter installations and service in homes to developing hazardous waste disposal sites and tracking systems. We'll need more and more consultants, inspectors, testers, and fix-it-uppers for our water, air, and pollution problems and controls.

Services related to fitness and health. It would seem that we have all the health clubs we need. However, there are a lot more coming: specialized organizations that concentrate in one area like cardiovascular workouts for the disabled, and nutrition evaluators for children.

Foods. The family farm is all but gone, but we're developing numerous smaller niche markets for entrepreneurs with green thumbs: naturally grown fruits, vegetables, and herbs, and also leaner beef, buffalo, fowl, and aquaculture are in demand as we eat healthier.

Personal services for the working family. This will include routine grocery shopping, maid services, general appliance fix-it operations, in-home computer repair, specialized and general "pick this up" and "take this back" services, home and yard maintenance. Time is getting so precious and our lives so filled that more and more families will hire out many of today's routine Saturday tasks.

Employment services. If you can't beat 'em, join 'em. Employment agenting for temps, part-timers, specialized professional areas, consultants, elderly, short-timers and flex-timers is growing. It's a low-capital-intensive business area that has a proven demand.

Retraining. It's all part of working smarter. Continuing education applies to almost all trades, professions, and skills. This is taking place in formal classroom studies, learn-at-home courses, conferences, week-long programs, 3-day seminars, all- or half-day sessions, and one-on-one tutoring.

Varying approaches to solving these and other problems is what the balance of this book is about. As seniors, we will be primary contributors in this complex problem-solving quest. What's more, we will be the leaders of the great opportunities.

2
A Most Fortuitous Occasion?

As little as 10 years ago, our youth-oriented culture would doubt that people over 40, much less 50 or 60 and 70, would be candidates for entrepreneurship. But then again, 10 years ago, who would have thought that in excess of 80 percent of all small businesses would be using personal computers?

A combination of factors is making senior entrepreneuring a fortuitous occasion. The slimming down of corporate America is freeing many middle management people to consider a career change. Our continued evolution from an industrial manufacturing to a service/knowledge/information based society is freeing us from monotonous repetitive tasks. The recognition that we're moving to a global marketplace is becoming accepted. All these major trends contribute to more areas that embrace the concept of senior entrepreneuring.

We're going to cover a lot of ground in this chapter. First we will establish what the traits and characteristics of a typical entrepreneur are. You'll be surprised at some of the points. Then we'll look at some examples of other successful senior entrepreneurs which leads us into an assessment of the assets that senior entrepreneurs have that allow them to attain a higher level of entrepreneurship than the average bear. Finally, we'll examine why seniors are taking to Seniorpreneuring.

What It Takes to Be an Entrepreneur

I'm going to give you the secret right up front, right here in the first paragraph. *There is no definitive set of characteristics to describe an entrepreneur.*

In fact, there doesn't seem to be a definitive set of characteristics to describe a Seniorpreneur either. Just having a business idea may qualify one to be an entrepreneur, but as you'll continue to learn, that isn't what makes a Seniorpreneur.

Having had both success and failure in my personal entrepreneurial activities—as well as tracking hundreds of investment opportunities of other entrepreneurs—I have continued to study entrepreneurs to determine if I can qualify the personal characteristics of entrepreneurial success. My conclusions to date are presented in this chapter.

Hardy, Ambitious Goal Achievers

Entrepreneurs are hardy, ambitious, goal-achieving dreamers. They spend their lives in stressful environments working to solve stressful problems. Some fail all their lives. Others just survive. A few become what we can describe as Ultrapreneurs (ultimate entrepreneurs) and create entire new industries—like Henry Bloch of Block Brothers, who revolutionized tax reporting, or Mary Kay Ash of Mary Kay Cosmetics, who opened the entrepreneurial door to women and created thousands of two-income families. Their one common bond is hard work.

So can we qualify a number of the success characteristics of a typical entrepreneur? Is there a definitive set of characteristics?

The answer is yes—and no. There is no single all-important set of personality characteristics or psychological profile of a typical entrepreneur. However, there are many areas of commonality—traits that can be identified and learned, abilities that can be cultivated, mindsets that can be adopted. In the end, you'll recognize that there is a great variety among types of entrepreneurs, that they have a diverse psychological makeup, but yet, how they achieve success defies the use of any single profile.

The next section is an assemblage of many of the traits currently used to define an entrepreneur. I have broadened and rearranged them to fit my definition of a Seniorpreneur from my book *Ultrapreneuring: Taking a Venture from Start-up to Harvest in Three Years or Less* (McGraw-Hill, 1993).

Characteristics—The Basics

The "perfect entrepreneur" has yet to be invented. It's impossible to arrive at a set of characteristics that are ideal for all situations. From all the various studies that have been conducted, both formal and informal, we know there are many characteristics that are proven, both desirable and acquirable. They can be set out in the following baker's dozen traits. If they were contained in one single individual, you would have the ultimate entrepreneur. I have listed them alphabetically, since it would seem that they are equally important.

Achievement	Honesty
Action orientation	Innovation
Commitment	Intelligence
Communication	Leadership
Energy	Risk tolerance
Goal setting	Self-confidence
Growth orientation	

Achievement

Achievement is generally considered the act of accomplishing or finishing something. For Seniorpreneurs, one would tend to add "successfully." They recognize that success occurs when preparation and opportunity meet. Preparation is up to them; opportunity ofttimes is not. They realize that by means of exertion, skill, practice, and with much perseverance they will achieve success.

The senior drive in achievement is for self-fulfillment, not for power or status. Seniorpreneurs realize that if they are successful, if they achieve their company and personal goals, then power and status will follow. Achievement comes from the execution of success plans that are acted upon and that achieve positive results, from seeking ever-larger, more-defined challenges. The people that back Seniorpreneurs, from team members to employees, to financiers to suppliers and customers, believe that the leader is an achiever.

Action Orientation

There is one Seniorpreneurial trait that underlies all the other entrepreneurial characteristics. This trait is that successful Seniorpreneurs are action based, always taking action. No matter what the movement, it must move. Sometimes this doesn't prove positive, but in the long run, taking action sure beats standing still. Occasionally, one has to take a step backward to move forward two steps. Seniorpreneurs realize—no—deeply believe and feel this. They know that even if their immediate action proves to have some faults, they're confident they will learn from a mistake, benefit from some new knowledge (not consider it a failure), and then will take corrective action.

This action orientation frequently comes naturally with Seniorpreneurial types. They seem to have a sixth sense about if and when actions should commence. Maybe it's street smarts. Then again, maybe it's from a thoughtful process.

Commitment

To this characteristic, Seniorpreneurs add dedication, determination, and persistence. These are the points that Seniorpreneurs need to overcome the odds, setbacks, and obstacles they face in securing their success. These qualities, perhaps more important than the rest, assist the Seniorpreneur in succeeding where entrepreneurs and others fail. They are the goal-attaining supplements to many other weaknesses. They are part and parcel of Seniorpreneurial commitment. Commitment is the willingness to take a stand for what one believes in. It requires that the Seniorpreneur generate a passion for success and a hatred for failure.

Persistence, which is an offspring of commitment, was once described by Ray Kroc, who was the driving force of the international McDonald's fast-food chain. He said:

> Nothing in the world can take the place of persistence. Talent will not...Genius will not...Education will not...Persistence and determination are omnipotent.

These qualities are what drives an entrepreneur.

Seniorpreneurs burn with a deep competitive desire to excel and win, to control their destiny, to shape their future by being deeply committed.

Communication

The greatest illusion about communication is that it has been accomplished. A difference between an entrepreneur and an Seniorpreneur is the Seniorpreneur's continuing questioning of the effectiveness of the communication process. It's called *feedback:* How do we know if what we're communicating is getting across? The answer is positive affirmation, or questions.

Good listeners ignore personal prejudices and listen with an open mind, not prejudging. Further, they listen for key points, ignore trivia, get important facts, and relate them to the main points. They avoid distractions, detect and interpret body language, read between the lines for what isn't being said, and avoid the temptation to interrupt.

When the listening session is over (which it never really is for Seniorpreneurs), they organize their thoughts into clear, concise statements and disseminate them via the spoken word, written instructions, and most importantly, positive-reinforcing actions. This is Seniorpreneurial communication.

Energy

Energy is a positive quality—a desire to get things accomplished, to get them done in the right way. It's an active quality, an urgent need to move from one position to another, to advance to a new goal, to accomplish a given task. Energy is never static, and Seniorpreneurs enjoy using it and get excited when they're put to an energizing task.

Energy gives Seniorpreneurs the drive that makes them challenge takers. It assists their natural tendency to be positive about setbacks and supports their tolerance for stress and the continuing business uncertainty that they live with.

Goal Setting

For Seniorpreneurs, goal setting is an obsession. Their goals are their dreams—dreams with a deadline, dreams being acted on. They realize that goals assist them in controlling their lives. They know that their goals have to be positive, have to be definite, have to be emotionally stimulating—something that turns them on, gets them excited, something that they really want to work for.

To them, goal setting is simply the long-term version of keeping track of time. Seniorpreneurs, more so than entrepreneurs, divide their goals into a lot of different areas, compartmentalize them into both small and large objectives. The goals are long range, while the objectives are intermediate targets with shorter time frames. Above all, they have a deep and firm recognition that goals are attained by action.

Growth Orientation

Very frequently, Seniorpreneurs have worked for large companies. Put another way, they have functioned in aging, mature companies that tend to stifle growth. It is for this reason, coupled with many of their other inherent traits, that they strike out on their own. They see the opposites of growth and aging business traits. They know that success comes from embracing risk, as opposed to avoiding it, that growth power comes from the sales and marketing that drives new companies and not from the controls of finance and legal departments inherent in large established companies. They appreciate value-added profit goals but not political game playing. To them, problems are opportunities.

Growth-oriented Seniorpreneurs are into quality—quality of people, of product, of service, of old-fashioned craftsmanship and caring. They understand that growth results from team building, hero making, by giving responsibility and sharing credit with others. Unlike yesterday's entrepreneurial lone wolf, today's entrepreneur is growth-oriented via people and establishing a growth-oriented organization.

Honesty

Today's buzzword for honesty is *ethics*. Ethics is simply a code of behavior that is governed by morality and law. It is based on a sense of right and wrong that is not dependent on what the law says one can or cannot get away with. Unfortunately, a lot of supposed business leaders and entrepreneurs lost track of many old-fashioned values in the 1980s. Was the cause a reflection of lost values in our society? Or, in some cases, the integration of global practices of many different cultures? The answer lies in the practical reality that humankind best functions when operating under some basic principles. Some things just aren't for sale at any price. Ethical, honest societies, by definition, have high value orientation, high personal standards of integrity, and an orientation toward reliability. They must avoid pursuing a lot of short-term gains in place of long-term successes.

Honesty, ethics, and honor mean taking responsibility that can be costly. You can lose a job, a customer, a supplier, even a lawsuit. But respect goes to those that stand up to their commitments or mistakes. Since Seniorpreneurs don't pass the buck, you know where they stand, and you know you can count on them in the crunch to do the right thing—to be honest.

Innovation

Seniorpreneurs are innovative because they are individuals or are part of small teams, as opposed to bureaucratic, massive projects. Innovation and bureaucracy just don't mix. Bureaucracies seek to minimize and control risk, where true innovation encourages risk. Entrepreneurs, although open to risk, want to hold tight rein over the innovation process and employees who may contribute. Seniorpreneurs manage risks by taking risks on a small scale, encouraging experimentation, and dedicating energy to fixing mistakes instead of finding fault.

Since innovation is making ideas happen, creativity is thinking up new ideas. Without new ideas there can be no great leaps in innovation, and without purposeful execution there can be no innovation. It used to be thought that a person who was creative or innovative had definite inherited or genetic traits. Now it's believed that these qualities can be learned, or at least encouraged.

The ability to create or innovate is not necessarily rare, just generally uncultivated. Creativity is simply thinking and making new discoveries; it is a matter of having reasoning processes and, for most Seniorpreneurs, having the right encyclopedic knowledge. Creativity when combined with innovation is the essence of successful Seniorpreneurship.

Intelligence

While there are many manifestations of intelligence, from advanced degrees to Mensa-level IQs, entrepreneurial intelligence is often thought of as coming from a rational, logical person, one who has the ability to recognize, understand, and analyze complex situations or problems. Often, these situations arise in areas where the Seniorpreneur has a large amount of technical knowledge and expertise or, at minimum, in-depth experience.

This expertise is then coupled with conceptual ability, gut feel, and a major dose of curiosity. Sometimes the creativity or innovation comes quickly, but usually it develops over an extended period of time. This Seniorpreneurial intelligence, blended with many other traits, as well as a recognition of one's own limits, combined with instincts and cunning, come together to create not only a new company, but sometimes whole new industries.

This Seniorpreneurial intelligence needs to be bound to an ability to assess the areas of expertise where one is lacking. Know your own limits and then surround yourself with other intelligent experts. Entrepreneurs often guard their intelligence, while Seniorpreneurs encourage its development.

Another entrepreneurial intelligence component needs to be a keen sense of humor. The pace is too fast, the hours too long, and the stakes too high not to be able to laugh along the way. Summed up, perhaps it's "street smart intelligence."

Leadership

A Seniorpreneurial leader is one who commits people to action. A Seniorpreneurial leader must convert followers into leaders and agents of change. The traits for Seniorpreneurial leadership are:

> *Foresight,* so you can judge how your vision fits the way your organization, and the environment in which it operates, evolves.
>
> *Hindsight,* so your vision doesn't ignore past traditions, business cultures, and mistakes, but still isn't afraid to take major new strides.
>
> *Global view,* so you can interpret the impact of new trends and potential developments.
>
> *Depth perception,* so you can peer into the details without losing sight of the whole.
>
> *Peripheral perception,* so you can track the responses of competitors to your new directions.
>
> *Re-vision,* so you can review your past visions to adapt to current and changing environments.

Seniorpreneurs recognize three leadership qualities. The first is that they know where they are headed. They have the master skills to be the best in their jobs. They carry and display a sense of direction and purpose that comes from addressing the larger questions and deal in the realm of "shoulds." This allows them to pursue lives of deep purpose and direction.

Second, they do things to get where they are headed. They deal in priorities with an end purpose in mind. They have a keen awareness that there are just so many hours in a day and only so many years in a productive life. Where managers do things right, Seniorpreneur leaders do the right things. They ask where they can focus their energies for the greatest results.

The third quality of Seniorpreneur leaders is that they inspire others to do the same—to know directions and use their energies for the best results. Leaders have a deep desire to benefit others and they feel a sense of failure if they succeed without pulling others along the path of success with them. The best leaders inspire people in their organizations with the vision of where they are headed as a group. They also display a caring about how others are growing as individuals.

Risk Tolerance

Risk is exciting—it stimulates "aliveness" in the person or people who are taking the chance. The willingness to take a risk means you are willing to go beyond a familiar niche. To even think about eliminating risk in growing a business is wishful thinking. Risk is inherent in the processes of committing existing resources to future expectations.

Studies have shown that successful entrepreneurial risk takers have a high level of self-confidence. For Seniorpreneurs, this includes a realistic vision of how to achieve objectives. They perceive and make meaningful connections between seemingly unrelated variables and are better able to relate the risk to a specific achievement. They don't enter into risks unless their internal perceptions have told them they can win. Seniorpreneurs don't like risk. The difference is that they understand it, they know how to make it work for them, and instead of intimidating them, it energizes them.

Seniorpreneurs take things in stride. They like risk excitement and aren't concerned with job security and retirement. Risk to them is more than money—it's their reputation that is at stake. They take the plunge in a very calculated, carefully thought-out manner, planning the odds in their favor with carefully defined strategies that include laying onto others as many of the risks as possible. This is accomplished by finding coworkers, investors, suppliers, and customers who are also willing to share in the risks. Sharing in areas and at levels that they are comfortable with, although most of these shared risk takers are also personalities that are seeking to stretch their personal development. All of these points come down to a highly developed, keenly honed level of risk tolerance.

Self-Confidence

Top entrepreneurs have a well-developed concept of self; in other words, they know who they are, they know where they came from, and they have a very good idea of where they are going. Many have suffered some type of identity crisis in their lives. While similar to entrepreneurs, Seniorpreneurs also encounter their share of hardship, but have learned to smooth out the kinks, pound out the rough spots, and become comfortable with the self into which they have evolved. However, they also have a self-awareness that keeps them from falling into the traps of arrogance, overconfidence, and lack of humility. Their aim is to achieve a level of self-knowledge that works well for them.

Self-confidence is the trait of envisioning victory from situations where others see only defeat, to find promise where others find grounds for pessimism, to see opportunity where others see obstacles. Seniorpreneurs have confidence in themselves and believe that they can personally make a major difference in shaping the final outcome of their project and consequently their lives.

Success Qualities

With these basic entrepreneurial characteristics in mind, what success qualities should a Seniorpreneur be trying to cultivate? Here are some answers.

Hard Work

It's never easy getting to the top and it's even tougher staying there. Very few people who have it made on a long-term basis did it without working extremely hard. They worked at least 60-hour weeks with a lot of Saturdays and many long nights. You need a highly cultivated work ethic; you'll never make it on 8-hour days. Eight hours are for survival, and anything over 8 hours is an investment in success.

Enthusiasm

For you, your business has got to be the greatest thing that you can do. Enthusiasm sells, but because once in a while business is tough, your enthusiasm is inclined to wane. This becomes apparent to your coworkers and customers. Maybe you need to take a little time for yourself or to spend "unbusiness involved." Pull back to pull yourself up, to regain your belief and enthusiasm in what you have chosen to do.

Creativity

In today's business world, you have to be creative in all areas. The things you did 5 or 10 years ago won't work today, at least not the same way. You've got to look for and develop new ways, new ideas. Use your imagination to solve problems and generate solutions. Cookie cutter and one-size-fits-all approaches don't work. Customize and innovate.

Flexibility

Adapt to change. It's a key characteristic because business is evolving and changing so rapidly. The market is always doing different things and there are new twists to learn. Look forward to change; welcome it with open arms. Sometimes it's hard to accept, but today, flexibility is a way of life and a Seniorpreneurial must.

Empathy

It is important that you show empathy to your coworkers, employees, suppliers, and most important, your customers. Everyone wants someone to understand and acknowledge their problems, maybe even display some empathy. People want someone to care about them, to be kind to them, to show some interest, build a relationship, or offer a solution. Empathy and kindness never go out of style; in today's cold, sometimes hard business world, it's a Seniorpreneurial key to success.

Knowledge

Knowledge in Seniorpreneurland is not power, but potential power. You must have the knowledge base, coupled with conviction and enthusiasm, to sell your dream. You've got to spend time and effort, on a continuing basis, obtaining more knowledge to be able to offer viable solutions to problems. Knowledge helps solve problems and problem solving is another key to Seniorpreneurial success.

Differentiating Factors

Along these same lines, what might be some of the factors that differentiate between entrepreneurs and successful Seniorpreneurs? These would include:

Entrepreneur	Seniorpreneur
First-time start-up	Prior start-up experience
Not sure where to go for advice	Knows where to seek advice
Doesn't know what advice is needed	Knows what specific advice is needed
Feels competent in all areas	Feels weak in certain areas
Seeks professional help in response to problems	Seeks professional help in anticipation of problems

Lacks key skills in industry	Has acquired key skills
Operations-oriented	Total business–oriented
Fairly well educated	Slightly better educated

These are the success qualities and some interesting factors for Seniorpreneurs. Study, absorb, learn, and above all, put them into practice.

An Age-Old Debate

Morris Massey is the creator of a videocassette entitled "What You Are Is Who You Were When." In some ways, it addresses an age-old debate as to who makes better entrepreneurs: the young with youthful drive and determination, or the older with experience and organizational and managerial skills?

Risk Is Back

Massey feels that what was right for entrepreneurs 20 years ago may not be right today, "A lot of entrepreneurs are not risk-oriented or aggressive in terms of research and development." He's right; risk-free orientation won't work in the 1990s, because opportunities change too quickly and the markets are characterized by world mushrooming competition. The Seniorpreneurial 1990s risk is team-oriented.

He also maintains that it's not age that determines people's belief systems or values, but "when we grew up." He contends that what was reality then remains reality now.

There Are Four Generations of Risk Takers

Massey suggests there are four different generations in the entrepreneurial field today: the olagers, in-betweeners, nuagers, and synthesizers.

The olagers, early fifties plus, tend to be conservative and traditional. They identify with their jobs, and their underlying belief system says, "He who dies with the most toys wins." As children of the Depression, the olagers consider overtime work an opportunity.

The in-betweeners, early forties to early fifties, believe you can have your cake and eat it too. They may be former hippies (thus challengers) with a foot still in the traditionalists' camp. They are the flip-flop group. They have been in midlife crisis since puberty and still can't make choices. They want choices, but can't make decisions.

Next are the baby boomers, the nuagers, late twenties to early forties. If you didn't like the above descriptions, wait till you read this. Nuagers are like the cast of the TV series *thirtysomething*. They talk, talk, talk, but never do anything. They grew up challenging the olagers establishment; however, they are not particularly responsible. They want "balance." Massey says, "They want to make it, but they don't want to sacrifice in order to get it." They consider overtime work an infringement, not an opportunity.

Last, and surprisingly not the least desirable entrepreneurial candidates, are the synthesizers. They're what's left, the group in its early twenties, currently called "Generation X."

They grew up in the decade of the 1980s when the most current entrepreneurial boom got its start. Massey feels this group is comprised of "responsibility-focused individuals." Assuming he means both female and male, he feels they have a "deep belief in themselves and a purpose in life." Recognize they grew up with the computer as a toy and consequently can synthesize many variables at once—an acknowledged entrepreneurial trait. Also remember they grew up in a time of major upheaval in the employment markets when a lot of traditional industries started to restructure.

Could their marching tune be, "We want success, and the best way to get it is by becoming entrepreneurs"? They grew up knowing, reading, hearing, seeing, and using—first-hand—the entrepreneurial success tools of the 1980s—Apple computers and Microsoft computer software. Those two companies' founders have become very rich, famous, and powerful heros for the synthesizers.

I doubt the age-old debate can be answered yet. But there's a lot of persuasive evidence beginning to surface that the olagers' theme song of "experience is what counts" is going flat. This is unless Seniorpreneurs make a concerted effort to stay abreast of the latest in technology advances, especially as pertains to their areas of expertise, as well as continue on a lifelong learning quest.

Seniorpreneurs Build a Mixed Team

While Seniorpreneurs have to have energy—a fire in their belly—a little gray on the sides indicates there's some season there. I'm tempted to wonder if the "risk-it-all attitude" is still valid. Then again, youth is being cocky and feeling that success always goes on. But in truth, Seniorpreneurs realize that business success comes in periods, no one does well all the time, and a big key is being prepared and then capitalizing on the opportunity, whether by chance or choice.

Actually, I suspect that the successful entrepreneurial team, perhaps led by a synthesizer, managed by an in-betweener, marketed by a nuager, and guided by an olager is probably the winning team for this decade.

Passion

The Seniorpreneur has one final characteristic that sets him or her apart from ordinary mortals. It's *passion*. And it's a passion of love. Seniorpreneurs won't succeed at anything that they don't love. Sure, they have a lot of help making a decision. But in the final analysis, they make the decision, they live with the problems, they make it work. Mainly because they have the key ingredients—the passionate desire and motivation—to face the situation and see it through.

In short, few start-ups or Seniorpreneurial ventures succeed without this passion. Yes it's true, many passionate entrepreneurs fail, and even some would-be Seniorpreneurs. But that's not the point. Almost none succeed without passion. Seniorpreneurs follow their hearts toward things they care about. How else can you expect to succeed if it's an area that doesn't move you? Simply, if you're a Seniorpreneur, you'll do what turns you on. That's how you capture Seniorpreneurial passion.

Successful Senior Entrepreneurs

The concept of seniors as entrepreneurs is new. However, the many examples of senior success are fact. This section tells some brief stories about usually well-known senior entrepreneurs. But you'll also find several who aren't so well known. A point of interest is that most of their stories now seem sure things, natural ideas for success. Nonetheless, keep in mind that at the time they formed their respective enterprises, the driving concept was usually not well accepted. They had studied the trends and became forerunners of change. You'll also notice that there is not much common ground for their businesses. They cover a wide range of entrepreneurial endeavors.

Roy Carver—Bandag Tires

He owned a villa in Cannes, France, and a 125-foot yacht with a helicopter landing pad as well as his own personal jet. He had built a worldwide business, from his headquarters in Muscatine, Iowa, which afforded him those luxuries. It all started when, at age 48, he acquired the rights from a European inventor to a new method of manufacturing tire retreads, mostly for trucks.

At age 54, after 7 years of continuing research and the expenditures of enough money to almost bankrupt his existing Carver Pump Company, he and his team of engineers finally figured out the keys to solve some sticky scientific and technical production problems. Then all that was left was to convince large users of retread tires that they should pay almost twice as much for his tires over competitive products. He did this by summoning a lot of marketing ingenuity. As an example, he offered to sell his tire at $20, about the same price as the competition, if the buyer agreed to pay an additional $20 each time a Bandag tire equaled the milage of the buyer's previous retreads. Since his often lasted three to five times as long, the customers quickly agreed to pay his $40 asking price.

Carver's Bandag, Inc. went from $3 million in sales to over $70 million in 9 years, and today has made many of his dealers millionaires.

Marion Isbell—Ramada Inns

In 1959, at age 54, Marion Isbell convinced a group of investors to consolidate their existing motel operations into one single chain. Two years later, when he was 56, this small chain of 25 motels became Ramada Inns. The company went international and also was listed on the New York Stock Exchange (NYSE) 10 years later when Isbell was 66.

Ramada Inns' head-to-head competition was Holiday Inn, established by 39-year-old Charles Kemmons Wilson in 1952. Ramada Inns' distinction was its restaurants, aimed at serving the general population as well as the motel guest. By the time Ramada Inns listed on the NYSE, its food and beverage sales accounted for 27 percent of total revenues. When Isbell retired at age 68, there were over 700 Ramada Inns worldwide.

When referring to hard work, which he felt was a key to his success, Isbell stated, "You can't learn it from books, and you can't learn it from school. It's something that's got to be burning inside of you."

Lowell Paxson and Roy Speer—Home Shopping Network, Inc.

Okay, fess up. Even if you haven't bought anything from Home Shopping Network (HSN), I'm sure you've been captivated by it on TV. The show and process were the general public's first exposure to the new world of "interactive media." Right there before your eyes, supplemented by enticing dialogue, was "such a deal." Millions of Americans pick up the phone and fork over hundreds of millions of dollars for TV merchandise. Paxson and Speer are the ones who brought it to you in the first place.

When they took their company public in 1986, Paxton was 52 and Speer was 56. Opening day, their stock started trading at $18 and closed at over $42. Not bad for a 4-year-old company whose 1986 sales were $160 million with $17 million in net earnings. In retrospect, their secret was simple. Unlike other TV merchandisers, HSN made it easy to purchase. Simply call the toll-free number listed on the screen, place an order, and purchase with a credit card or send a check. With the claim that merchandise was offered for up to 70 percent off retail, who could resist?

Paxson and Speer brought the shopping mall to your house. They added a lot of show-biz glitz and do it around the clock. Paxson summed it up by stating: "What happens is, you watch, we create a need and then, hopefully we fill it." I sum it up as Seniorpreneuring "street smarts."

Anthony Rossi—Tropicana Juice

At age 78, Tony Rossi finally accepted an offer he had rejected three times from the giant food processor Kellog's, and sold Tropicana Juice for $495 million. The third time, just a year prior, the offer had been $382 million. A hundred million isn't bad extra profit for holding out for a year when you're over 75.

Intense devotion to every aspect of his business was his secret. He attempted to control every aspect of his operations by owning the subsidiary businesses. From the processing plants to the packaging suppliers to the shipping (literally via company-owned ocean-going tankers), he designed and owned the equipment needed to supply the best orange juice available on the market.

Before Rossi patented an aseptic vacuum-packing method, orange juice drinkers outside the citrus belt could get it only by squeezing their own oranges. Rossi, starting as a small store grocer, brought orange juice to the masses and used his considerable fortune to fund his Aurora Foundation. His "code list" for success was: ambition, persistence, creativity, and common sense.

Carl Sontheimer—Cuisinart, Inc.

Sontheimer retired, at age 55, in 1969. That lasted about 2 years. One of Carl's sayings was, "If you aren't passionate...don't even bother." One of his passions was cooking and while attending a trade show in France, he acquired the sole U.S. importer rights to a food processor he would name "Cuisinart." It took another 2 years to gain U.S. "UL approval" along with a dozen patent improvements to the original design.

Sontheimer eventually gained all the rights to Cuisinart, but the path took some interesting entrepreneurial twists. One was when a dock strike completely dried up his product supply at Christmas time. His solution, when he held 60 percent market share with a product priced at almost twice the competition, was to market a gift box with a certificate promising delivery at a later date at a price of $225. That's called Seniorpreneuring passion at its best.

William Gore—Gore-tex

The first field test of what would become famous as Gore-tex laminated fabrics took place when Bill, age 58, and his wife used it on a tent camping trip in Wyoming. The first tent didn't pass all the tests, but it provided the basis to continue experiments to perfect the process. W. L. Gore & Associates, although generally known for its laminated fabrics, has seen success as a major manufacturer of synthetic fibers. Gore-sponsored products are used in astronaut suits, sportswear, vascular grafts for arteries, artificial heart valves, and artificial knee ligaments. The Gore-tex material is accepted by the body as natural tissue grows into its open pore spaces.

As if the Gore-tex product line is not enough, Bill Gore also conceived an unusual company operating style. There are no traditional management charts with a president followed by various vice presidents and officers and then a long list of lesser employees that would be typical for a company that earns multimillion dollars a year in annual revenues. Highly unstructured with no titles, no rank of command, and lots of voluntary job commitments, Gore's "lattice organization" features "associates" who create their own job descriptions. They form teams, set mutual goals, and let natural leaders evolve.

His management structure is not without problems, and it takes a while for employees to adjust. Gore states, "Hierarchical structures stifle freedom and creativity. People will be tremendously productive and innovative when they are given the opportunity to exercise their talents freely. Our associates are probably twice as productive and three times as creative as people in other companies because they have more freedom." This may not work for you, but as a Seniorpreneur, you may wish to devise a management structure (or unstructure) that fits our new technology encompassing work life. Gore provides an example that you can skin (or Gore-tex) a cat in many ways, including the company environment in which its done.

John Hanson—Winnebago Motor Homes

Although it wasn't the first equity money for Winnebago Industries, John Hanson took his company public, at age 52. An initial $1000 investment became worth $1 million in 6 years. John semiretired 6 years later but just couldn't stay out of the action. He came back at age 65 and resumed control.

When John was questioned if he could have started his company when he was younger, he stated, "Impossible. Not enough knowledge, experience. It would have been an absolute no-no." That's an endorsement for Seniorpreneuring if I've even heard one.

The point that these Seniorpreneurs *started* their companies at these usually thought of as older ages is important. Many didn't reach "success" for 5 to 10 years *after* founding. Here are a few more examples of Seniorpreneuring in action.

It Takes All Kinds

George Demestral, when in his sixties, was pulling burrs out of the coat of his hunting dog. The result was the thistlelike surface now called "Velcro," used in hundreds of everyday products to hold or close.

William Hersey had his book *Hersey's Short Course for Short Memories* published by Prentice-Hall on his fifty-third birthday. It went on to sell hundreds of thousands of copies.

Helen Santmyer became famous at the age of 88 when her 1300 page book *And the Ladies of the Club* was chosen as the main selection of the Book of the Month Club.

Julia Montgomery Walsh was in her late fifties when she started her own investment firm with three sons (Julia Walsh and Sons). When she sold it, the firm employed 35 brokers with over 4000 accounts.

Judy Reis liked to cook. In her fifties, she opened a restaurant, which went on to become one of Chicago's finest. And speaking of Chicago, department store founder *Louis Goldblatt* retired at age 69 and then started an artificial-flower-marketing company that grew to over $35 million in annual sales.

Mary Rittenhouse, at age 59, founded Part-Time Parents, a baby-sitting service that employed women who sought part-time work. It went on to expand to provide care for invalids and semi-invalids. She ran the company well into her eighties.

Coralee Kern was in her fifties when she formed Maid to Order, a domestic house-cleaning service. Divorced with two children at home, Coralee was told by her doctor that she was too ill to go out and earn a living. Her cleaning service idea provided her with a nice retirement.

At age 63, *Florence Butcher* started a tour group company. Over the next 23 years, she arranged 130 tours all over the United States, and her last trip was at age 86.

We can't leave out *Colonel Harlan Sanders*, who at age 72, started Kentucky Fried Chicken.

What do all these senior entrepreneurs have in common?

Senior Assets

Senior entrepreneurs have one distinct advantage over other entrepreneurs: *senior assets*. Senior assets advance the successfulness of Seniorpreneurs. They provide senior entrepreneurs with a multiplicity of advantages. These senior assets, identified as "age assets" by Joseph and Suzy Fucini in their book *Experience Inc.* (Free Press, 1987) are commitment, confidence, freedom, insider's knowledge, objectivity, reputation, resiliency, and resourcefulness. They set the scene for Golden Entrepreneuring.

Commitment

The Seniorpreneur, with years of business experience, is better able to define precise goals and make realistic projections about the time, effort, and capital required to achieve success. Because of this experience and realism in accessing the challenges, they are able to approach their businesses with a deeper sense of commitment than younger entrepreneurs.

Confidence

Seniorpreneurs, because they have a track record of successful accomplishments upon which to build, hold a deeper level of self-confidence in their ability to pursue their projects. On the basis of this high level of confidence, they feel they can accomplish the tasks before they make the commitment.

Freedom

Seniorpreneurs have several distinct advantages that many younger entrepreneurs are lacking in that they have a higher level of financial freedom, less worries over career commitments, and their child-bearing responsibilities are for the most part past. These freedoms allow a higher level of risk taking from a less incumbered personal position.

Insider's Knowledge

A large majority of senior entrepreneurs tend to get involved in an industry with which they have had a great deal of experience. This intimate familiarity with an industry's inner workings allows them to recognize emerging trends and opportunities before less experienced entrepreneurs see them coming.

Objectivity

Nothing teaches like experience, and age gives us a more realistic view of ours and others' limitations. Because of this hard-earned objectivity, senior entrepreneurs are much more likely to team up with and seek outside advice with other professionals to complement their own expertise.

Reputation

With longer career histories, Seniorpreneurs have had more opportunities to build strong and abiding professional reputations than younger entrepreneurs. This is a valuable asset in attracting both employees and investors.

Resiliency

Seniors have seen it all, or at least weathered more ups and downs than young entrepreneurs. This gives Seniorpreneurs an overview that makes them able to see beyond temporary setbacks and better equipped to bounce back from mistakes, which can then be turned into additional learning experiences.

Resourcefulness

Resourcefulness is what sets entrepreneurs apart from other mortals, and Seniorpreneurs are granted an extra dose of "street smarts." It's the best way to sum up the experience that allows Seniorpreneurs to reach into their repertoire and extract innovative solutions to their business challenges.

It's not that younger entrepreneurs don't also have some of these assets; it's just that experience is usually present in much greater depth in the combination of senior assets. As an example, younger entrepreneurs may have a deep sense of commitment, but they usually lack the strong professional reputation that makes the difference in getting the tasks accomplished quicker and more efficiently. Senior assets make Golden Entrepreneurs really shine.

Seniors Are Better Qualified for Entrepreneurship

Seniors are well qualified to undertake entrepreneurship for many reasons.

- Past education and experience help them find and identify better opportunities faster.
- They are not as likely to get caught up in just the national and international headset, and they pay more attention to the many local opportunities around them.
- Their experience in "knowing the road" allows them to travel it faster, with fewer mistakes.
- Having been around a little longer, seniors frequently have made more contacts that give them greater access to capital.
- Having a more settled lifestyle and being more financially secure means that many seniors have smaller salary needs.
- Having a broader perspective on life and business, seniors are more likely to seek outside counsel than younger "know-it-all" entrepreneurs.

- Senior entrepreneurs are likely to have larger, higher quality, better formed networking contacts. They know people with both knowledge and skills.

The rewards of Golden Entrepreneuring are many and include:

Enhances lifestyle

Increases income—part and full time

Creates a sense of belonging

Promotes accomplishment and continued learning

Broadens horizons and outlooks

Creates great opportunities for new friends and acquaintances—even prospective mates

Improves physical activity

Raises return on investment—possibly higher than going market rates

Why Seniors Are Taking to Entrepreneuring

At the beginning of this chapter, I made the statement that there is no definitive set of characteristics to describe an entrepreneur. I then went on to set out a number of characteristics that have proven common to many entrepreneurs. I also offered some stories of successful senior entrepreneurs and explored some of the assets that distinguish seniors for entrepreneurship. When you combine all these points, it's easy to see that entrepreneurs come in all shapes, styles, and sizes. The same holds true for Seniorpreneurs—with one exception.

Seniorpreneurs have the major advantage of street smarts. Their experience elevates them above younger entrepreneurs. It gives them advantages and affords them opportunity. How they choose to use their senior street smarts is up to them individually. However, it's difficult to deny that having senior street smarts isn't a major positive for seniors to take to entrepreneuring.

3
The Problems (as They Are Perceived)— and Advantages— in Senior Entrepreneuring

The Beginnings of a National Challenge

When we think of seniors, the images we most often conjure up is that of gray or no hair, stooped over with a cane or in a wheelchair, slow thinking and even slower body movements. The challenge is to continue to dispel this thinking.

As mentioned in Chapter 1, the country may have to support a campaign to break the concept of seniors into two broadly defined age groups: those aged 50 to 70 known as *junior seniors,* and the balance over 70 known as *seniors.* Obviously, even this can be treading on thin ice, as we all know of 80-plus-year-old seniors who are healthier and mentally quicker than most 30 year olds.

Many, many people know about an organization called AARP (American Association of Retired Persons). Few recognize that the lower age limit to be a member of AARP is 50. Even fewer yet know that 47 percent of AARP's current 33 million members are from 50 to age 64!

That's 15 million people (currently thought of as seniors) who fall under the common "retirement" age of 65. And starting right about now, there are 76 million baby boomers who are about to turn 50. It's *guaranteed* that they don't think, and won't accept, that they are "seniors" in our present context of "old age." The traditional thoughts and feelings about what age is old is changing. People at age 50 are definitely not "seniors" in the traditional sense, and people at 65 are not old seniors in today's and tomorrow's societal values.

Older workers are mature. We're responsible, we have most of our family problems behind us, we aren't hindered by children who need daily care, we've been around and appreciate what it takes to run a company or provide for jobs. We have a good attitude and don't think the world owes us a living.

Many of the "new seniors" are people who have been downsized with lots of energy, money, health, and ambition—people who are seeking a new way of life. They are fed up with the "security" of large corporations and now are considering the security of entrepreneurship. Hopefully, this book will help change our society's attitude about "seniors" as well as be the initial guidebook for our burgeoning Seniorpreneurial effort.

The Perception Is Changing

Parade, New York, publishers of the Sunday supplement magazine *Parade*, conducted a national survey in July 1993 that conformed to the U.S. census data for men and women aged 18 to 75.

They asked the question "What does it mean to be old?" Sixty-six percent, which is two-thirds, said old age begins at 70. Twenty-eight percent considered 80 and older as old. Not surprisingly, among those over 65, only 8 percent thought of 65 as old, while those under 25 said old is 40 to 60.

Interestingly, and contrary to the general movement in the business world, 93 percent said that if healthy, the elderly should be allowed to work as long as they choose. Ninety-one percent said that Americans don't take advantage of age and experience. That finding was reinforced by 96 percent expressing that they thought young people could learn from the elderly, and 87 percent thought that there was too much emphasis on youth.

Old Perceptions Die Hard

Age is an attitude and most seniors realize this. How seniors deal with age is also an attitude, and the prevailing attitudes about seniors are changing. However, some stereotypes remain, and they must be confronted by seniors contemplating entrepreneuring. These preconceived attitudes include that seniors are set in their ways, inflexible, opinionated, unable to change, and have values so diverse from today's youth that there is an ever-widening generation gap.

Each of us can relate to some if not all of these perceptions. We've thought or felt some of them personally—especially as applied to our own parents or elderly friends and acquaintances. While many are true characteristics, and others are stereotypes, they aren't necessarily representative of the new crop of seniors. Nevertheless, old ideas pass hard, and a Seniorpreneuring challenge is to work to dispel what I consider to be modern-day myths. In the next section, we'll explore some of the above perceived problems and discover how they really are myths.

Problems Turned to Myths

Set in Their Ways, Inflexible, Unable to Change

I had an occasion several years ago to get involved with a project that is typical of a lot of today's existing senior company owners. Two gentlemen, both in their mid-fifties, had very successfully founded and operated their company for almost 20 years. It had provided both of them with a much better than average monetary lifestyle. They had worked very hard at their business when they were younger, and it had paid off handsomely. At the time I met them, they were in the process of selling their 50/50 mutually owned company. Why were they selling? Health concerns and feeling overwhelmed were the main reasons they gave. Wanting a different lifestyle which allowed them more leisure was another.

But to my way of thinking, the primary reason was burnout. As I got to know both of them better over our 2 plus years of negotiations, I came to believe it was their inability to cope with a changing business environment. Their business had become very highly regulated, more than most. They had strict FDA rules to comply with, and they had state and local regulations within which they had to operate. As with all businesses, they had federal, state, and local tax laws to observe. But the one issue that really got to them was the increasingly complex environmental regulations.

There's more. These gentlemen operated seven sites in five different states plus their headquarters in a sixth state. Their business required an immense amount of detailed daily paperwork—a lot of forms that had to be filled out, filed, turned into the home office, and refiled with the various governing bodies they reported to. They also had to track a detailed site-specific client list which was tied into a national database. But do you know, even though they did a super job with maintaining paperwork compliance, it was all done by hand. Not one fax machine, not one modem, in fact not even one PC computer throughout their whole operation. Imagine, a multimillion-dollar enterprise in 1992 that hadn't entered the modern world of time- and labor-saving new technology devices. Bottom line, here were two seniors who hadn't faced up to changing times and innovations that could have resulted in even more profit and perhaps even extended their productive business life. Thank goodness for them, they had made enough money and invested it wisely so that they could live very comfortably. It is my estimate that over the last 5 years of their operations, and considering the price that they finally sold their company for, they lost at least $6 million because of their resistance to change.

As senior entrepreneurs, we need to guard against this resistance to change. The reality, at age 50, of having 20 years of very productive life remaining leaves us with little choice. Simply remember what your work life consisted of 10 years ago, how daily duties were executed, and what job devices were at your disposal. Maybe this job you had 10 years ago doesn't even exist today. All this points to the fact that learning new job skills is now a daily, ongoing process. It means that Seniorpreneurs have to go back to school, learn new skills, update existing knowledge, read, listen to tapes, ask questions, and generally be on a constant search for knowledge.

Being Opinionated

If you want an opinion, if you really want to know how to do it right—in fact, the only way—ask a teenager. Teenagers know it all. Right after the teenager is a senior. All seniors have strong opinions on just about everything, as opposed to teenagers on "everything." For seniors, this may be rightly so. They have lived through a lot and have a databank of personal experiences to back up their opinions.

But Seniorpreneurs are different. They're a little mellower. Sure they have opinions, but the wise ones know to research the subject matter a little deeper before strongly voicing their opinion. They recognize that in our fast-paced society, they may have missed some development that can affect their decision. This doesn't mean that they are not strong-willed. They are and they have a right to be. It's just that Seniorpreneurs are into teamwork and team sharing and team building. They may voice their opinion. However, in many cases, their interest is in building shared opinions, seeking a consensus for the best possible customer and company building solution.

The Generation Gap

Let's take a look at some icons of the different generations. Try spiked purple hair, earrings, and baggy pants with a waistline below the hips. Or BMWs, vacation condos, and gold credit cards. Then there were gold chains with Nehru jackets, guitars and love-ins, free-speech and hippies. And who can forget the Beatles and Woodstock, Elvis and ducktails with sideburns, Frank Sinatra, the crooners, and big bands? Do these help you identify with generation gaps? Haven't you been a part of these from both sides?

Seniors are frequently accused of not only not understanding the generations that follow, but of also not caring about the youth of today. If this applies to you, change is essential to achieve Seniorpreneurial success. Seniorpreneurs need to work with people of all ages in many ways which include as employers, coworkers, suppliers, and customers.

Some of our current generations pose greater challenges than others. We seniors can contend with the baby boomers who are directly behind us. We've been living with them for quite a while now. We know that they will soon catch up with us in their more conservative thinking and actions.

The thirtysomething generation is pretty quiet and passive compared with the enormity of numbers represented by the boomers. But the next generation is really a puzzle.

Generation X Is Upon Us. Generation X, as they're being called, are today's late teens to age 30. They are perhaps the most difficult to understand. They are comprised of the smallest group of entry-level workers in American business in 50 years. They also face what is described as "McJob" entry-level jobs—low-paying jobs requiring minimal skills.

How They're Perceived. Many surveys have shown that Gen Xers are perceived as self-centered, not wanting to work hard, not willing to pay their dues, aren't loyal, and want something for nothing. Expert opinion suggests that they got this way for several reasons. As youngsters, they were told to stay out of the way...while the older people were doing more important things, like finding themselves. They were cheated out of time with their parents, who were consumed by career ambitions. Quality time to them was a few hours on weekends. Now they want quantity time—they don't want to live to work, and they want time to do things they really enjoy. They don't harbor the boomer's rebellion against authority; rather, it's a cynical feeling of disdain and distrust.

The predictions are that the Gen Xers, as they advance to leadership positions, will refocus politics on the rootless poor, restrengthen the American family with a commitment to traditional values, and emerge as no-nonsense, conservative, political leaders. They will make up for what they didn't have as children and favor investment over consumption, endowments over entitlements, the needs of the very young over the needs of the very old.

The Value They Contribute. I suggest the Gen Xers bring some valuable viewpoints to business. They are more realistic and practical than some previous generations. They recognize that for the first time in American history they may not be as successful as their parents—in monetary terms. They have grown up in the information age and this has made them pretty savvy consumers and market-wise employees; they're not easily fooled. They have a high level of awareness of environmental issues and God knows, they know a lot more about computers than we'll ever pick up—not to mention possessing a higher comfortability level in using and accessing high technology.

How to Relate. Our Seniorpreneuring challenge is to learn to identify with them, and here are some hints. Remain flexible. They're a generation starved for attention; they'll respond well to your spending some extra time with them. Get them involved, and let them know they have an impact. Listen to their ideas and you'll be rewarded with productive and happy employees. Beside that, you'll learn something and that's what successful Seniorpreneuring is all about.

Adapting to Technology

Fax machines, cellular phones, personal pagers, PC computers, the Infobahn: the buzzwords of new technologies, the bane of seniors. How do we cope with all these advances that seem to pop into our lives, especially in the business world, on almost a daily basis? The technology changes seem to move so quickly and indeed they do.

In the high-tech hardware world, a new piece of equipment takes a year to design and ready for production. During its first year in the market, it is purchased by users who pride themselves in staying state-of-the-art and who pay a premium to do so. The second year, the average consumer/user who stays state-of-the-industry comes on board and pays an average of 30 percent less than the previous year. By year three, the product is frequently on its last leg, discounted 60 percent from its introductory price, and most likely 50 percent slower, less efficient, or less capable than this year's state-of-the-art equipment. By year four, the product is almost useless, and the dealers won't even service it—doomed to the closet like eight-track tapes and PC-ATs.

Seniors, brought up with a World War II mentality of conserving and finding a use for everything, "recycled" as much as possible before the word became popular simply because we were taught and forced to conserve. We have a tough time walking out of a room and leaving a 60-watt bulb burning. Now we're supposed to leave our offices at night with an energy-consuming computer and monitor left on.

The changes are difficult to face, much less accept. But as Seniorpreneurs, we must learn to accept these changes, especially with technology used in the workplace. We've learned, usually quite readily, to accept "fast-food" and 7/11 stores. The primary reason is that they are a convenience or a time saver for us. They allow us to satisfy a hunger pain, grab a quick bottle of aspirin, and still make the first inning of our kid's or grandkid's Little League game.

If we approach the new technologies with the same mindset of benefits as fast-food and convenience stores, it helps posture new technologies. They also save us time. If anyone should be able to value saved time, it should be seniors. We need to take advantage of every time-saving device we can identify. If it makes our jobs easier, takes out the drudgery of routine, so much the better. And that's just what a lot of the new business appliances do: save time, eliminate routine tasks, simplify fact and data finding, crunch numbers quickly, and transmit and process paper and information as well as voice contact faster. The bonus is more time to use our "white-haired wisdom." Seniorpreneurs take the time to learn how to use new business technologies to their advantage.

Advantages of Age

Some sage said that problems are really opportunities in disguise. We've just explored some of the more common so-called problems for seniors in entrepreneuring. Let's look at some of the considerable opportunities or advantages in undertaking an entrepreneurial effort as a senior.

Prudence

Most of us over 50 have been through some major times of recession. Maybe not monetary depression, but at minimum, periods in our personal life where money was in very short supply, ofttimes, not by our own cause. It could have been a temporary layoff or a sizable period between jobs, or when a spouse was unemployed when least expected. As a consequence, we have learned how to do with less and stretch out limited resources. We know that lean times sometimes happen and we don't panic. We simply dig in and wait out the slow period with prudence.

Delayed Gratification

Along with this prudence, seniors also understand the meaning of "delayed gratification." Most of us have had money responsibilities long before today's easy credit. We can all remember that when you wanted to buy something, the normal practice was to save for it, to put forth some extra effort, build some desire to seek a monetary goal that required some continuing effort to achieve. This carries over to many other areas of life and reinforces patience, persistence, and the rewards of delayed gratification.

Patience and Persistence

Senior patience levels can frequently overcome the younger generation's higher energy levels. Patience comes with years of living and experience. It is the recognition that things don't always happen the way we want, when we want. Persistence is another learned trait. It's stick-to-it-ivity that is earned by patience, and both are desired and needed to succeed entrepreneurially.

Money Smarts

Seniors usually have some extra money set aside that can be used as start-up capital. Frequently it's used to kick-start a project. Maybe it's used to support the due diligence stage of investigating the feasibility of an endeavor. It may not be an actual investment and can be used in the form of reduced or no wages during the start-up period or during the always common cashflow crunches that go with entrepreneuring.

An item that is just as important as actual money can be the fact that other major cash drains have passed. Those like children who are reared and gone. It's not only the expense of supporting kids, but also the distraction. With this distraction out of our daily lives, it leaves more room for concentration on the business at hand. This higher level of concentration with fewer disruptions can enable us seniors to progress toward the stated goals faster, thus saving some more financial expenditures.

Contacts

There's one other area that can be applied to money smarts. It's the old adage: it's not what you know, but who you know.

The senior advantage here is that with 20 to 30 years of business activity, one should have a good Rolodex. This is a valuable asset which enables you to make more contacts easily, access some at higher levels, and tap your established lines of influence. It's sort of like cashing in on some old chits.

Customer Service

It may sound old fashioned to refer to "old-fashioned customer service." However, the trend is back. Companies of all sizes are making a lot of noise about their service. We seniors can remember living in those days, of enjoying the fact that someone seemed to care about us as individual customers. We can also remember the withdrawal and sense of frustration we felt when self-service became the "in" method of merchandising and sales. As seniors we have a big step up on younger generations which don't have an appreciation of the subtleties of providing and receiving good customer service. With a society that rightfully continues to improve and employ the technology of computerized customer tracking, the time has returned to personalize and improve old-fashioned customer service, backed by superior technology.

Success Wisdom

Many seniors who are undertaking Seniorpreneuring have already been successful in their business lives—some as owners, some as managers, and some as responsible employees. We have learned what makes a successful business and what works for us as individuals. Seniors are better at communicating—making ourselves clearly understood. It's a wisdom that is learned and earned through many experiences in life in general as well as business life. Success wisdom gives one the power to judge more correctly, follow a sound business course of action, eliminate many previous mistakes, and reach our entrepreneurial goals faster and in a more personally rewarding fashion.

Work Ethic

Seniors have been taught to work hard. This work ethic says that a day's pay deserves a full day's work. Good or bad, it's ingrained in our generation of senior workers.

Conclusions

The general populous is adapting to the fact that the old perceptions of seniors are changing. We're recognizing that 65 isn't old anymore, that retirement should be an individual choice, that semiretirement is commonly desired, and that lifelong learning is truly replacing early-life learning.

We seniors have learned that attitude really does affect one's outlook on every level, that today's extended life usefulness means that we must cultivate our desire and ability to be flexible in our opinions, adjust our understanding and caring capacity for younger generations, and strive to accommodate new technology. The result of these attitude changes coupled with such senior attributes as patience, persistence, contacts, and a strong work ethic will continue to open everyone's eyes to the value of Seniorpreneuring. It's all part of your work smarts, street smarts senior advantage.

4
Senior Entrepreneurial Opportunities Abound

Let's contemplate the possibilities. Look at the convergence of new industries: information, CATV, electronics, digital (computers + software), telephony (TV + phones), edu-tainment, electronic board rooms. We can even throw in some more specifics: interactive cable, CD-ROM, fax machines, portable/personal everything (phones, faxes, pagers, computers, day-timers), high-resolution TV, and we haven't even walked into the kitchen yet (new-style sinks).

When we look at the end results, we find that these new industries come about from recognizing a need—or creating a need—to serve the desires of users, customers, everyday homemakers, and businesspeople. The fulfilling of such a need makes our lives simpler, helps us get more control over our home and work environments, or connect with other people and places. This fulfilled need expands our choices in where we live, how we work, how we look after children and elderly parents, and how we manage other demands of our modern life.

Even with this short but mind-expanding list, we haven't included a whole potpourri of ordinary everyday business opportunities. Simple but much-needed businesses like boutique retail stores, computer data entry, simple home services such as lawn mowing or window washing, apartment finders, secretarial services, household appliance repair, or just a plain old-fashioned auto mechanic who can tell us that the strange noise we hear isn't our car's computer about to fall out onto the street.

If you'd like to further boggle your mind with the overwhelming number of possibilities, grab the Yellow Pages for any reasonably sized city. You know, one that's 3 inches thick. Mine, for Denver, interestingly, begins with "Abdominal Supports"—which you almost need to lift its 2104 plus pages. It ends with a listing for Zoos, which is preceded by "Zippers—Repair." Now I never thought about there being a place of business listed in the Yellow Pages showing me where I could get a zipper repaired. Spend a half-hour paging through your Yellow Book. I guarantee that besides getting your fingers all black, you'll be absolutely amazed at the different types of entrepreneurial endeavors we have in any city in this country.

The biggest problem that the senior contemplating entrepreneuring faces is the selection of a business enterprise from the vast number of choices. This chapter intends to assist you in identifying opportunities and assessing your skill levels and the skills you may need to operate a new endeavor.

Small Is Back

For America, small was beautiful well into this century. We were a country built on individual proprietorships, small shop owners, small family-owned businesses and farms. Then we turned to worship big—big business, big corporations, big farms, and big problems. Now the worm is turning again.

Between 1980 and 1990 the *Fortune* 500 companies shed some 3.5 million jobs. At the same time, our economy created some 23 million jobs. So while big was shedding, small was gaining in a big way. In a closed economy in which smaller companies depend on larger companies as customers, the decline of large businesses could be serious. But America is no longer a closed economy. Small companies are now just as likely to be exporters and even more likely to be innovators than large ones. Now it is possible to produce a product anywhere, using resources from anywhere, by a company located anywhere, to be sold anywhere.

The 1980s saw a return to entrepreneurship. There has been a continuing increase in new incorporations. Where many small companies used to be founded because the entrepreneur had a long-term vision of what might be, today a large number of companies are started out of frustration, by people like yourself who are frustrated with their current jobs because the big companies are downsizing, restructuring, and putting new initiatives on hold.

This opens up a lot of opportunities. When big companies have trouble fighting foreign competition or keeping pace with rapid product innovation and technology change, their difficulties create a vacuum into which a lot of smaller companies can enter with a rush.

We've come back again to entrepreneurship, to people starting their own businesses. We're more willing to take risks because so many of the big companies are not as stable as was supposed. For large companies, the biggest fixed investment has become people instead of fixed assets. Downsizing is prevalent, and starting a company has become a more viable career path.

This trend has opened the door for entrepreneurs. The big companies have discovered that small companies can adapt to change faster, grab market share faster, create new products and services faster, bring them to market faster, start selling faster, cut fat, trim overhead, go lean and mean with growth-oriented management that is more alert and better equipped to capitalize on opportunities. Small companies thrive best where the rest of the globe hasn't yet dared to venture. Small growth companies can plow income back into operations because the larger reward is the ultimate buyout by the biggies.

Two things are happening. First, the size of economic units that do things is getting smaller, and second, the number of these units is increasing. It's a fundamental shift in the economic structure that is irreversible for the foreseeable future. Big companies will never look like they did in the 1960s and 1970s. Their profitability and market share will come not from hiring more people, but from using fewer people and using them smarter.

John Naisbitt in his book *Global Paradox* (William Morrow, 1994) addressed this subject from the context that the bigger our world economy, the more powerful our smallest players. He contends that while people want to come together to trade more freely, they also want to be independent politically and culturally. He suggests that the more people are bound together economically, the more they want to otherwise be free to assert their own distinctiveness.

The entrepreneur is almost the most important player in the building of our new global economy. So much so that big companies are decentralizing and reconstituting themselves as networks of "intrepreneurs." Large multinational companies are breaking up to become confederations of small, autonomous, entrepreneurial companies—"deconstructing" themselves, and the ultimate in deconstruction is the sole performing entrepreneur.

Information is power, and as more and more information becomes available to the solo entrepreneur, through constantly improving telecommunications systems, the entrepreneur is empowered as never before. In the years ahead, all big companies will find it increasingly difficult to compete with—and in general will perform more poorly than—smaller, speedier, more innovative companies. Big company subsidiaries are beginning to show that power belongs to the lowest possible point in the organization.

A "kinder and gentler" corporate America is evolving into a "leaner and meaner" economy. It's forcing every company to reevaluate its strategies and search for new ways to win market share and maintain growth. This big corporate mindset, with downsizing firmly in place, is beginning to recognize that without all those layers of middle management to battle through, entrepreneurs become the dominate source of new ideas, methods, products, and services to strategic partner with, acquire, manufacture, market, and distribute for. Small is back in a big way.

Make Time to See the World through Different Eyes

If small is back, what's driving it? It's the birth of a new medium which will dominate mass culture during the first half of the twenty-first century. Called the information highway, it most likely will be the senior's biggest continuing challenge. The challenges are recognizing it, accepting it, dealing with its increasing daily intrusion, and most challenging, learning to use it.

Let me see if I can help you grasp what you're going to be dealing with.

First, you have to get the current complex electronic world out of your mind. Forget about the mumble-jumble of what type of computer or software to buy, forget about 500 channels of TV and what's going to be on them, forget about the half a dozen different on-line services to choose from or will it be phone or cable hookups—maybe even direct satellite reception, and the multiple other choices that are currently invading our dizzying communications-telecommunications world. That's all going to get sorted out. If these are your areas of experience and expertise, you might even be a part of the sorting process. For now, open up to the fact that in the near future, your personal computer (yes, you will have one) will be an affordable, portable, notebook-sized *consumer appliance,* as easy and familiar to use as your microwave. Remember, that too was a challenge when it first resided in your kitchen. You even had to reference a cookbook at first. Multiple technologies will drive the development of the information highway, forced by the entertainment industries.

Here are several examples.

The newspaper of the future will actually be a computerized assistant that can, for example, read your calendar, then provide you with articles and ads about the place that you are going this weekend. With a multimedia and interactive paper, you will be able to touch a photograph or ad, opening a window to a slice of video. You will be able to send as well as receive. You will be able to instruct your personal notebook to clip and file whatever you desire or need, even send copies to a friend.

Here's another example. Do you wonder what 500 channels of TV will carry? TV will have *content* knobs instead of *channel* knobs where you can control the content of what you are watching. Suppose you have chosen a documentary which has portions of interviews with prominent persons. After watching the program, or during if you desire, you may wish to bring up the full interview. Ultimately, you will also be able to log into that person's "electronic mailbox" and ask direct questions which where left unanswered in your mind.

The Seniorpreneur's challenge is sorting through this maze of new technology and identifying ways to Seniorpreneur it in areas that we are experienced and comfortable with.

The Revolution Is Coming in Double Time

Pure, plain, and simple, economics will drive the technology revolution. The technology business world recognizes that there are a lot of technically illiterate people out there. They realize that if the technology being developed in the think tanks, laboratories, and workshops of the nation's cable television, telephone, and computer companies isn't user friendly, it will take a lot longer for the economics to work. The technology revolution taking place is fast becoming more and more user friendly.

The big leaps of basic technology acquisition have been accomplished. The challenge now is applying them. The information highway hardware is being built around a sophisticated system of fiber-optic and coaxial cables, microwave transmission stations, and telephone lines. It's feasible because of "digitizing"—the same technology used to transfer music to CDs. It's enhanced by "data compression, which currently allows 500 channels to be squeezed onto existing cable lines. With a fiber-optic system, 50,000 channels or more can go on. Microwave's transmission potential appears to be equal to fiber-optics and eliminates the need for investing in cable infrastructure. The applications for third world countries to leap forward are real. The former Soviet Union countries and some South American countries are currently installing microwave cellular phone systems when they have never even had a wired telephone. Leaping from a few hardwired phones to handheld units for the populous is a giant information availability leap.

An economic reality is that the people who need it most (it being knowledge and information) get it first. The people who need it less get it second but for less money. For Seniorpreneurs, there are a wealth of opportunities to become involved in the double time revolution of implementing technology and information transfer. This applies at various levels of sophistication all over the globe. Pick the one you're most comfortable with and love the most. It's really not seeing the world through different eyes as much as *participating* with corrected lenses.

Seniorpreneuring—The Basic Challenges

> "Okay, so there are going to be many opportunities for us seniors tomorrow. What about today? How can I sort out what is and what is not a good opportunity?"

The balance of this chapter and the next chapter will help you with this. We'll start out with some market guides and tips, and then in the next chapter we'll get into the how to's.

While the most important aspect of a senior-led company is management, a most important challenge is marketing. Consequently, analyzing the many opportunities requires analyzing the market into which the prospective product or service is going to be placed. It is the most factual way to qualify a prospective opportunity. Because marketing is so strategically important to many aspects of a company, it is discussed in various chapters of this book when it is subject-applicable. In this section, some of the more important facts are brought out with regard to some basic marketing problems. Study them and use the checklists when analyzing a prospective Seniorpreneurial opportunity.

Opportunity Testing Marketing Guides

Even for established companies, the process of putting a new product on the market is a high-risk adventure. This is doubly true with a new company. The following are some areas that should be carefully examined.

Be First. Being first is important. There is a need to ascertain, sometimes called guessing, the customer's wants and needs. Seniorpreneurs try to gather validated market research that supports their ability to create and sell a product or service that fits buyer demands and to do so at a price that the buyer is more than willing to pay. This customer-pleasing product or service needs to be on the market before the competition. Getting to the market with just what's needed doesn't do any good if you're second.

Product development is a lengthy, time- and dollar-consuming process. By validating the following points, the Seniorpreneur can save on all of these areas:

1. Is the product wanted and/or needed?
2. Can the market segment be tapped?
3. Can the company produce what is needed?
4. Should the product be manufactured internally or contracted out?
5. Can it be sold competitively and profitably?

Seniorpreneurial marketing involves not only sales skills, but also distribution, consumer testing, pricing, packaging, promotion, and everything else that gets the product or service to the consumer. Simply put, Seniorpreneurial marketing is the process of discovering and translating consumer needs and wants into products or services, creating demands for them and then expanding the demand. Marketing is the performance of various business activities that direct the flow of goods and services from producer to consumer. Many manufacturing companies are manufacturing oriented instead of being Seniorpreneuring marketers who manufacture in order to have something to market. Preferably, to be the first one into the market.

Five Quick Seniorpreneuring Marketing Tips

1. Target the buyers and develop a product/service especially designed to appeal to them.
2. Determine the distribution network that most effectively gets the most product/service out to the greatest number of consumers at the highest profit levels.
3. Develop unique advertising, promotion, and pricing strategies.
4. Modify what doesn't work.
5. Use your senior experienced street smarts in all these areas.

Three Quick Seniorpreneuring Competitive Strategy Tips.
Businesses don't choose the kind of competition they face. It's determined for them by laws, regulations, finance, technology, and the structure of their particular industry. However, what sets the Seniorpreneurs apart is that they realize that they can determine the product/service market niche. They do this by reviewing:

1. What is the competition offering? Is there a market niche for a specialty offering? Something that is cheaper? That lasts longer? Has a longer warranty? Is of better quality? To edge out a competitor, create a market niche.
2. In Seniorpreneurial marketing, develop advertising, promotion, distribution, and a sales force to create more efficient selling methods.
3. For Seniorpreneurs, market timing is the secret, when to make the move. The larger the company, the less likely its product will continue to be a marketing target. Aggressive Seniorpreneurs get shot with arrows in their backsides. Followers get fatal arrows in the front. Lead, don't follow; it's safer.

Finally, Seniorpreneurs have to really guard against *marketing myopia*. This is where companies do not offer customers what they need but only what the company wants to sell. This is what happened to the railroads when they didn't recognize that they were in the transportation industry. Or more recently, when IBM stayed in mainframes and didn't offer work stations fast enough. Seniorpreneurs know instinctively that they have to lead, to be first. What they have to watch out for is that they don't get set in their ways and that they stay current with the reality of the market trends. The way to do this is by judging the opportunity against the Seniorpreneurial marketing techniques that we have just discussed.

Senior High-Tech Qualifiers

Two Approaches

While there are many approaches to developing viable senior business strategies, there are always two criteria that need to be balanced. One is the need to reduce risk; the other is the need to be able to enhance company value.

One approach is to start with newly developed unique technology and then seek market opportunities that may be exploited using the technology. This approach is best used with leading-edge, state-of-the-art technology when the life cycle of the opportunity is very early and because few companies are involved. As the technology is developed and as it matures, many competitors get involved and commit a lot of resources to the technology. This then makes it a lot more difficult to identify large, fast-growing markets.

Another approach is to first identify the market opportunity and then seek out the technology (or skills for a service area) that are required to enter the market. The anticipation is to capture a significant market share, hopefully the leading position. Having an experienced, solid, and basic understanding of the market and, more specifically, the target market requirements allows the Seniorpreneur to be able to push development a lot faster and with much less risk. This is considered a more sophisticated approach, since it begins with an envisioned product or service in mind and proceeds with a definition of the market opportunity. Some venture capital firms purposely cultivate this type of approach by providing seed financing to a prospective entrepreneur to back the process of writing a business plan to explore technical and market viability.

Market Opportunity. Since markets are made up of buying customers, a market profile is simply a customer profile. Therefore, good market definition can come about and prove meaningful only if there is a thorough understanding of the potential customers. This means that good opportunity assessment must include addressing market issues. The key points in defining a market opportunity include:

A determination of the potential customer's needs. The best product or service is one that solves a problem.

A determination of the potential value by analyzing the financial impact the proposed product or service will have on customers. Will they make or save money because of the product or service you envision?

A determination of the very important ingredient called distribution. Using what channel, how, and from whom do the customers purchase your intended product or service? Where do they learn about new ideas?

An essential point, if applicable, is a clear understanding of the regulatory environment. What is the impact on you and your potential customers? This is becoming extremely important in today's "greening" of our society.

A determination of the competitive scene, both current and potential. "Me too" products result in a lot of business failures if they don't have a distinct competitive edge. Seniors shouldn't make me-too mistakes.

A lot of good product or service ideas fail because they haven't been judged according to these key points. Overlooking or misjudging them means that even the best will not succeed if the customer cannot assess the product or service or it does not fill their needs at an economic advantage. The senior experience factor should play a large part in correctly accessing these points.

Once the Seniorpreneur has a firm grasp of the customer's needs, a superior product or service definition can be developed. This can include detailed technical performance criteria, customer expectations, and solid pricing definitions. The last helps with production pricing and determining production costing targets.

Technical Approach. With customer needs determined and a product or service definition in hand, Seniorpreneurs can proceed with selecting the best technical approach. In doing so, they should consider the following:

> Having a versatile "core" technology or service that can be used in a number of ways or in different markets. This gives the Seniorpreneur the opportunity to change directions, to broaden the commercial potential, and to identify other applications.

> Using technologies and services that are well defined and well understood by decision makers in a particular industry. This can be critical to reducing risk.

Basically, there are three sources of technology from which the Seniorpreneur may choose; they can be ranked by degree of risk. The least risky is using technology that is already in existence—one that is owned and well understood by the potential customers. The second choice is using an existing technology or service that the Seniorpreneur does not own (but may license) and that is well understood by the customer. This is a top choice for seniors. The third and most risky choice is to develop or acquire a new technology that requires a lot of customer education or further development.

Although these qualifiers are especially pertinent to high technologies, they have broad applications in any arena. Seniorpreneurs considering any opportunities should judge their project against these known and proven successful qualifiers.

Partnering Strategically

When seeking and examining opportunities, the Seniorpreneur should review the strategic partnering or strategic alliance possibilities. They can add leverage and value to the endeavor. With mean, lean, focused flexibility, small companies are attractive to large companies as they strive to develop networks of suppliers. Large companies, while able to throw large amounts of money at research and development, are not entrepreneurial environments, in that they just can't hold onto a primary entrepreneurial characteristic called "in touch with the market." They don't know how to innovate and cash in on their innovation effectively.

Big companies have an increasing need to acquire, form joint ventures, and cast strategic partnerships with small companies. There are two primary reasons. First, the rapid pace of technological change confronts large companies with an increasing number of technologies to be mastered. The most practical way for them to do that is to engage the skills of small companies that focus on niche markets.

Second, large companies in a competitive global economy realize they must return their focus to what they do best—marketing and distribution. This heightens their need to rely on small suppliers. In turn, small companies are helped as they gain access to capital and channels of distribution which are global in scope. Big companies need small companies for one basic reason: Small is more innovative.

Acquisitions Make Them Larger

Big companies are seeking large growth potential, large market-size potential, and synergism related to their mainstream business activities. They accomplish new business market entry in two ways: internal development and acquisition. Internal development is usually marked by major time consumption in product research and development. It requires large dollar expenditures because of the big business "cover your backside" attitude, and it is normally used only if the new product or service is similar to existing lines. Acquisitions are often used to diversify into foreign product areas. This is where the acquirer is less familiar with the business but believes it is a growing area.

Strategic partnerships, also called strategic alliances, increased substantially during the 1980s. During the 1990s, the partnering parade will strut even taller and faster. This trend is being driven by the fact that for big companies, product development is less important than the ability to compete. The focus is on yield per employee, the time to market, and return on capital. Increased worldwide competition means it's no longer possible to rely solely on in-house resources and the traditional research and development mechanisms. Licensing and acquisitions are a new key—a key that can be very attractive for Seniorpreneurs. Big corporations excel in mass manufacturing, distribution, and marketing. Seniorpreneurs excel in fast-paced innovation.

Seniors, especially those who have been downsized, have an advantage in accessing companies for acquisition and strategic partnering, since they are frequently intimately knowledgeable about the holes in the big companies' business activities. Further, Seniorpreneurs may have some valuable connections in their old large company that will allow them to walk right in the door with their Seniorpreneuring idea. It's the invaluable senior networking asset at work.

Seniorpreneurs Can Do It Faster and Cheaper

If the Seniorpreneurial team can identify a niche product or service, they can better afford to develop and market-test it than can a large company.

They can do it faster, cheaper, and with a lot more flexibility. Their challenge is to start the process and then seek out a strategic partner who can bring a variety of resources to the table. Large companies are constrained by a bureaucracy that tends to retard the process of innovation. By entering into strategic alliances with a Seniorpreneurial company, larger firms can "jump start" their innovative process to gain new technologies that otherwise may take them years to develop in house.

Most commonly, this means that large companies finance the growth of the Seniorpreneurial company. They make systematic investments and gain a window on the technology or process to integrate into their market applications of the future. For the Seniorpreneurs, they get to exercise their bold new idea, and probably realize partnership economies of scale in manufacturing, marketing, and distribution.

The biggest problem with strategic partnerships is negotiating the initial agreement. It requires a keen focus on the integration of planning with a lot of attention, at the outset, on what the partners expect to achieve and what each will need to put into it to make it work. A lot of issues arise. Who will lead the effort? Who is responsible for maintaining open lines of communication? At what stages do which experts get involved? Does this change the leadership? What financial returns are expected? Are there limits on other joint partners? What risks may arise for both parties? The list is almost endless.

Large companies aren't very good at being partners; they're more accustomed to operate as owners. They have a tendency to treat their acquisitions as buyout candidates. Obviously this can be good for the small company in the long run; however, it can cause problems in the short term. Generally, the large company doesn't spend enough time with the smaller company after the initial agreements are signed. Attempts to avoid this should be negotiated upfront. Clear definitions need to be established as to which party is to do what, by when, with an airing of expectations brought forth.

Confirm Two Points. Two additional points stand out. First is that from the very beginning, it must be agreed that an arbitration clause or completely acceptable mechanism for coping with disagreements can be cast. Second, there have to be strong feelings of trust on both sides. This has to include "I like you and I know you like me" attitudes and beliefs. Strategic partnerships are like marriages; loss of trust or faith easily results in divorce.

The natural aim is that both partners achieve their mutual end results as initially anticipated. For the Seniorpreneurs, this may even be the ultimate reward of being bought out, when the major kinks in the product or service have been ironed out. For large companies, their reward may be that they have a product or service that now needs their boost of big-time marketing and distribution. In a way, strategic partnerships can be likened to marriages of convenience.

Qualifying a potential strategic partner is another one of the tools used in analyzing a Seniorpreneuring opportunity. The larger partner almost always brings financial assistance, but if strategically chosen the partner may provide a major bonus to credibility—not to mention acquire the Seniorpreneurial company. That's one way Seniorpreneurs gain added value for their companies.

Using a Senior Advantage in Making the Opportunity Decision

Picking the right business opportunity encompasses many areas. It's not just identifying strategic partners, and it's not just validating marketing. For the Seniorpreneurs, it means choosing an opportunity that suits their capabilities and provides an enjoyable, challenging, and fulfilling work environment, as well as a meaningful return on the risk investment. Then the work will seem like fun and will lead to success. If you enjoy and find fulfillment in your work, you are more likely to do an outstanding job. And if you do an outstanding job, you are more likely to succeed. These points are also important to the Seniorpreneurial investors. They need to be excited about their investment, which in turn helps energize the Seniorpreneur.

Many people choose business opportunities the wrong way. They don't attempt to match their capabilities and desires with the business they select. They see only the imagined financial rewards. Maybe they don't properly investigate the income potential and the strengths of their competitors. Too often they rely on hot business tips or on recommendations of a friend or relative. More often than not, these poorly thought-out business ventures end up in failure.

Basic Questions Checklist*

Long-term viability needs to be considered for any project; this screening process gets grounded in looking at the project's goals. Seniorpreneurs have this long-term concern in mind whether they are intending to sell off or harvest the enterprise. But along with assessing the longer-term viability, one needs to assess the immediate prospects of getting the company off the ground. The following checklist of questions should prove helpful as an overview for initial analysis.

Basic Feasibility

1. Can the product/service actually work?
2. Will it be legal?

Competitive Advantages

1. What will be the specific competitive advantages?
2. What are those of the existing competitors?
3. How will the advantages be maintained?

Buyer Decisions

1. Who will decide to buy, and why?
2. How much will each buy, and how many people are there?
3. Where are these people located, and how will they be sold?

Marketing

1. How much will be spent on advertising, packaging, and selling?
2. What share of market can be obtained by when?
3. Who will personally perform the selling functions?

*Karl Vesper, *New Venture Strategies*, Prentice-Hall, Englewood Cliffs, N.J., 1980, p. 159.

4. How will prices be set, and how will they compare to those of the competition?
5. How important is location, and how will it be determined?
6. What channels will be used—wholesale, retail, agents, and so on?
7. What specific sales targets should be met?
8. Can orders be obtained before starting the business? How soon?
9. How will returns and service be handled?
10. How will pilferage, waste, spoilage, and scraps be handled?

People

1. How will competence in each area of the business be ensured?
2. Who will have to be hired, and when?
3. How will they be found and recruited?
4. How will replacements be obtained if key people leave?
5. How will attorneys, accountants, and other advisers be chosen?
6. Will special benefit plans have to be arranged?

Control

1. What records will be needed for development of product/service?
2. Will any special controls be needed?
3. Who will take care of it?

Finance

1. How much will be needed for development of product/service?
2. How much will be needed for setting up operations?
3. How much will be needed for working capital?
4. Where will money come from? What if more is needed?
5. To which assumptions are profits most sensitive?
6. Which assumptions in projections are most uncertain?
7. What will be the return on equity and sales, compared with figures for the industry?
8. When and how will investors get their money back?
9. What will be needed from a bank, and how will they feel about it?

Benefit from This Checklist

A Seniorpreneur can really benefit by addressing all the points in the above checklist. Answers and comments will provide the basis for a lot of the information that will be needed in assembling the prospective company business plan, which is discussed in more detail in Chapter 8.

Taking Aim at the Future

Entrepreneurs, mostly acting on their own—but some within established businesses (called intrapreneurs)—have done more to shake up American business in the past decade than at any other time in U.S. history.

Entrepreneurs in small businesses have also acted as an important economic shock absorber by making an unexpectedly significant contribution to new job creation. Several decades ago, scholars and forecasters were predicting that the millions of baby boomers who would enter the work force in the 1970s might compel the government to become the employer of last resort. Almost no one suspected that small business, which for many years had been a far less conspicuous job creator than government and big business, would be the major producer of new employment. But that is what has happened. The facts are well documented: job creation in the United States by small business has continued unabated through regional, national, and international rolling recessions. Employment in Western Europe, by striking comparison, has been stagnant during most of the same period.

To be competitive in a global economy, America is learning to pare the size of its manufacturing labor force and substitute more competitive factory automation. It's estimated that less than 10 percent of the labor force will be engaged in manufacturing by the turn of the century. The reality, which is continuing to become more accepted, is that the productivity gains that are being put into place by automation are extracting a painful cost in employment displacement. Small business is taking up a lot of the slack.

People today want to become entrepreneurs. Lots of new ideas are being tried out, touching off a creative entrepreneurial boom, a lot of it driven by women. A great deal of former big company executives are now getting their piece of the rock by participating in stock ownership plans. In other cases, management buyouts have created a new group of employee-owned companies.

In many instances of new technology, competitive efficiency depends more on design of a product or service process than on sheer size, speed, or delivery. This is where Seniorpreneurs excel. A lot of these design efficiencies and innovations can be made with a minimum of capital. This is a secret to the kind of contribution Seniorpreneurs can make. Even though it continues to be a challenge to innovate in an increasingly complex global environment, a secret is to explore the service areas or exploit market niches. With the speeded-up pace with which both consumer markets and industry markets change, just the ability to respond quickly favors smaller, more adaptive companies.

Today's reprogrammable computer-driven machines are making small-batch production runs more economically feasible. Ingenuity and skill can overcome sheer size. Computer-aided engineering, computer-aided manufacturing, and computer-aided ad infinitum really lower entry barrier costs for smaller enterprises to be competitive. Simple but highly capable low-cost PC systems enable many companies to install sophisticated management systems to assist them in staying on top of what's happening in their companies. They can track hundreds of thousands of inventory items, all of their production, management, and sales costs. They can intimately track sales orders to assist in keeping inventories low and receivables current, which in turn eases cashflow. "What if" scenarios are simply run on a variety of readily available spreadsheets, and large databases store gigabits of marketing information many times gleaned by tapping into a variety of modem-accessible sources.

Reviewing the Opportunity

We've covered a lot of ground in the process of determining and qualifying valid Seniorpreneurial opportunities. Guidelines and checklists have been furnished to help quantify the process; what at first glance appears to be off-the-wall thinking has been explained to show the Seniorpreneur, the Seniorpreneurial team members, and those who finance Seniorpreneurial projects some new insights to uncover and analyze Seniorpreneurial opportunities.

When all is said and done about analyzing business opportunities, when all the numbers have been gathered and the assumptions confirmed, when the due diligence is close to being completed, there are still some bottom-line feelings that will tell you "go or no-go."

These come from the gut, and ofttimes it's hard to remove the emotion involved. But that's the point. Emotion is what makes successful Seniorpreneurs. If you *feel*, and your research seemingly justifies, that the opportunity is a good one, then check your enthusiasm level. Seniorpreneurs use this all the time. Do you *feel* enthusiastic about the choice you're making? Are you excited about its potential? Do you have a *feeling* that its success is intricately woven into your existence? Do you *feel* that the opportunity is an extension of yourself? Do you *feel* that you will be excited every morning when you face the daily challenges? Are you sure you can retain an interest in learning, improving, and changing? Will the opportunity keep you motivated?

Motivation is more than just another capability. It is *the* single capacity that can, and will, help you overcome a lack of other capabilities in other areas. It's what makes your potential opportunity valid, keeps you fascinated, preoccupied, and yes, even obsessed.

With age, you gain a sixth sense about yourself. You gain confidence both in yourself and what you do. You know better what will work and what won't. By this time, you should have learned to listen to and trust your feelings. You have a great advantage compared with people in their thirties. They're opinionated, stubborn, and rather anxious, much like you were at that age.

By this time, you have a pretty good idea where your strengths and weaknesses lie. You should capitalize on that. Make two lists, one for "what you do well," and one for "what you don't do well."

These are the "gut" questions that need to be answered. A long stream of "gut-level yesses" will confirm your *feeling* about the validity of this being your Seniorpreneurial opportunity.

5
Should You Start, Buy, or Franchise?

Choose a job you love and you will never have to work a day in your life. ORIENTAL PROVERB

Starting a business, buying an existing business, or becoming a franchise business owner are the three key topics in this chapter, but the proverb stated above is the backbone for our discussions. If you enjoy and receive satisfaction from your work, you are more likely to do a better job, be more successful, make more money, and have more fun. As a senior, you don't need any more hassles. You've had them all. Now is the time to love what you do day to day, have fun, and savor the enjoyment of being in business and making money.

We've covered the pros and cons of becoming and being an entrepreneur, and we've looked at a variety of entrepreneurial influences and opportunities. You most likely will continue to weigh the possibilities. We'll be covering a lot more details. For now, we can delve into the alternatives of starting a business, buying an existing operation, or purchasing a franchise. Many of the areas and issues we have explored hold true when applied to all three. These include pick a growing industry, choose one you have some experience in, conduct thorough due diligence, pay close attention to your marketing plans, and develop strategic objectives.

However, throughout the rational evaluation process, learn to listen to your heart, assess the feelings in your gut. If what you're hearing and feeling isn't setting well, then don't waste more time with that particular opportunity. Explore a new path, seek a new area, and keep in mind that you don't want to "work" another day in your life. Seniorpreneuring is for having fun.

Starting a Business

We've already covered numerous factors that should be considered when you are choosing or starting a business, and the majority of this book is aimed at those themes. A lot of the information in this chapter is cross-applicable whether you are starting, buying, or seeking a franchise. I would expect any Seniorpreneur to use the information provided regardless of the start, buy, or franchise determination. Consequently, this beginning section will be most helpful by summarizing, reviewing, and previewing some fundamental information.

Pioneering Can Be Tough

Starting a business can be tough. It's even tougher to be a pioneer or an initiator. Preferable is to let someone else pioneer and after it has been shown to pay, do it bigger, better, and faster. Let the other person take the initial time and dollar risk. When you pioneer, you usually have to spend a lot of effort and advertising dollars making your customers aware of the fact that they have a problem as well as the fact that you have a solution. If you let other people pioneer, they can carry the heavy front-end awareness load and you can catapult your improvements into a ready-made market. If you're going to copy something, make sure you're imitating a winner. Go beyond the present level of service or the current way of doing things. Regardless, always seek to solve a problem or meet a need that is currently unmet. Here are some more points to take to heart.

Seek Longer-Term Opportunities

If you're starting a business, you want a product/service that allows an opportunity for long-term success. One where you can keep building for 10 years or more. Avoid competing against a well-entrenched business unless you have something unique with a lot of customer-added benefits. Recognize that it's highly unlikely that you will succeed with exactly the same plan that you begin with, especially if you're pioneering.

Find a Gap

When you're conducting your market assessment, look for a "gap" where you can find a better way of selling, advertising, or marketing. Do this with an underutilized product or service that you can market to an overlooked audience.

Don't Guarantee

Watch out for operating companies that require you to have "guaranteed sales." They can be bad news. This is where you place your product for sale with a promise that if it doesn't sell, you'll take it back. What you are liable to get back is a lot of unexpected, damaged, mishandled, unusable inventory along with a large return freight bill.

Think Diversity

Diversity is the best insurance against adversity. The best kind of diversity moves a company into an associated business. A good-fitting diversification offers existing customers an additional product or service they need.

And Contemplate These Points

- If you sell something just once, you had better have fat margins.
- Favor a business in which you get paid up front or let your sales drive your overhead. It's better to lose a few sales because you don't have the equipment or staff than close your company because of high expenses.
- Quality and reliability are to a product company what full-service is to a service company.
- Many new ventures fail because their managers place their personal interests ahead of their customers.
- Seasonal, supercyclical businesses that have a lot of competition should be avoided.
- Climb aboard a growing trend and be cautious about peaking trends.
- Avoid getting bogged down in major schemes that will solve one of the world's primary problems. Avoid wasting time on super-big deals because they are generally time wasters. The same is true for ventures far outside your normal operation and expertise areas.

Buying a Business

How do you go about the process of buying a business? This section begins by addressing the advantages of buying an existing business and then examines: discovering where to find a business to buy, valuations, due diligence, negotiations, and the close.

Four Golden Rules for Buying a Business

1. Don't buy without having or putting excellent management in place.
2. Restrict buys to businesses you can truly understand. You must have available or be able to bring in someone with a total grasp of the market and its environment.
3. Go for something worth having—the bigger the buy, the greater the benefit if it succeeds.
4. Never overpay. The lower the premium, the better the buy. The less paid per dollar of sales, the greater the chance of making money.

Six Advantages of Buying

1. When you buy a business, as opposed to starting one, you bypass certain start-up problems. They're frequently costly and time consuming and usually unforeseen. Customers are already buying in an existing business and many operating methods are already proven.
2. Some guesswork is eliminated regarding items such as location, facility size, forms of advertising, and pricing.
3. The business may be a bargain because it was a forced sale, or because of health or family problems.
4. Historical operating information is available from the owner regarding competition, demand, seasonal fluctuations, and other variables.
5. There are some existing trained employees who can help you learn.
6. There is an established group of proven suppliers and service people.

Where to Find a Business to Buy

One point needs to be made at the early discussions of buying a business. The point is that the process takes time. Very seldom are successful business purchases made on the spur of the moment. Too much is involved and too much is at stake to enter into a hasty buy.

Where to Start the Search

Start the search process with yourself by selecting an industry in which you have some familiarity and experience—preferably, one in which you have worked and have some in-depth industry knowledge. You will find that you feel a lot more comfortable and have a greater sense of security if you're not a complete beginner.

Most likely, as a Seniorpreneur, you will select an industry that is at least 10 years old, preferably 15 to 25 years old. It should be a proven business and not a fad so that when you're ready to sell or move on, there will be ready buyers. Additionally, it's easier to get good background information on established industries. You can easily determine key operating ratios, industry norms and standards regarding financial information as well as marketing practices. Established industries make it easier for you to determine the industry trends, up or down, as well as seeking out niche areas and whether the industry is consolidated or fragmented. Fragmented industries, those with a lot of small to medium-sized competitors in local or regional markets, are ideal for consolidation. If your forte is management, these types of niche markets inside a larger industry can be ideal for you to exercise your management expertise by ever-increasing acquisitions. This allows you to generate cashflow and increase value by consolidating purchasing, distribution, and marketing efforts and management functions.

How to Find Out Information on an Industry

Family, friends, and acquaintances are always good but go only so far. At some point, you will need some real hard data to support your gut-level feelings about the industry you're interested in. One of my long-standing favorite ways to get up to speed on an unfamiliar industry is by accessing a publication know as *Business Rates and Data*, published by Standard Rate & Data Service. It's available in many libraries. This publication lists the names of 16,000-plus trade journals organized by industry. Many industries have six to ten publications, and every industry has a least two or three magazines. *Rates and Data* supplies you with complete information on each publication. You can phone the chosen magazine and get recent copies, order a subscription, talk with the publisher, editors, writers, and ad managers and tell them that you are a buyer of a business in their industry. Ask questions and solicit their input and assistance. They know the ins and outs of the industry. You'll find that they enjoy sharing information if you're not a pest and your approach is direct and sincere.

Ask them questions built around these points:

- Who are the top industry leaders and who should I be talking with?
- What have been the biggest technology trends in the past 5 years and what do you think they will be in the next 5 to 10 years? And why?
- What are the most significant profit opportunities, both now and in the next 5 years?
- What are the biggest problems that the industry is confronting in the next 5 to 10 years?
- Do you know of any companies for sale?

If you can, get copies of the last 6 months, or better yet, the last year's issues from a half dozen industry-related publications. With these in hand, you can quickly become a knowledgeable industry expert. You can find out where the various trade shows are held and which ones are the biggies. By reading the editorial columns, you can find out the major industry and political directions. The classified advertising will often have a section on companies for sale and the advertising in general will tell you what's "hot."

Purchase or review a copy of the *U.S. Industrial Outlook*, which is published annually by the Department of Commerce. It contains overviews on the historical, current, and future trends of 145 major industries. It's an unbiased, factual source of good data and information which you can use to cross-check your other findings.

Obviously, one should review the normal business publications like *Business Week, Entrepreneur, Inc. Magazine, Forbes, Fortune, Success*, and *The Wall Street Journal*. Libraries have back issues, and librarians can help you identify other reading sources via accessing various periodical indexes.

How to Get a Deal Flow Going

The biggest secret in creating a deal flow is networking, networking, networking. Nothing beats word of mouth in the variety and speed with which you can generate leads and information. It takes a concerted effort on your part. It's a participant endeavor, and the more you put into spreading the word, the more leads you will gain.

Herein lies one of the largest downfalls for persons seeking to start or buy a business. They just don't get exposed to enough deals to increase their chance of finding a top-notch opportunity. Seeing 10 or 20 deals in a 6-month time span sounds like a lot, but experienced deal hunters want to see three or four times that many. I see 400 to 500 business plans a year and turn down twice that number over the phone. That is a common number with many national venture capital and investment banking firms. Some see several thousand.

It's always been surprising to me how fast word flies when a new business idea is born. It's not unusual for me to receive four or five business plans from different parts of the country within a 3-week time period, each of which thinks it has spawned a concept that no one else has thought of. I learned a long time ago that when I receive that many plans, about the same new business idea, from such a diverse area, I most likely will not choose to invest in the new idea. It's very difficult to choose a winner in any area, but it's double trouble when you have dozens of people trying to do the same thing all over the country, simultaneously. The lesson here is that you need to generate as large a deal flow as possible. The more choices you have, the better your chance of finding a good one. The greater your deal flow, the more knowledge you gain about the business, the more sophisticated you become in your due diligence techniques, and the better educated you are with questioning and probing to identify a deal that exactly matches your criteria.

Remember one caution if you are able to generate a large deal flow. Be careful not to develop a "no" complex. When you're exposed to many deals, it becomes easy to overanalyze them and find too many reasons to say no. Don't get bogged down in information overload and detailed due diligence on multiple deals at the same time. It becomes difficult to keep all the facts straight, and you end up confusing yourself so much that you get dejected and give up on the cause. You're looking for a good deal on favorable terms, so keep your objective to "get" a deal in mind.

Start with Classified Ads. Classified advertisements always get response. You can place your own as a potential business buyer, including specifying the type of business you're interested in, the size, the geographical area, or other particulars. Use national publications if you're open to relocation (*The Wall Street Journal* Thursday under "Business Opportunities") or a regional or local publication in your immediate area.

Responding to ads from others can be frustrating. Many sellers are reluctant to advertise and retain brokers to front their sale. You then have to wade through the qualifying process, usually to find out that the target company is overpriced or about to go under. Other advertisers are just shopping their company. They may be trying to determine if their company is salable and at what price. Or they may be feeding their ego, and you'll find out, after much time and discussion, that they aren't really serious sellers. But responding is the name of the game, and the experience will teach you how to quickly qualify your interest in a particular deal.

Expand with Professionals. Every business works with professionals in the form of attorneys and accountants. These professionals are the ones who often have the inside scoop on many different business opportunities, and they frequently have it early, sometimes even before the business owner knows they have a business for sale. How can I make that kind of statement? How can an accountant or attorney know a company is for sale, sometimes even before the company owner? Let me give you two quick examples.

Accountants may know because they work with many different companies and have experience in the early warning signs that a company is in financial trouble. They can see that the management is losing interest in getting out and selling because of consistent quarterly revenue declines. They may detect that additional family members brought into a family-owned business really aren't equipped to run the business, and are causing the margins to decrease. It means that at some point in time, the family founder is going to have to face the fact that they may be better off selling out rather than trying to pass on the legacy.

The attorney may have the inside scoop because he or she assembles the will of a company owner who is in failing health. Another attorney example is when a divorce situation requires a settlement that could result in the owners simply deciding to change their lifestyle for a few years. But don't limit your professional search to business attorneys and accountants. Contact divorce, real estate, estate, and tax experts as well. Ask attorneys for referrals to other attorneys and accountants and vice-versa.

Where Else to Go. Here are a number of other deal sources.

Salespeople. These are the ones who are on the road, on the go, selling their wares to the company that you want to buy. They come from suppliers of the products or services. They come from the suppliers of supplies. They don't want to lose a source of business and would welcome the opportunity to tell you about the industry and the companies they feel may be for sale. They are a great underground source for information.

Bankers. Just like the accountants and attorneys, bankers often have the inside scoop on a potential sale or a company that is seeking additional financing. Get bankers' names from accountants and attorneys just like you'll ask the bankers for names of accountants and attorneys. Although commercial loan officers can be helpful, you usually will need to get a little higher up the executive ladder to get solid leads. Banks are also good sources for bankrupt companies or those that may be operating under court liquidations.

SBA. The Small Business Administration office can assist in several areas. One is the liquidation officer who may have a group of illiquid loans that need financing or management assistance. The SBA SCORE program may also have some leads, as will the management assistant officers at local offices. Making contact with the SBA when you're in a deal-finding mode will help you establish some personal contacts that could prove beneficial should you determine to obtain SBA financing when you find the right deal.

Cold Calls. It's always surprising how well this works. Simply identify a company in your industry of choice and cold-call the owner. You'll be pleasantly surprised at how often people will be happy to sit down with you and tell you about their business. Once in the door, you can glean all types of information from the status of their operations about who they know who may be open to selling.

Other Government Sources. Although I feel that private sources are the most knowledgeable, there are numerous government sources with which you can network to increase your deal flow possibilities. Try your local chamber of commerce office, especially if it has a community development department. The same goes for your city or state economic development offices.

Business Incubators. Find out if you have a local business incubator, innovation center, or business development center (BDC) in your community. Such centers always have entrepreneurs who are seeking financial or management assistance. What better opportunity for a Seniorpreneur than to tie in with a young entrepreneur who has a great idea and needs some experienced street smarts help.

Don't forget colleges and universities. Many have business departments that also include student programs that do research for small companies. They help business owners write business and marketing plans as well.

Business Brokers. These range from individuals to large nationwide firms. The services they offer are both to buyers and sellers. Their one major advantage to a buyer is that they have basic information on a variety of deals. Most of the time, their biggest problem is that they have more buyers than sellers and you can get caught up in a bidding war with another buyer.

Venture Capital Groups. At last count, there were over 100 venture capital groups around the country. Most of these organizations are nonprofit and exist solely for the purpose of promoting entrepreneurship, venture capital, and networking with business-oriented professionals. They hold monthly meetings that are open to the public, and thousands of entrepreneurs have made valuable contacts through these organizations. To obtain a directory, contact: International Venture Capital Institute, P.O.

Box 1333, Stamford, CT 06904. The author is cofounder of The Rockies Venture Club, 190 East 9th Ave., Suite 320, Denver, CO 80203.

Some Deal Flow Closing Thoughts. Creating a deal flow is not easy. It takes time and personal attention to get the deal flow off on the right foot and then extra effort to stay in the race. One of the mistakes that many deal seekers make is spending a month or two to get their deal flow activities going and then finding a deal that appears attractive and stopping. After a couple of weeks of investigating what initially appears to be the deal of their dreams, they discover a major problem that causes them to abandon the deal. If they haven't paid attention to the continuing deal flow generation process, they suddenly find that they don't have anything else to look at. Don't ignore your deal flow generation. You may be at this for up to a year or so and any interruptions cause additional setbacks. Besides, you might find two that you just can't live without or that make a great combination that far exceeds your initial expectations.

Due Diligence

Due diligence refers to the process of attentive application to the care of investigating all aspects of a prospective project. It's sort of like the old-fashioned habit of kicking the tires when you are thinking of buying a car. The legal definition is the "exercise of reasonable care" in the investigation of a project or company.

For the Seniorpreneur, it means digging around and finding out as much information as possible about the potential of a proposed project or possible purchase of an enterprise. The following provides a basic checklist from which to start.

Due Diligence Checklist

- Company identification
  a. Name (dba's, previous name/s)
  b. Any trademarks, patents, copyrights, royalty agreements—issued and pending (obtain copies)
  c. Affiliates, subsidiaries
- Location—branches
- History—founders (when established and by whom), what past changes in ownership, legal status (proprietorship, partnership, corporation "state"), other states in which qualified to do business,

class and number of shares issued and outstanding, any options/warrants (obtain copies of articles, bylaws, amendments, minutes, organization chart, other pertinent company documents)
- Is a current business plan available? (policy/procedures manual)
- Product/service information—What is principal product/service, obtain information on profit margins, unit costs, return policies, liabilities, substitutes, quality control, names of trade journals, details of advertising (obtain copies of brochures, price sheets, warranties, discounts)
- Industry information—Is it expanding/contracting, average size of companies, fragmented/concentrated, regulatory atmosphere, foreign competition, standing of company (size by employees, sales, profitability, as appropriate for local, regional, national, and international)
- Competitive information—who, where, strengths/weaknesses, age, areas, position in industry (who are leaders, what's their advantage), trends, develop a product-to-product comparison, copies of any market research
- General management—who owns what, key employees, experience, who manages what, who does buying, any specialists, who will stay/leave. Is there management succession?
- Marketing (see "Marketing Checklist" below)
- Source of goods sold—manufacturer, assembler, distributor (list of suppliers, terms, time involved, purchase commitments, relationship, problems)
- Distribution information (How is product distributed, by whom?)
- List or obtain the following information regarding the premises occupied by the business (this applies to all locations):
  a. Physical description
  b. Location—city, state, area, and so on
  c. Type of construction—cinderblock, wood, metal, and so on
  d. Total land area/total building area
  e. Age of building/s
  f. Taxes, insurance, maintenance costs per year
  g. Rent/lease cost per year—how long is lease?
  h. Is lease triple net or gross?
- Obtain the following for financial analysis:
  a. Profit and loss statements for the last 3 to 5 years
  b. Balance sheets (same)
  c. Tax returns (same)

    d. Credit reports
    e. Ratios
    f. List of payables (perform aging)
    g. List of accounts receivable (perform aging)
    h. Inventory list—how valued (LIFO/FIFO)
    i. Capital equipment list—depreciation schedule
    j. Leasehold/building improvements
- What is the company's reputation among:
    a. Employees
    b. Customers
    c. Suppliers
    d. Competition
    e. Banks
    f. Distributors/marketers
- Any legal problems (past, present, anticipated)
- Documents (obtain copies of all agreements that obligate the company (contracts, leases, purchase order commitments, letters of intent, insurance policies)
- Apparent reasons for growth/lack of
- Employees—number now, average last 5 years, unionized, longevity, obtain résumés of owners/officers and key employees, salary schedules, benefit/bonus plans, employment contracts, polices on sick pay, overtime, vacations, and the like
- Obtain list of independent contractors and what they provide (include accountants, attorneys)
- What are the corporate opportunities for expansion and growth?
- Reason for selling company (age, finances, liquidity, other)
- What is the fit with your (buyer's) existing operations, experience, knowledge?
- Terms of sale: cash/credit—how much monthly?

Marketing Checklist

1. Is there a written marketing plan?
    a. What is the basic product/service strategy?
    b. What major changes have taken place in the past 5 years?
    c. What major changes are contemplated in the next 5 years?
2. Competitive comparison—terms, discounts, credit policies
3. What are the products or services?
    a. How old, how many, are they related, how are they sold?

    b. Details on the product or service lines in order of sales and profitability.
    c. Competitive comparison, by line.
    d. What are the primary trends in the industry?
    e. Discuss breadth and depth of market strategy.
    f. Importance of service, quality, price.
4. List product or service features—pros/cons.
5. What are the major causes of returns?
6. What's the seasonality or selling cycle, if any?
7. What does product development produce, who does it, how often?
    a. Describe research and development efforts, budgets, results
8. What is pricing policy and terms, what/who dictates it, competitive standing.
9. Method of distribution, at what costs, terms.
10. Who are the actual customers (original equipment manufacturers, resellers, end users)?
    a. Who are significant customers?
    b. List major customers (new/lost) last 2 years.
    c. Obtain a list of current, active customers.
11. What are the market trends?
12. Are there other major/minor markets?
13. Describe marketing area (can it expand, be changed, new areas—geographical trading areas, local, regional, national, international).
14. What is marketing group [who heads, main policies, promotion programs (effectiveness)—how to change, any marketing research, selling/advertising budgets, how do you pay—salary, commission, bonus, combinations]?
15. What are advertising practices? (Obtain copies of ads and ad budget.) What public relations activities take place?

Valuations—The Discussion Goes On

For generations, the discussions have raged on and on as to the proper methods of valuing a business: Is it art or science? The answer is a combination of both, with science weighing in heavier in some cases, and art in others. We'll explore both sides and then draw some conclusions.

  Closely held private companies are difficult to value because they cross over so many different factors. These include assets (and how they are valued), earnings (current, historical, and future), net worth (with consideration to accounting methods), management (how people will transition), cashflow (and its sustainability), intangibles (trademarks, market share, location), and the viability of the industry itself. Buyers approach each of these differently depending upon their individual perspectives, needs, wants, and financing.

For Seniorpreneurs there may be multiple considerations in the valuation process. One can be the amount of financing available. Another may be the expertise, networking, or acquisition value added. Even the primary point of return on investment may get skewed. Are you looking for a current and reasonably steady return in the form of a paycheck, or are you focusing on a major return when you have added your management expertise to grow the operation and merge or sell it out?

As you will see, the valuation process can be very complex. So complex, in fact, that books have been written about it. I can only briefly overview the subject in this chapter and refer those with a deeper interest to their accountant, local library, or better yet, their friendly bookstore. For those with a mathematical bent, the challenge of figuring the various models can be intriguing. For you bottom-line folks, be sure that someone runs the calculations because you don't want to attempt a buyout without solid valuation figures. Use your Seniorpreneuring street smarts.

The Scientific Approach

Despite the art versus science arguments, buyers must look at not only how much they can make, but also what's the downside, how much they will lose if the deal goes bad. With this in mind, there are two traditional scientific methods of valuation: assets and earning power.

Valuations Based on Assets. This valuation process can be approached from four basic ways: actual book value, adjusted book value, liquidation value, and replacement value. Combinations of these plus a few other tricks are commonly used by company "raiders," but that's another subject. What we are discussing here are pretty straightforward, industry acceptable deals.

Actual Book Value. This is the simplest method, but the most unreliable. Too many variables are involved. Actual book value is just the plain acceptance of the total amount of assets less the total amount of liabilities with the result being the actual book value shown on the companies financial balance sheet. An example of one variable would be the value placed on an asset. The balance sheet may show that a computer was purchased for $4000 and that there has been no depreciation taken. If it's 2 years old, you know it's not worth four grand. Or maybe the books show $45,000 in receivables and further investigation shows that $20,000 of these are more than 6 months old. Then again, the figures may show

$50,000 of inventory, and an inspection indicates that $15,000 of that has so much dust on it that the underlying goods have deteriorated to zero value. Regardless of the true value, book value gives one a scientific starting place for bringing in the art.

Adjusted Book Value. This is simply taking the book value and adjusting it for large differences. These may come from totally disregarding some items, determining market value of others, using liquidation value on some, maybe depreciating the machinery, and adding appreciation to land value. This is the most common process for all asset valuations: using a commonsense valuation on all assets and liabilities to achieve a current adjusted book value figure.

Liquidation Value. You can be sure that banks and other loan sources will use the liquidation value method regardless of what you may be furnishing as collateral. Simply put, it's how much money can be raised if everything is sold, *today*. But wait. We have to carry this one step further. After we have sold off everything, how much will be left over after we also pay off the liabilities, including the cost of hauling off the junk that didn't sell? The money that's left is the company's liquidation value.

Here's a rough schedule for debtor liquidation values. Some of the percentages may surprise you.

Land—40 percent of current market value

Buildings—25 percent of current market value

Machinery-equipment—40 percent of current market value

Inventory-raw materials, finished goods—50 percent

Goods-in-process—nothing, zip

Accounts receivable—80 percent up to 90 days, nothing past 90

Liquidation value is obviously bottom line. For a buyer, it's a figure you use in negotiations.

Replacement Value. This is also a benchmark valuation. How much would it cost to replace all the assets under current market pricing? This type of pricing always causes lots of discussion between buyer and seller since many times items can be purchased used that will serve the purposes just as well as new items. This is also the area where leasehold improvements get negotiated.

Valuations Based on Earnings. At first blush, one would also assume that this is pretty scientific—just take an earnings figure and multiply it by some factor. Presto, a price/earnings ratio. Life for the buyer or seller should be so simple. Which earnings (pre or after tax)? What multiplier (Dow Jones, S&P, or one of six others)?

Usually, the decision to buy a company is based on the assumption that the company's value will increase, because the new management can increase the earnings. Herein lies the fallacy. Supply and demand of closely held companies enters the picture. So does state of the industry. So do current return on investment (ROI) trends or expectations. And these factors can all change, depending on if we're discussing past, current, or projected earnings.

I think that negotiating private company sales between private buyers on the basis of evaluating past earnings is a major mistake. It's a tool used in the *art* of buying, nothing more.

The problems stem from qualifying *all* expense items. Are they realistic? Are they consistent? For example, high advertising cost from 2 years ago, which weren't repeated in the current year, may mean that current-year sales are at good levels. However, if the advertising hasn't been kept up this year—thus an expense saving—next year's sales could crumble. Same with maintenance costs. If they are low this year, will they be three times as much next year because of neglect? Additionally, depreciation, amortization, and inventory write-downs can all be adjusted to affect the bottom-line pretax and taxable earnings.

The only way to use a price/earnings ratio in determining valuation is to carefully "recast" the profit and loss statements and then, use the results only to factor into the *art* of the valuation. Recasting is a process of examining each expense item and adjusting it to what would appear to be a normal-year operating statement. Unless you're well versed in accounting, and experienced in recasting, my suggestion is that you take any prospective seller's financial statements to an accountant and ask him or her to work with you in the recasting prior to putting much faith in valuations based on earnings.

Future Earnings Projections. This can be an especially valuable exercise—in fact, a needed part of any buyer's valuation. It is very relevant when the existing company is losing money or marginally breaking even, and the intention is that new management cannot only turn it around, but make it very profitable. The new buyer may intend to substantially change the company's direction, integrate it with another company for manufacturing, marketing, or service providing purposes. The historical figures may provide a basis, but the changes and additions become the center of focus. The projected future profits, usually done as "best-, expected-, worst-case" projections, are useful in determining the value of the company to the buyers.

What Else Goes into a Work of Art? As you have begun to see, the process of valuation can be quite complex. What follows are some additional valuation methods that you should consider. Value, like beauty, is in the eye of the beholder. The more ammunition that you have on your side, in the form of science, the better positioned you will be to disarm a seller with persuasive numbers as to your justification of the value of their business.

Cash Flow Projections. Here is where we separate the kids from the Seniorpreneur. Cashflow studies help you determine the amount of cash that you will have available to service debt, determine salaries, perquisites, dividends/interest, and total return on capital invested.

Comparable Sales Value. This valuation method comes from the real estate business. The approach is to gather information on similar businesses and compare their sale value with the one you have identified. The problems with this method stem from finding truly comparable companies. Factors such as size, public versus private, forced or free-will sale, all enter into the validity of this type of valuation. Again, add this to our art list.

Excess Earnings Method. This is a simple concept. If you make an investment, you expect a return. The return, expressed as a percentage, should be determined as an excess amount of earnings. Here's more detail. Excess earnings are earnings above and beyond what you would expect from an investment of a similar risk level. If the current rate of CDs is 5 percent and you invested $100,000, you would expect a pretty sure $5000 (or 5 percent) return. That same amount of money invested in higher risk Dow Jones stocks would be expected to earn some modest percentage over CDs—say, a total of 7 percent, or $7000. If you invested the $100,000 in a business, common thinking would suggest you should receive a higher return—say, 10 percent or $10,000—because the risk is considerably higher.

But you should also consider some other factors. If you are going to be the person who will manage the operations of the company, you can rightfully expect to receive some compensation in the form of salary. If your $100,000 investment is just part of the purchase price (down payment) and a lending source has also put up some funding, you want to make sure you subtract the costs of servicing that debt in the form of the interest paid.

Other factors of expense should also be considered, but you can see the idea. You need to "recast" the operating statements to be sure that the earnings are in excess of all the expenses incurred, including the costs of all the monies invested which are expected to provide a return of excess earnings. Again, add this method to our art.

Income Capitalization. This method also comes from the real estate industry and it carries a good deal of credibility. First you have to assume a rate of return—let's say 10 percent. This means that each year you will receive 10 percent of the money you invested each year.

Should You Start, Buy, or Franchise?

Consequently, you will get your full investment back in 10 years. But you have to be careful to factor in taxation, all-cash versus debt financing, and interest or cost of money. Use your accountant to assist you with this combination scientific/art valuation.

Additional Miscellaneous Methods. Over the generations of buyers and sellers of companies, a lot of hybrid methods of valuation have been concocted, mostly to benefit the persuasive powers of either the buyer or seller. I'm not discounting these, as many of them are applicable in a specialized situation. However, they are not necessarily mainstream but do bear mentioning their names. They can include:

Discounted cash flow. This complex method requires a lot of time to calculate where you end up looking at cashflow and not pretax profits.

Fair market value. This is defined as the price that a willing buyer will pay, and a willing seller will accept, in a situation where neither party is forced to act. It can apply to the total final agreed price of the company as well as to individual assets.

Net worth plus. In this method, you take the replacement value of the fixed assets, then add in the subjective value of intangibles (goodwill, customer list, patents, etc.). The total, less any liabilities you assume, is a starting point for negotiations.

Rules of thumb. These can be helpful for quick checks on the reality of initial asking prices. Use either one or both. Normal pretax earnings times four to five. Or take normal annual cashflow times four to five.

(Reader note: You'll find an additional section on financial analysis helpers in Chapter 12, referring to pricing ratios and equity valuation.)

Fashioning the Art

I opened this section commenting that the discussion goes on as to what methods should be used to determine a proper valuation for the purchase of a business. After reviewing the multiple choices presented here, and they don't include all the possibilities, one can see that the valuation process can rightly be considered a combination of science and art. Numbers (the science part) tell part of the story, but subjective evaluation and interpretation weigh in heavily (the art).

Consequently, the Seniorpreneur uses these combinations, plus street smarts, to determine a fitting valuation. What you're really looking for in this process is to establish a range of values: top and bottom figures as to what you feel the company may be worth; figures that you can use to compare against the seller's asking price. You would feel pretty bad, if 6 months after you bought, you discovered that you had unknowingly paid 25 percent more for the company than it was worth.

The valuation process to determine a proper price sets the stage for you to take the next step in purchasing an existing business: negotiation. This is the subject of the next section.

Negotiation

There are many good books totally devoted to the subject of negotiation. If you haven't done much negotiating in your business life, I'd suggest you pick up several different ones and spend some time educating yourself in more depth than this book can provide. There are many theories on the forms and techniques as well as the how tos. You're sure to find some that suit your style. These will give you a feel for the details. I'm going to pass on some time-proven basics that apply to all negotiations and especially as related to negotiating business deals.

Negotiation Is an Art

Just like there is an art and science to valuation, there is art and science to negotiating. The science side is helpful when you're massaging the numbers. However, the most important point in successful negotiating is to remember that it is the *art of compromise.* As selling is the art of persuasion, since you need to talk to persuade, many people also feel the compulsive need to talk, talk, talk, sell, sell, sell when negotiating. Negotiating is not selling. In order to reach the compromises in successful negotiating, you also need to *listen.*

The negotiations to buy a business start a lot sooner than most people think they do. They start at the time a prospective purchaser has the first contact with the seller. Actions, attitudes, smiles, the way you dress, and the way you sound set the initial scene for negotiations. Right up front, at your first contact with a seller, employ the art of negotiating by becoming a listener. People love to talk about themselves, and company owners are surely no exception. Sellers usually want to tell you their success stories and the good times they've had in the business. Don't disappoint them; encourage them to talk. Try to adopt a 20/80 percent mindset. Spend 20 percent of the time talking about yourself and posing questions to them. Let them exercise their tendency to talk 80 percent of the time. They'll naturally want to talk about their business—after all, it's your initial mutual point of interest. Make it your secondary challenge to get them to talk about themselves. This familiarity campaign will pay off in the long run.

They expect you to ask questions at the start. Take advantage of this and get them used to answering questions. The secret is not to ask just business questions. Find ways to also draw them out on personal opinion and philosophical issues. Gather as much information and observations about them as individuals as you can. Remember, they are the seller (they need to talk), and you are the buyer (you need to listen).

Qualify Yourself Quickly

I've seen more deals lost right up front by ignoring this point. Sellers, although eager, are always suspicious. You would be too if you had spent a large part of your life devoted to building a business. Yes, they want to sell, and they have a price. On the other hand, there's always a part of them that wants to be sure that what they've built, what they have a heavy-duty ego involvement with, gets a qualified caretaker. Someone who loves their business as much as they do.

Buyers should never approach sellers with a secretive attitude, displaying what seems to be a hidden agenda. This causes a lot of additional grief when the time comes to get down to the serious stuff of cutting the deal. Make it easy on yourself at the very beginning. Furnish the seller with a copy of your résumé or bio at your first meeting or exchange of information. Let them know what your interests are in their business. Don't hold back when they question you about your knowledge, background, experience, and connections. Your driving agenda is to create a win-win forum in which to negotiate. Be prepared, attentive, relaxed, focused, interested, and charming. In the first meeting, your primary objective is to establish a positive rapport with the seller. The second objective is to establish that you are a qualified buyer.

Don't Discuss Price or Terms

The first personal meeting is not the time to discuss price and terms or to exchange financial statements. Obviously if the sellers offer theirs, you should graciously accept. Your focus should be on gathering due diligence materials to fully explore the risks and opportunities. If they ask you about your reaction to their listed or quoted price, simply reply that you do not know because you have not analyzed the business. I emphasize *business,* not the deal.

Part of your interest in the early meetings is to qualify the sellers. Are they truly motivated to sell? Do they have a timetable? Do they have a valid reason? Do they say they're "thinking about selling"? Ask what they intend to do after they sell. What do they plan on doing with the proceeds? Seldom will a serious seller say that is none of your business. Ask how they got started. Ask about the major decisions they've made. What big problems have they faced? Draw them out to determine their true motivations. Avoid controversial subjects and proffering your opinion. Remember, they're the seller. They talk. You are the buyer. You listen. It may take more time than you estimated, but you're establishing rapport and learning.

After you've made the tour of the facility and gathered some initial due diligence materials, set a time for the next meeting. Make every attempt to have this second meeting in a week to two. If you have already determined that you really aren't interested, say so and bow out gracefully.

Getting into the Nitty-Gritty

In your second and subsequent meetings, your primary goal is to continue your due diligence efforts. Keep in mind that your strategic goal is still to establish a comfortable relationship with the seller. Come prepared with a checklist of questions. Don't be afraid to take notes, but do so openly, on a large tablet, and don't use a tape recorder.

When you have reached the point where everyone seems comfortable with the exchange of financial information, realize that this is a two-way street. Obviously, you need a good deal of information from the seller. (Refer to the financial part of the checklist in the due diligence section.) You also need to be prepared to furnish some information on how you intend to pay for the purchase of the business. This may mean that you have a semi-prearranged commitment letter from a lender or that you have other backup materials sufficient to substantiate your payment ability.

At some point in time, you are going to have to get into the serious points of working out the deal. Most likely this won't happen until you have pretty much completed your due diligence and hopefully not until you have established a good rapport.

Getting the Deal Done

You can look at the negotiating process as taking place in three periods:

First—Get comfortable

Second—Get information

Third—Get the deal done

This third step is when you introduce the subject of terms and price.

After spending a good deal of time together in steps one and two, you will have a good sense of what the seller is expecting. If the price has been a nice round $1 million figure, your continuing comment has generally been "Based on what I know so far, your price is reasonable." You have not argued the price, you have not attempted to take anything away from the seller, you have not made the mistake of saying "That's too much."

A big negotiation key is to get the seller to be the first to name the price. If you are forced to start this discussion, always start by naming the terms and then lead into the price. During the first two steps you should have gotten a handle on the seller's wants and needs—answers to points such as how much debt is on the books, how important the club memberships are, the cars, other perks, or a continuing consulting agreement. These are all psychological points that can affect the hard dollar issues like tax implications to the seller.

Begin a "get the deal done meeting" with a presentation of a written offer by presenting and emphasizing each point, starting with the terms. Start off with the perks, and obtain verbal agreement on each one. Never lump these benefits into one figure. These are benefits you are giving up. By leading off with the perks and benefits that you are willing to give, the next steps are to offer your downpayment and term payments (we are assuming that like the vast majority of all private deals, there will be owner-carryback involved). This process causes the full price to come out in a logical process.

By using this presentation process, you have effectively structured the deal. When you go back and make compromises on the benefits in the front or middle part of the offer, sellers fast realize that each time they say no, they are giving up some benefit.

Any resistance, at any point, means you don't have a really motivated seller or you haven't gotten to the bottom of his or her real need. For each resistance point, ask point blank "What's wrong? I thought you wanted...Talk to me...I must have misunderstood...What do you really want?" *Stay mindful that if price is the only point, you probably don't have a truly motivated seller.*

Use rational examples from your valuations studies. Point out your thinking step by step. Compare other deals for the educational value of alternative investment returns. Most important, remember that the art of negotiation is compromise and the key is to listen. Last but not least, if you haven't got a bonafide seller, walk away and go to your next deal.

There you have it. My keys to successful Seniorpreneurial business buying negotiation. Make it your intention to provide a win-win deal by listening.

Franchising

If starting a company sounds too risky and buying an existing company just doesn't hold any appeal, you may wish to consider the franchising alternative. To an extent, much of the idea-generation process of putting together a business plus the inherent problems of transforming an idea or concept into a viable business is accomplished when you buy a franchise. You get the excitement of forming a new venture, save time in developing the operations, and to some extent, reduce your investment risk.

As is true for many of the more complicated subjects addressed in this book, there are full books devoted to the subject of franchising. I suggest that you read several. I'm going to review some basics and then offer you a different perspective. This perspective approaches franchising from the opposite side, from the side of the franchiser—the seller to the franchisee. This serves a dual purpose for Seniorpreneurs. If you feel you have an idea that may merit being franchised, these points will help you assess its potential. This way you can get a feel for franchising from the inside-out.

New Franchise "Watch Points"

In recent years, there have been between 200 and 300 new franchise companies established each year. Just as in starting any new business, a large number of these franchising concepts don't survive. It's easy to be attracted to a new franchise concept. The idea is usually fresh and seems a natural. But a new idea alone isn't going to make a franchise successful, especially long term and especially as a Seniorpreneur investment. Here are some of the areas you should specifically look for when you are investigating a new franchise concept.

Some Basics

First some basics. Check with the local Better Business Bureau (BBB) and state attorney general's office. This may be in your area, the franchiser's area, or areas where there are existing franchises. Ask the BBB if there are any complaints on file or recent actions against the company. Most states require that a franchiser register with the state. Ask if that's been done and if not, ask the franchiser when it will be done. Don't invest until this has been accomplished.

A second basic is to inquire if a federal trademark registration has been filed. This item shows up on the UFOC (more on this next) Item

Should You Start, Buy, or Franchise?

13, and the last thing you want to get caught in is a trademark infringement suit or to have to change on-site signs and business materials.

The last basic is what is termed a uniform franchise offering circular (UFOC), commonly referred to as the franchise "disclosure document." This is a document that the federal government requires all franchisers to furnish all prospective franchisees. It is a very important document, and you should read and attempt to understand it completely. It's not a bad idea, after you have semi-determined that you have a serious interest in a particular franchise, to have your attorney and accountant review the UFOC. Legal counsel can clear up your legal obligations and the accountants can assist you in analyzing the financial condition of the franchise company.

After you have gotten acquainted with the basics, there are some additional areas that bear particular note when dealing with any franchise concept. These areas have been given increased attention through a revision in the federal guidelines in the UFOC document as a result of the concern of past violations by a few franchisers.

- The franchiser must furnish the document, including a standard franchise agreement, a minimum of 10 days prior to the franchiser or a sales representative making an offer to sell you a franchise.
- The complete investment must be expressed in terms of the maximum and minimum costs to open and operate a franchise for a reasonable period (3 months) including preopening costs disclosed in chart form.
- A detailed outline must disclose information on the franchise training program, including the opening assistance offered by the franchiser.
- Each prospective franchisee must be given reasonable time to review the operations manual as part of the disclosure process.
- Detailed information must be provided regarding site selection, the preopening process, training, and operation of the franchise.

The list of other areas you should question or be concerned with includes such items as:

- Who are the principal owners, officers, and management? What is their experience and background?
- Verify existing franchisee earnings claims by reviewing the basis and assumptions, the numbers of units that exceed the claims, and cautionary language.

- What are the full initial costs and what do these cover? What are the continuing licensing fees, and are you required to purchase supplies solely from the franchiser?
- If the product requires servicing, who is responsible for the guarantees and warranty?
- What is the franchiser's attitude toward you? Is it concerned about your qualifications? Does it seem interested in a long-term relationship? Are there renewal rights? What about resale rights?
- Carefully review the financials. Look for continuing income from royalties to show that the existing franchises continue to support the franchiser.

Ideal Characteristics of a Franchise

The following is a list of the ideal characteristics of a franchise. If you think you have an idea or concept that may be franchiseable, compare it to this list.

- Is it a stable, nonfad concept, that encourages repeat business?
- Is it recession proof, something that people always need? People buy franchises in good times (when they have money) and during bad times (when they need jobs).
- Is it in a rapidly growing segment of a rapidly growing industry? Or will it create a rapid growth segment (niche) of a stable mature industry?
- Can you compile and write a simple, clear, concise operations system guide (this includes marketing, operations, advertising, and training guides).
- You need a solid trademark—name, process, item, slogan.
- You need to be able to "document" the best advertising methods.
- Can you monitor it long-distance (keeping track of operations and offering assistance)?
- The location should not be so unique that it won't work elsewhere. You will need to be able to document the location finding process.
- Is it a cash business, or one needing a minimal amount of start-up capital for inventory, receivables, and custom fixed assets?
- Does it have the potential of being number one in a national niche? Rarely has the market-segment leader been overtaken in franchising. (However, some concepts are viable for only regional franchising.)

Should You Start, Buy, or Franchise?

- Copycat franchise ideas can capture significant market share. However, the growth curve is considerably reduced.
- Your product or service has to be distinct: quicker, cheaper, bigger—better in more than one way.
- Your product or service must have a difference that can be easily and quickly communicated.
- The concept must be timely and be able to adapt to changing market conditions over a 20-year period.
- Will it be an enjoyable place to work, own, or manage?
- Can it be competitive from the start?
- The business itself has to be easily teachable.
- It must be a business that lends itself to others operating it.
- It must lend itself to simple licensing procedures. However, some successful franchises can be created that require a specialist as head of the franchise—for example, medical, dental, legal, insurance.
- Will the franchisee be proud of the product or service?
- Does the idea/concept lend itself to being a nationally accepted franchise? This spurs national growth and creates a market for resale of the franchises.
- Is it one in which the franchiser gives real value to the franchise, especially in combining the operational lessons to a number of units?
- Have you proven that it works? You need a profitable track record. (It takes only one or two, not ten or twenty units.)
- Can you financially support the initial growth period?

The largest myth about creating new franchises is that the franchiser's money comes from selling franchises. Wrong. Successful franchises are built by collecting royalties—by building an ever-increasing, value-added stream of income by providing goods and services to the franchisee.

If you think you have a franchiseable business, check the Yellow Pages for the names of franchise consultants in your area. Contact them and request information about the franchises that they have started or worked with. Ask for specific names that you can contact. Then contact several and inquire about their feelings in having worked with the particular consultant. After you have positive feedback, and only after receiving this feedback, recontact the consultant.

There are quite a few so-called franchise consultants that simply charge large fees to prepare the complex documents needed to start franchising. They may not be qualified to determine the viability of the proposed franchise concept itself. Good franchise consultants can conduct feasibility studies that will assist you in determining the franchise potential of your business.

The top franchise service concepts for the last half of the 1990s will address areas such as:

Education-driven child care

Medical billing and management

Services for our aging population—in-home care, transportation and shopping, how to complete paperwork

Fitness and health services

Personal services for working families—shopping, maid and house cleaning and caring, computer repair.

Seniorpreneurs Love Their Job

We have covered a lot of information in this chapter that has included a number of checklists and points for you to ponder when you consider the advantages and disadvantages of starting, buying, or signing up for a franchise business. This has included approaching the deal from the science side as well as employing art. The best advice, when all things have been carefully considered, is to step back, take a few deep breaths, and ask yourself if you can really love this job. If the answer is yes, just like the Oriental proverb, you'll never have to work another day in your life.

PART 2
Getting Going

6
Building the Inside Seniorpreneurial Team

The Seniorpreneur has to seek out the team members individually while pursuing business goals. This and the following chapter help define the challenges and provide suggestions and solutions for Seniorpreneurial team building. The clues in these chapters apply to Seniorpreneurs who are building small enterprises as well those conceiving large far-flung operations.

A long, long time ago, back when there were downtowns (not malls), grocery stores (not hyperstores), banks (not ATMs), the scale of our world was a lot smaller, more intimate, and personal. Your grocer probably knew you had fried chicken on Sunday and your paperboy (not person) knew you wanted your paper inside the door. This was because these people were your neighbors and friends. Business was personal because life was personal. Mass marketing and info-highway satellite communications take out the human relationship and replace it with anonymous and impersonal contacts. This is a point to remember when choosing your team. Attempt to put together a *personal* team—one that relates to people and not just numbers. This is a superior way to make a Seniorpreneurial team standout.

One or More Seniorpreneurs?

In Chapter 2, we explored the characteristics of entrepreneurs and Seniorpreneurs. We uncovered the traits that contribute to Seniorpreneurial success and what drives the individuals themselves. Our concentration in this chapter is to determine if a whole Seniorpreneurial company needs to be comprised of Seniorpreneurial types, or just part of it, or if only one Seniorpreneur is needed. Basic instinct tells us that it's probably just one or, at most, a couple of individuals with specialized management talents, like inventors or marketing types. The lead Seniorpreneur—and the quality of the team—is *the* most important factor to success.

This basic instinct is correct: only one is needed. However, for Seniorpreneurial companies, that one person must be supplemented with a team that is entrepreneurially oriented. Team members can't just be run-of-the-mill, ordinary managers. They have to be superior in their chosen management discipline, confident of their talent and ability to get the job accomplished on time, within budget, and with spectacular results.

The Seniorpreneur management team needs to be sure that when problems arise, they get addressed and solved. The positive mentality seeks out the problems, identifies the causes, works together to solve them, and goes on, ever-mindful of the ultimate goals.

Staff

When lead team members have been selected (a topic addressed in more detail in the next section), they then become responsible for selecting staff personnel, organizing their tasks, and putting systems into place.

Senior-guided companies tend to create an invigorating work environment in which a lot of the key people as well as staff employees exercise their will to succeed. The results can be spectacular. Enthusiasm builds on itself and is part of the excitement of being associated with a Seniorpreneurial project. But how do you make sure you are hiring people who have this unseen quality to succeed?

Hire the Well-Qualified

Although there is no sure way of enhancing your chances, one good approach is to hire overqualified personnel. This is a tough assignment when you are operating within a limited budget, but it can make a big difference in the final outcome. One way to reduce hiring mistakes (and there will be some) is to attempt to develop well-defined job descriptions. Management's challenge is to be sure that new employees understand their jobs, are able to perform them, and are supplied with a super support structure. If this is not done properly, the results will be mass confusion and lack of work productivity, not to mention rehires.

Rehires in all personnel, especially in staff positions, are extremely time- and dollar-consuming. It takes a minimum of 3 months for new staff employees to learn their jobs. Many times, in reality, it takes closer to 6 months before you can count on them as building blocks for new responsibilities. This ability to hire, organize, and manage is an important quality to look for when putting together the top team members. One caution: Overqualified people tend to instigate too many controls when the company is still small. This overregulation can destroy the missionary zeal that senior-managed companies seek.

Seniorpreneurial Management Types

It's commonly acknowledged that entrepreneurs see opportunity where no one else knows it exists. This ability to retrieve something meaningful from a lot of unrelated places is usually backed with a good deal of creative drive. For true success, entrepreneurs need someone to back up their innovation, someone to keep the pieces glued together. They need managers—managers to help find them money, to account for it once it's found, to prepare legal documents for their endless stream of deals, to prepare the brochures and coordinate the sales trips, to be sure that the products are getting produced and shipped, and that they work when they arrive at their destination.

This ever-roaring entrepreneur, who is always creating work, needs other bodies to sort out the pieces, solidify disorganized plans, and implement the whole. Managers differ from entrepreneurs in that they are thorough and don't get distracted from the task at hand. Entrepreneurs live for the great achievements which lie ahead; managers, while optimistic about the future, are pleased with their accomplishments to date.

While not risk-averse, managers typically don't have a high level of risk tolerance. They're seeking a balance among challenge, risk, and reward. They want, need, and deserve equity, a piece of the action. They make the team stronger by creating better business plans with more concrete market and product research along with systematized launch strategies.

There must be depth, maturity, and experience in the industry in which the company operates. It's best if Seniorpreneurs have had prior profit center responsibility; if they don't, there had better be plenty of it in other team members. There also needs to be an intimate knowledge of the market and a well thought-out strategy for penetrating the market. The management team is the most important consideration in the investment decision, and the Seniorpreneur needs to assemble a top-notch team.

Getting Intimate with the Management Team Requirements

Since Seniorpreneurs come in lots of sizes and shapes, and with varying talents, the blend and unique fit among the founders are what is most important. The object is to take the talents of the Seniorpreneur and combine them with the capabilities of equally talented and committed partners. Mix in the wishes that they can work well together and that the critical mass can seize and execute the opportunity, and the chances for success are dramatically improved.

The functions of a management team differ for different companies, depending on the nature of the business. For instance, a high-tech product company may need a large research and development department, whereas a service firm may not. In another example, a company that subcontracts all its manufacturing most likely won't need a production manager; however, it may need a quality control expert. Specific management abilities function in specific designated areas. The following is a general list of guidelines, qualifications, and fundamentals outlining abilities by various members of a management team for a variety of Seniorpreneuring companies.

Administrative and General Management

Communication. The ability to communicate clearly and effectively to all parties and the public in both written and oral form.

Making Decisions. The ability to take input from the team and implement changes.

Negotiating. The ability to solicit differences from all sides, balance opinions, and arbitrate fairly for mutual benefit.

Planning. The ability to identify obstacles, establish attainable goals, and develop and implement action plans.

Problem Solving. The ability to gather and analyze facts, anticipate trouble and know what to avoid, understand how to implement solutions effectively, and follow up thoroughly.

Project and Task Management. The ability to properly define and set goals, organize participants, and monitor a project to completion.

Operations Management

Inventory and Quality Control. The ability to establish suitable inspection standards, maintain accuracy, and set realistic dollar benchmarks for raw, in-process, and finished goods.

Manufacturing. Demonstrated experience in the process, openness to continuing improvement techniques, people power, machinery, time costs, and quality needs of the customer.

Purchasing. The ability to seek out the most appropriate sources and suppliers, considering cost, delivery time, and quality, and to effectively negotiate contracts and manage flow, balancing current need and dollar resources.

Financial Management

Capital Raising. The ability to determine the best approach, form, debt/equity structure, short- versus long-term needs, and financing sources.

Money Controls. The ability to design, implement, and monitor all money management needs and to set up systems for overall and individual projects.

Ratios Applications. The ability to produce detailed pro formas for profit and loss (P&L), cashflow, and balance sheets, and to analyze and monitor all financial areas.

Marketing Management

Evaluation and Research. The ability to conduct thorough studies using proper demographics and to interpret and analyze the results in structuring viable territories and sales potential.

Planning. The ability to provide promotion, advertising, and sales programs that are effective with and for sales representatives and distributors.

Product Continuation. The ability to determine service and spare parts requirements, track customer complaints, and supervise the setup and management of the service organization.

Product Distribution. The ability to manage and supervise product flow from manufacturing through the channels of distribution to the end user, with attention to costs, scheduling, and planning techniques.

Support. The ability to obtain market share by organizing, supervising, and most important, motivating a sales force.

Engineering and R&D Management

Development. The ability to guide product development so that a product is introduced on time, stays within budget, and meets the customer's basic needs.

Engineering. The ability to supervise the final design through engineering, testing, and manufacturing.

Research. The ability to distinguish between basic and applied research, keeping a bottom-line balance.

Personnel Management

Conflict. The ability to confront differences openly and determine resolution with teamwork.

Criticism. The ability to receive feedback without becoming defensive, and to provide constructive criticism.

Culture. The ability to create an atmosphere and attitude conducive to high performance, rewarding work well done, either verbally or monetarily.

Development. The ability to select and coach subordinates and pass this ability on to peers.

Help. The ability to determine situations in which help is needed.

Listening. The ability to listen without prejudging, really hear the message, and make effective decisions.

Legal Management

Contracts. The ability to comprehend the broad procedures and structure for government regulation and commercial law, including warranty, default, and incentives.

Corporate. The ability to comprehend the intricacies of incorporation, leases, distribution, and patents.

This list covers the basic qualifications, abilities, and characteristics that the Seniorpreneur should take into account when assembling a management team.

Five Basic Management Functions

It's the Seniorpreneur's responsibility to ascertain if prospective team leaders are proficient in the following basic management functions:

1. *Set objectives* in clear, concise terms.
2. *Organize,* analyze, and classify work, and group these into an organizational structure.
3. *Communicate* with and motivate people. This skill is essential, because it is the people who in the final analysis get the job done. How well they do it depends on the quality of the communication and degree of motivation.
4. *Follow up,* measuring performance and results.
5. *Develop* good people in present jobs as well as in anticipation of future advancement.

With the qualifications and functions defined, the Seniorpreneur can turn to the tasks of identifying, interviewing, and putting together a team.

Seniorpreneurial Hiring

In a company founded by seniors, it's not unusual for two or three key people to be preidentified; however, it's also not uncommon for there to be two or three big holes in the team lineup. This may also apply to some key middle management people, who may be critical right from the start, who have not been identified or retained. This section provides an outline for organizing new hires and gives some helpful hiring tips.

The Search Process

Jon Fitzgerald, President of Health Industry Consultants Inc. in Denver, Colorado, heads one of the country's top executive search firms in the health industry. He has also worked with the author in conjunction with the Senior Entrepreneur's Foundation. His firm has a guide for the steps involved in a comprehensive executive search. It provides a good outline for a Seniorpreneurial company to use as a guideline when it must go outside its inner circle to find and qualify potential top-management candidates. In an abbreviated form, the following describes the executive search process from a human resource manager's standpoint.

Step One—Company Review. The first step is to write down a profile on some company basics. This includes gathering information regarding products/services, market share, and competitive information. It also entails assessing such items as working environment, management style, organizational structure, reporting relationships, and compensation packages, as well as listing the candidate's ideal qualifications. Additionally, interviews are conducted with key people in the company. These initial familiarity sessions help the senior search team assess the existing and potential chemistry needs between the Seniorpreneur and the management candidates as well as providing a written outline to guide the search process.

The Seniorpreneur should also consider these factors prior to initiating a search. The Seniorpreneur should prepare a "brief" that addresses the company's intended positioning in its industry, the "style" of the company, and the "feel" of the management. With these points in mind, the fit with a prospective employee can be better balanced.

Step Two—Planning. A forecast of completion dates for each hiring step is drawn up. This causes the existing team to establish some time and task benchmarks.

Step Three—Research. Research is undertaken to gather data on areas in which additional team members might be identified. Resources include competitive sources, university affiliates, management directories, "who's who" directories, and industry directories. For Seniorpreneurs, this step takes some extra effort. They have to force themselves to look outside their normal circle of business contacts and uncover and explore new sources. The list may be over 100 names.

Step Four—Recruitment and Evaluation. The Seniorpreneur now initiates prospective candidate contact, making preliminary interest inquiries and soliciting résumés. Extensive telephone interviews are conducted and some initial personal interviews may be held.

Again, for Seniorpreneurs, this takes an extra effort. It requires the commitment of blocks of time to concentrate on soliciting candidates and the preliminary interview process. There's a hidden benefit in this step. It is that the Seniorpreneur makes new personal contacts and many times gets some scoops on the latest happenings in the industry.

Step Five—Documentation of Results. An initial report is prepared that summarizes each candidate contact, and then a review is completed to reduce the list. Relocation sensitivity is determined and additional promotion of the employment opportunity is presented to the candidates.

Step Six—Interview Cycle. This step requires interaction among the candidates, the top search executive, and personal interviews, as well as additional phone discussions. Information is exchanged all around, and preferred types of interviews or tests are conducted, including psychological interviews when required. In-depth reference audits are also performed.

This step is the most difficult for Seniorpreneurs. Parts of it require an unemotional attitude, and ofttimes Seniorpreneurs have a hard time backing off their natural sales enthusiasm and just presenting the facts about the company and the position.

Step Seven—The Hire. This is the final elimination. Salary negotiations are conducted, an offer is extended and (presumably) accepted. Many times, the Seniorpreneur is the lead in this step.

Step Eight—Termination of Search. Backup candidates are notified that the search is completed.

The Seniorpreneur may wish to have an executive headhunter conduct all or part of this search process. The executive search by a headhunter can take from 2 to 6 months, with costs varying from hourly fees to set annual retainers, all plus expenses. Most venture capital firms have established contacts with favorite executive search firms as well as a large collection of industry contacts.

Seniorpreneurial Interviewing Techniques

You are about to make a decision you may have to live with for years. Don't do it lightly. Hiring decisions are supercritical for Seniorpreneurs, whether for top team members, middle management, or line employees. You can't afford the loss in time by making a bad hiring decision. Each employee is part of the value-added process; when you consider that every person takes 3 to 6 months to get up to speed before he or she can make continued meaningful contributions, you realize that attention to detail applies in hiring just as it does in all Seniorpreneuring steps.

It's important that you spend some time prior to an interview to square yourself away and get into the proper frame of mind:

Keep in mind the position to be filled.

Read the résumé immediately prior to the interview.

Know in advance what questions you wish to ask.

Give the candidate your undivided attention.

Choose a quiet, private, comfortable location.

Your Attitude

Be impartial. First impressions can be prejudicial.

Use the candidate's name frequently.

Think of candidates as interesting; learn something.

Smile; be friendly.

Treat the candidate as you would wish to be treated.

Meeting the Candidate

Introduce yourself by using your name and title.

Mention that you're going to take confidential notes.

Ask questions in clear, concise, conversational tones.

Don't ask "yes" or "no" questions.

Ask open-ended questions: who, what, when, where, how.

Attempt to determine the candidate's goals.

Avoid snap judgments; draw the candidate out.

Don't sell; interview.

Give the Facts. Review the facts about the position, good and bad, including job requirements, hours, working conditions, job security, opportunities for advancement, benefits, and pay. Make no promises you can't keep; don't exaggerate. Remember, this is a high-stress situation for the candidate; speak slowly.

Asking Questions

Keep questions clear and concise.

Ask one at a time.

Start with easy ones.

Ask what candidates have done, what they want to do, what they can do, what they are willing to do.

Pay attention to their answers.

Pay attention to their questions.

What You Want to Learn

Are interviewees industrious or lazy?

Are they alert and observant?

Are they open-minded or opinionated?

Are candidates enthusiastic self-starters?

Are they willing to learn new things?

Are they thorough, and do they display common sense?

Are interviewees honest, and do they take pride in the job?

Interview Guide

Some further techniques are presented in the following guide. The "ask yourself–ask them (prospective employees)" question format is very effective. The Seniorpreneurial team members should spend some time prior to an interview with the candidate's résumé in hand to formulate some specific questions. This is a critical step that will assist you in getting below the surface of the individual to determine if he or she really fits your company's needs.

Ask yourself	Ask them
1. *Attitude*	
Can compete without irritation?	Ever lose competition, feelings?
Can bounce back easily?	Uncertain about making a living?
Balanced interests?	How can American business improve?
What is important?	Are you successful to date?
Loyal?	Describe best boss?
Take pride?	Favorite duties/least favorite?
Team player?	Feelings about coworkers?

Ask yourself	Ask them
2. Motivation Settled in work of choice? Work from choice/necessity? Make day-to-day plans? Make long-range plans? Leisure for self-improvement?	What ambitions do others hold for them? What done to improve job skills? Mortgages, debts pressing? Will job help get what's wanted?
3. Initiative Self-starter? Complete tasks? Follow through? Work independently?	How got into line of work? Work better alone or with others? What likes/dislikes in job? Do supervisors let you work alone?
4. Stability Excitable/even-tempered? Impatient/understanding? Show likes/dislikes freely? Use words showing strong feelings? Poised/controlled? Impulsive/erratic? Perform under pressure? Enthusiastic about job?	What disturbs you most? Get along with people you dislike? What childish actions irritate? Describe unpleasant work. Describe pleasant work. What do you most admire about spouse? What do you most admire about others? What irritates you about others?
5. Planning Ability to plan/follow up? Ability to coordinate others? Ability to fit into company? Think of new improvements? See whole or details?	What part work like best/least? What part is most difficult? How spend typical day? Where will you be in 5 years? If manager, how run job?
6. Insight Realistic in self-appraising? Desire for self-improvement? Problems of others' interest? Reaction from others? Will take constructive action?	Tell me strengths/weaknesses. Weaknesses important to do something about? Size up last employer? Most useful criticism received?
7. Social Skills Leader or follower? Learn new ways to deal with people? Make friends easily?	Do with spare time? Start any groups? Prefer new or old friends? How go about making friends?

Rate a candidate in each category. Keep in mind: "What is this candidate telling me on a personal level? What kind of person is he or she?" Other parts of the interview should cover education, previous experience, and other matters related to specific qualifications.

You're in a search posture when interviewing. Your charge is to gather facts, establish feelings, and confirm information which will lead to a critical decision. Seniorpreneurs are always seeking ways to add value to their enterprise. Putting together a top-notch team by effective interviewing is one of the best value-added tasks.

Your Board of Directors

Here's an area where Seniorpreneurs can really shine. Because they have a longer work history, they should have more contacts, and these contacts should be of higher quality. The result is that their company will really stand out from a company established by younger entrepreneurs. A highly visible, well-qualified, and supportive board of directors is an important executive tool available to the Seniorpreneur.

The Difference between Good Boards and Bad Boards

A good board of directors is composed mainly of outsiders. A startling statement? For many entrepreneurs, yes. Those who have a little experience understand that selecting outsiders for the board often goes against the grain for the CEO. It's true that there could be outside members who don't have a stake in the company. It's understandable if one dislikes involving outsiders in important policy decisions. Thus CEOs tend to enlist people who are involved in the day-to-day operations of the company, such as the key management team members. This is a *bad* board of directors.

Most entrepreneurs will deny this, but employees and managers tend to rubber-stamp the CEO's decisions and inhibit rather than encourage frank comment—not to mention that they may be too close to the situation. It's called self-preservation. It's hard to be objective when one's own job may be at stake. Therefore, it's in the Seniorpreneurial CEO's best interest to choose board members who will give independent, unbiased feedback, and who will not be afraid to disagree or say no.

Another good reason to limit insiders on the board is to preserve the CEO's own infallibility. No one has all the answers, but when the CEOs can't come up with answers it can weaken their leadership position in the eyes of management. It's not a good idea for subordinates to know when CEOs are frustrated and unable to come up with the solution to a problem or to discover they are not the great leaders they seem. All of us, at one time or another, face a decision we just don't know how to make. Strong boards of directors can serve as psychological support teams to help Seniorpreneurs make the important decisions.

Determine the Outsider's Role

Outside board members serve a very important function in a Seniorpreneurial company. They are outsiders only in that they do not actively work in the company as employees or managers. A board member could be a major shareholder (most valuable), a business associate (valuable), a retired chief executive (valuable), or an investment banker (good). Also acceptable, but lower on the ladder, are lawyers, accountants, and suppliers with a financial stake in the company. The common feeling is that potential board members should be reviewed very carefully, since they may have personal interests at odds with the company's best interests. Other excellent candidates for the board are persons engaged in businesses different from the company's, who can appreciate and understand the risk of running a Seniorpreneurial enterprise.

A good board member plays many roles—from assisting in formulating long-term policy and plans, to critiquing existing financial, production, or marketing practices. But the board member's most powerful role is that of confidante, mentor, and peer to the Seniorpreneur. With a good board, rather than the president making decisions alone, the directors become involved in setting company policies and strategies and reviewing operating results.

Overall, board members should demonstrate respect for the Seniorpreneur. They should like the Seniorpreneur and want him or her to succeed. They should have unquestioned integrity, good judgment, relevant experience, problem-solving skills, and a capacity for taking action and handling risk. That's why a good board is hard to find.

An Informed Board Is a Helpful Board

One of the prime responsibilities the Seniorpreneur has to the board of directors is to keep it informed. Directors must be given information on a timely and continuing basis. They must have meeting agendas and pertinent background information sufficiently in advance of scheduled meetings to allow them time to prepare for the meeting. They must be furnished with monthly financial statements, including comparisons to budgets. At all meetings, they must be given detailed reports on the company's progress.

Although most directors may know what is expected of them, it would be a good idea for the company, usually through its legal counsel, to furnish each board member with a copy of the *Corporate Director's Guidebook*, published by the American Bar Association. This book provides an overview of the functions and responsibilities of the corporate director and will help the directors perform their directorial functions responsibly, as well as adhere to the company's bylaws and any governmental regulations. Consider it a *must read*.

What to Expect from a Board of Directors

The Board of Directors Does Not Run the Company. The board of directors does not run the company; management runs the company. The board sees to it that the company is well managed.

The Board of Directors Does Not Develop Company Strategy. The Seniorpreneur and management team develop company strategy. Board input can be indispensable, however, in coming up with ways to test and evaluate management strategy.

The Board of Directors Enhances Company Performance. The board of directors can turn its attention to immediate needs, such as controlling costs, or it can apply its expertise to planning ahead to future needs, such as defining and penetrating a new market. The board must be flexible enough to deal with all matters in the best interests of the company.

Directors Should Be Experts in Their Fields. It's up to the Seniorpreneur to assess the management team's strengths and weaknesses and the company's direction, and then select the best candidates for board positions. The intent is to fill or supplement voids in the management structure and thereby help improve the company's performance. The Seniorpreneur will probably be pleasantly surprised to find the high caliber of outside people who not only are flattered but would gladly serve on a Seniorpreneurial board of directors. The ideal board is composed of top-notch people who are experts in the industry, such as a scientist with an interest in business dealings who would benefit from the experience.

Directors Must Attend Meetings. At the very minimum, board meetings should be held quarterly. The frequency of meetings depends on the needs of the company. According to national surveys conducted annually since 1971 by Korn/Ferry International, one of the world's largest executive search firms, boards meet an average of eight times a year. Seniorpreneurial companies may find it necessary to schedule meetings 10 to 12 times annually. The Korn/Ferry survey also determined that the average outside director devoted more than 150 hours annually to company business.

By contrast, a survey by *Venture* magazine found that 38 percent of private companies held board meetings only when needed, 29 percent held monthly meetings, 25 percent held quarterly meetings, and only 8 percent met semiannually.

Directors Get Paid. As far as compensation goes for directors, no two companies do it the same. Compensation can take many forms, including annual retainer fees and hourly or per-meeting fees, plus expenses. In a recent Korn/Ferry survey of 31,000 companies, meeting fees for outside directors ranged from $100 to $1000, with an average of $534. In addition, many firms have established annual retainers of $5000 to $10,000. For Seniorpreneurial companies there may be no fees at all, although $100 per meeting seems to be a common practice.

Another form of compensation, especially for cash-short companies, is the issuance of stock in lieu of money. This practice can prove to be a disadvantage over time, as it makes outside directors insiders. If a director is also a shareholder and the company is faced with a decision that may adversely affect the value of the shares, that board member may not be totally objective.

Directors Can Get Sued. By way of explanation, in 1977 Congress passed the Foreign Corrupt Practices Act (FCPA) as a part of our securities regulations. This act stated that officers and board members should create an environment whereby middle and lower levels of management, as well as employees, understand the nature of corporate accountability. It urged board members to be cognizant of their responsibility to monitor the totality of corporate performance. This well-intended legislation was probably the forerunner of many lawsuits, especially against public companies.

Most of these lawsuits are nuisance suits, but they are very expensive to fight. There were hundreds of such suits filed up to the mid-1980s against both private and public companies. This resulted in skyrocketing premiums by liability insurance companies. Many insurance companies just plain stopped writing officer and director policies, and many fine outside director prospects turned down offers to serve on boards of directors.

In response to a major outpouring of protest from the business community, many states passed legislation that limited officer and director liability. The SEC compliance became stricter; tighter financial accounting rules to promote more control were instituted. The increased adverse publicity resulted in companies policing themselves more carefully, and court awards were reduced. These cases were no longer plums for the lawyers seeking to make big, quick bucks, because plaintiffs had to prove that the company, its management, and more particularly, individual directors, were purposely negligent in performing duties, or committed willful acts of omission, especially fraud. The result has been that these types of suits have really subsided and, in fact, liability insurance is now again becoming affordable.

Makeup of the Board

There is no standard operating procedure regarding the number of members that must constitute a board of directors or the mix of outside directors versus management members. It depends on the scope of the company, egos, and personal preferences of the Seniorpreneurs. Five directors on the board is a good number for several reasons. It's an odd number, which avoids tie votes, the rigged taking of sides, and bitter personality battles. Three members may not allow for sufficient diversity of opinion or fill weak areas in management. Two outside directors seems to satisfy the vague FCPA rules and the court's feelings about the need for outside objective input. Using two inside managing directors and rounding a board out with one outside major shareholder may be ideal. For a Seniorpreneurial company, five directors is ordinarily sufficient and, as the company grows, it can easily expand to seven. Thus a company can add expertise from either inside or outside to fit expanding needs without the board becoming cumbersome and overly expensive.

Committees of the Board

Because of the proliferation of liability suits against companies, management, and boards during the last decade, as mentioned earlier, companies were compelled to become more accountable. Committees were established to validate accountability. Many entrepreneurial companies today maintain committees composed of board members, management, and outside experts. These include:

Audit Committee.   Comprised entirely of outside directors, the audit committee reviews the company's internal accounting procedures and controls. It also chooses and interrelates with the outside audit accountants.

Nominating Committee. This committee reviews the performance of the directors and recommends nominees for directorships.

Conflict-of-Interest Committee. Composed at least of two-thirds outside members, the conflict-of-interest committee oversees significant transactions among the company, its subsidiaries, and members of management.

Compensation Committee. This committee reviews management compensation, including salaries, bonuses, perks, and stock incentives.

Executive Committee. The executive committee serves as a mini-board acting on behalf of the full board to see that policy is implemented.

The Board of Advisers

The board of advisers is not set up as a committee of the board, although in some corporate structures it is considered to be one. One or two board members may head the advisory committee and act as a buffer between the advisers on the outside and the board itself.

As a rule, the formal setup of the board of advisers is accomplished through an amendment of the bylaws. The advisers are appointed by the board of directors, but they are distinct from the board. In most companies, advisers may not be officers, directors, or employees of the company. They are experts in various fields whose function is to consult with directors and company management on technical, management, and economic factors that affect the company. Well-chosen advisers add prestige and credibility to a Seniorpreneurial company, especially when it comes to fund raising.

It should be noted, too, that members of the board of advisers serve at the pleasure of the board of directors and receive compensation as determined by the board, often only in the form of consulting fees. They are also provided with indemnification by the company.

There are no requirements for formal group meetings by the board of advisers and, in fact, it's not unusual that advisers never meet as a group. Individual members of the board are consulted as necessary in their areas of expertise.

Team building is not restricted to insiders and full-time employees of the company. Seniorpreneurial companies cannot afford to have all the needed management disciplines in house. Consequently, the next chapter addresses some other important *outside* team members.

7
Assembling the Outside Seniorpreneurial Team

Unlike many other types of entrepreneurs, Seniorpreneurs recognize that their inside team members don't necessarily complete the picture. They know they need and depend on some outside players also. There's even a greater difference. Seniorpreneurs know that these outside members are not just ordinary professionals, but people who must be integrated into and support the Seniorpreneurial concept. These outside team members are always highly qualified, very knowledgeable in their areas of specialization, and motivated to ensure that the Seniorpreneurial effort succeeds.

Consultants and Advisers

The old adage that too many cooks spoil the broth doesn't apply when it comes to hiring consultants and advisers for Seniorpreneurial companies. No matter how professional a management team may be, and no matter how well staffed the company, there are usually areas of the business that can use outside expertise. That's why consultants were born.

A consultant is a person with specialized expertise. Consultants are often retained on a one-time basis for a specific problem. Advisers, discussed later in this section, may also serve as consultants, but are expected to have a broader knowledge of the business. Advisers are usually retained to advise the company's management team on a longer term. They can be especially useful when working through the Seniorpreneurial approach.

What Consultants Are Really For

Bringing in a consultant is not the same as hiring another person on the staff of the company. Consultants should be retained only for the period of time required to assist the management team in identifying, isolating, and solving problems or deficiencies. The consultant's function is to bring a particular problem into focus and zero in on the solution.

If there is a marketing problem, the marketing consultant may advise the company when to put the product on the market, whom the product should be directed to, and where the product is likely to receive a good reception. Or a consultant can provide expertise on product packaging improvement or production techniques. There are countless situations in which management could be served by help from an outside professional.

A consultant or consulting firm is not someone management turns to in desperation; rather, he or she should be used as a source for helpful guidance. In the case of a Seniorpreneurial company, many consultants like to get involved during the conception phases. If they really know their craft, they can be very helpful in starting a company off on the fast track.

Consultants Can Come from Anywhere

Anyone can set up shop as a consultant. Some people who call themselves consultants are simply self-promoters. Some work on a temporary basis. They are often people with good management skills who are between jobs, or they can be former CEOs who offer expertise in their particular fields.

There are tens of thousands of private consultants in the United States today. Most work on their own, but there are also consulting firms that employ as many as several hundred people. These range from national to international in scope. Their clients are usually major companies. They prefer long-term projects and their fees are commensurately high. Many major companies operate on this premise: the higher the fee, the better the consultation. The question is whether the consultant's expertise and experience fit your company's needs. Look for proven professionals in their field who have successfully helped others with problems similar to those facing your company.

Hire When Ready!

When enlisting the aid of a consultant or consulting firm, you should first be convinced of the need. Management consultants are generally hired for the wrong reason; once hired, they are generally poorly employed and loosely supervised.

Therefore, it is important that the company do its homework before hiring a consultant. Most consultants have an area of expertise and a specialty. Some may claim broad expertise, but their experience may actually lie in a special industrial or technical area. The company should find out this information in advance. The fact that a consultant has an excellent background in one field does not make him or her an expert in another field. The company should also determine in advance the precise problem needing a solution, thus eliminating some consultants from the running.

Consultants Are Not Always Necessary

Properly utilized, a consultant can appreciably help a company's operations, but too often management may already have the answer to a problem and need only to convince key people. The consultant can serve that purpose, but at a price. Consultants also are often asked to explore areas that the company has no intention of pursuing. Yet another misuse of company money is to hire consultants to research information that is readily available.

A sharp management group can solve many consulting chores without paying unnecessary consulting fees. For instance, suppliers can usually advise a company whether it is more advantageous to buy or lease certain assets, or how to go about computerizing a business with the right kind of hardware or software. Insurance company agents are trained to determine the most efficient insurance and employee benefit plans. Advertising agencies and marketing firms interested in working with the company will usually provide sound, useful information for free. All it takes is a little talking to the people a company does business with or plans to do business with. Remember, a consultant is not the only one who can supply answers.

Consultant is not a magic word. Consultants should not be left to their own devices. Management has an obligation to stay on top of consultants' activities as well as to make certain they get the necessary support from the company's staff. Consultants should be encouraged to develop solutions within a reasonable period of time. It's your time and money.

How Much Should You Pay?

Consulting fees can take many forms. They are often open to negotiation, but some consultants are firm in their charges. Much depends on the complexities involved. Fees can be based on hourly time or a weekly amount. Some consultants ask for a fixed fee or retainer. Many companies prefer to have consultants work in house, but some consultants will work only off site.

The ideal way for the company to approach the consultant situation is to contact several possible consultants. Brief them on the problem. Secure proof of their expertise and get information on several similar projects they have worked on. Besides asking for credentials and a résumé, request specific proposals on how your project could be handled. Before reaching the final decision, be sure you feel confident working with the consultant and satisfied that the four items listed below will be received.

A realistic and reasonable charge for services

A determined attempt to produce results

A cooperative attitude toward the people involved

Maintenance of a continuing relationship

The effort and time involved in securing the services of the right consultant for a particular need will pay off handsomely. The chemistry must be there, for with it comes the confidence and security the job will be done right.

There are many sources for locating consultants. They can be found through the Small Business Administration, colleges and universities, and professional placement services. Bankers, attorneys, and accountants are very good resources. Some of the best sources may be recommendations from other companies; if you put the word out in your daily networking, you should get solid results.

Some Advice on Advisers

As mentioned earlier, advisers differ from consultants in that they are usually connected with your project for longer time periods. The best advisers—the most dependable ones—are those people or consulting firms that have been through the Seniorpreneurial battle from beginning to end more than once. You may have to search, because there are not many out there. What's more, even though the advisers may have been through the process, they'll find it different every time. Markets change, financing methods change, and the exit strategies change.

Advisers are best used if they are integrated into the Seniorpreneurial process as early as possible. It really helps if they can have a handle on the progress as it ramps up and carries on. They should be able to temper the eagerness of the Seniorpreneur and the management team, ignore minor pitfalls, offer encouragement, act as sounding boards, and help get on with the show. Advisers are best used in strategic planning, in helping to form policy, and in identifying other professional outside team members.

Accountants

Although it's not a strict requirement, and there is no law that states so, it is very advisable that a Seniorpreneurial company have an audit-capable certified public accounting (CPA) firm involved with it from its opening stages. For the small company, hiring an auditing accountant to verify the controller's figures may seem like paying to have the same job done twice.

Generally, start-up and early-stage companies do not have a need for a detailed or complex accounting system. In all probability, a part-time bookkeeper or controller could easily handle the accounting.

It's easiest to look at the accounting function of an early-stage Seniorpreneurial company as having three distinct parts: a bookkeeper/controller, a chief financial officer (CFO), and an audit accountant. The controller is the on-site, most likely full-time person who is a full-charge bookkeeper. He or she sets up the books and keeps them going, hopefully in a very accurate way.

The chief financial officer will most likely be a part-time consultant or adviser. As the company grows, it may be the intention to bring this person in on a full-time basis. Regardless, the CFO will most likely have an accounting degree and may also be a registered CPA.

The audit accountant is optional, but for very reasonable cost should at minimum be used as a consultant at the start-up stage. This adviser will assist in making sure that the initial accounting systems are properly set up so that the company's books will be in order for an eventual audit.

Compilations, Reviews, and Audits

The following are brief descriptions of the three types of reports that CPA firms issue. The reports can be confusing, but a Seniorpreneur needs to have a good understanding of the differences.

Compilations. A compilation is the simplest of the CPA reports, generally performed for internal use only. The purpose is to give the accountant a general understanding of the nature of the company's business, the accounting records, and company policies. The CPA reads the company's prepared financial statements and makes sure that they are in appropriate form, free from clerical errors. The figures are supplied by management, and the CPA does not express any opinion about them.

Reviews. A review is a report that goes beyond the compilation. It provides some assurance about the reliability of the company's financial statements. The CPA reviews the accounting principles and practices of the company and its industry, and analyzes and compares expected trends, past results, industry data, and internal projections. The review may also contain some of the specific procedures that would ordinarily be performed in an audit. The CPA firm will state that it has reviewed the financial statements but will not express an opinion about their validity.

Audits. An audit is a confirmation of the creditability and reliability of the financial statements of a company. An audited financial statement is prepared by an outside audit accountant (who is a CPA) to guard against company manipulations in the report. The accounting firm reviews and evaluates the effectiveness of all accounting procedures and internal financial controls. The accountant must attest (issue an opinion) to the legitimacy of the company's financial statements and to the company's financial position for the period covered. This is the toughest type of accounting report.

Be Prepared

Companies in the early stages of doing business should start making preparations for long-term existence. They should start this process right from the beginning of corporate formation. If a CFO is not part of the start-up team, a qualified adviser should be in place.

At minimum, a bookkeeper or controller should be on the job, but need not be a full-fledged accountant. The position includes responsibility for day-to-day bookkeeping functions and coordination with the outside accounting team. As the company grows, there will probably be an increasing need to bring in a full-fledged accountant.

Seniorpreneurial Considerations with Regard to Audit Accountants

Audit accounting is a subject warranting a closer look. Audit accountants must be completely independent of the Seniorpreneurial company.

They must not have any financial or ownership interests in the company, and they cannot take stock for fees. They work in teams, and their job is to look for trouble in the books, so they tend to be suspicious. They seem to trust no one, especially in the company. They can be expected to cross-check every item because that's what they're paid to do.

There are many ways to qualify an auditing firm. One of the best is to get recommendations from a trusted business friend who is familiar with audit accounting. Seek information from your advisers and attorneys. A word of caution to Seniorpreneurial companies contemplating going public as a harvest strategy: Any CPA firm can work the numbers game, but not all CPA firms can play the public company Securities and Exchange Commission (SEC) numbers game to the benefit of the client. If your harvest strategy includes going public, or being acquired by a public company (both of which require audited financial statements), you should carefully consider using an SEC-qualified CPA firm from the beginning. Select promising candidates and request proposals for final evaluation. Ask questions such as the following.

What are the firm's areas of expertise?

Do you have useful investment contacts?

Who will work with your company day to day?

What are the billing methods? Hourly? By job?

What is the billing cycle?

When can someone begin?

How long will it take?

Will the firm give you an estimated total cost in a written proposal?

Familiarity Is a Must. Every effort should be made to hire audit accountants familiar with the company's type of business and industry. Familiarity helps because audit requirements differ vastly from industry to industry. For example, the inventory of an oil pipe supply company occupies many acres of outdoor storage, whereas the inventory of a fast-food franchise is turned over (consumed) every day. Similarly a manufacturer of high-tech small parts may fit 3 months' inventory in a few fireproof file drawers. Bookkeeping, payable, and receivable methods and standards vary from industry to industry. This results in special rules being applied to different types of companies and to their various stages of development. The audit accountant must have the skill and knowledge to work through these differences. That is why familiarity is a must.

GAAP Must Be Observed. GAAP is an industry term. It stands for *generally accepted accounting principles.* GAAP dictates the principles for presenting audit information. As an example, accounting methods of private companies are generally aimed toward decreasing taxable income and depreciation. Inventory booking and write-downs are adjusted accordingly. Private companies frequently switch back and forth from cash to accrual accounting methods to assist tax adjustment. These practices are not allowed for companies which function under GAAP. All accounting for public companies must be done on an accrual basis.

Although the process of auditing an existing company that has not been previously audited can be costly and time-consuming, it can be done, providing the company has maintained fairly complete financial records. However, getting into the verification of inventory may be a different matter.

Inventory verification within GAAP can be very complicated. For most auditing, there are pieces of paper that provide an "audit trail"—something that shows what happened when, for what number, and for what amount between what parties. The audit accountant can verify these facts. Sometimes it involves writing to suppliers or customers to request verification that on such-and-such a date, they sold or were owed X number of items at X costs or X number of dollars. It almost always requires that the company's bank verify the amount of money in various accounts or in loans on certain dates. But until some sort of time machine is perfected, it will be very difficult, if not impossible, for the audit accountant to verify that on such-and-such a date, X number of some part were sitting on some backroom shelf and included in an inventory count. How do they know for sure that there were 28, not 29, pieces? This is why, at minimum, having an audit accountant monitor an inventory check becomes so important. That way the audit firm can certify that it did indeed physically observe all inventory. The audit trail is complete.

Time Costs Money. A Seniorpreneur with the goal of selling a company should seriously consider enlisting the services of an audit accountant to monitor and audit inventory procedures from the very start. The cost will be considerably less than that for a fully audited financial statement. It won't eliminate the necessity of a full audit if a buyer insists, or if the company intends to exit via going public, but it will save time and dollars, not to mention making the company much more creditable for acquisition, sale, or merger.

An audit for a small existing company can take from a few weeks to possibly 6 months. It depends on the problems that the auditing process may uncover. Previously unaudited companies, if they haven't conducted their accounting according to auditing standards, are typically beset with such deficiencies as poor accounts payable systems, uncollected accounts receivable that haven't been written off or down, unreconciled bank accounts, notes payable with double assets pledged as underlying collateral, and incorrectly recorded depreciation expenses.

Accounting ethics require strict adherence to due diligence procedures. For instance, if the company purchased a major piece of equipment, the accountants will have to see copies of purchase orders, invoices, receipts, and canceled checks. Areas that can present very complicated problems for previously unaudited existing companies include personal financial dealings (by officers and directors) that were placed through the corporation. Even when the company extends its officers advances and loans that aren't by nature wrong, special schedules may have to be filled out.

All these issues take time to resolve, and the costs vary according to the time expended. An acquiring company may require an audit before it hands over the check. Wouldn't it be nice to say, "No problem, we're audited," instead of waiting for weeks or months to seal the deal while getting an audit performed? It makes sense, both timewise and dollarwise, to consider setting up the Seniorpreneurial company's books for audit right from the start.

Attorneys

The Difference between Large and Small Legal Firms

Like shoes, legal firms come in different sizes and styles. Many of them specialize in various types of legal services. It's up to company management to choose the firm that best fits the company's requirements as to size, compatibility, competency, and potential worthwhile business contacts, including investment contacts.

A large legal firm is not the answer for all companies. True, a large firm may have several hundred lawyers with many areas of expertise. On the surface, that may seem advantageous. Many large companies prefer such firms, as they can call upon the services of different specialists in one office. That arrangement may serve the purpose of a diversified, multinational company with many divisions and different companies under its corporate umbrella. A Seniorpreneurial company, lacking that corporate makeup, wouldn't need a firm with all those attorneys, and faces the possibility of getting lost in the shuffle.

Large legal firms with many partners and associates traditionally also have many young, inexperienced junior associate attorneys. These are usually assigned to work with small companies on a day-to-day basis. Since the associates must often clear their advice with a partner, dealings can become frustrating for the Seniorpreneurial management as well as time-consuming and costly. These new, bright young lawyers, although capable and intelligent, lack experience, and they can make a lot of mistakes. It's a learning process for them, but it's usually the Seniorpreneurial client who pays for their mistakes.

Depending on the benefits and prestige derived from engaging large law firms as opposed to small ones, it may be preferable for the Seniorpreneurial company to work with a smaller legal firm. For one thing, the company will get closer attention. Junior associates or paralegals become involved usually to help out only on routine matters. Many small firms can be fully competent to handle all the corporate information, including a good surface knowledge of SEC rules and regulations for the Seniorpreneurial company contemplating going public as an exit.

Getting Along

Too often the attorney's image is that of a necessary evil. Attorneys have been typecast as arrogant, nonresponsive, and overpriced. In fact, some of them are very nice, but rarely do they come cheap. However, in the eyes of reasonable entrepreneurs, the price is right if it helps get their Seniorpreneurial company results.

There must be no secrets kept from counsel. The more a legal firm understands the company's industry, its management team, and its aspirations, the more helpful it can be, and the less frustrating for all. Forthrightness will also save time, which translates directly into dollars when dealing with legal counsel.

Specific Questions to Ask Prospective Attorneys

Before interviewing for counsel, management should prepare a list of questions for a potential law firm or attorney to answer to assist the CEO in the selection process. The questions below can prove helpful in making the decision.

> Do you have particular specialty areas, and are they compatible with our company's industry?
>
> Who will be our day-to-day contact?
>
> What is your billing procedure?

… Assembling the Outside Seniorpreneurial Team

Can you give us your best estimated total costs, including expenses and fees, for a particular project?

Do you have any useful investment contacts such as underwriters, brokers, or private investors?

When the interviewing and cross-checking of references are complete, the most important selection criterion comes into play. It's called "comfortability." Are you comfortable with the personal rapport between you and counsel? Do you sense a good level of mutual respect? Will you feel comfortable working with this person on tough problems under possibly stressful conditions? If your answers are affirmative, trust your gut and go for it.

What Lawyers Are Selling, and How They Charge

Attorneys typically bill by time; they count not just hours, but minutes, including phone minutes. Their rationalization is that they do not sell products or services, but knowledge and past experience which can be invaluable to the client.

Although hourly rates vary considerably from less than a hundred dollars to several hundred, a good round figure for the primary senior contact member of a law firm is about $150 per hour. Junior associates may bill from $75 to $125 per hour, and administrative functions (typing and copying) may cost from $35 to $60 per hour. These are give-and-take figures, but every minute counts.

Ethical law firms usually provide an estimate of the total costs on a project basis. It's safe to assume that the final amount will seldom be less than the estimate. Although some firms are willing to put a cap on a project cost, they usually leave an out for themselves for unanticipated exigencies. The entrepreneur can make book there will be something.

It's also unrealistic to assume that legal counsel will work on a contingency basis for normal Seniorpreneurial legal needs. It's best to plan on a deposit or an advance of at least the first month's work or first stage of work. Rarely will a law firm perform any substantial work prior to an initial payment, usually made at the time of the signing of an engagement letter.

Other Forms of Payment. Generally speaking, the legal profession is not adverse to taking a limited flyer with the company. Many attorneys like Seniorpreneurial companies, not only because they generate handsome fees and are fun to work with, but because they can take a portion of their fees in stock. The structure of the legal business in itself does not generate capital appreciation or equity buildup. Consequently, accepting stock as part payment allows lawyers to become more intimately involved with the company and gives them an opportunity to invest without actually putting out any hard cash.

Paying stock in lieu of money can create problems. For one thing, it can dilute ownership among shareholders in the company. It can cause disagreement among the partners of the law firm too. Especially in larger firms, it often happens that partners who are not directly involved with the project may not feel as positive about the company's potential. They would prefer cash to restricted stock that has no guarantees.

The strongest argument against stock as payment is the potential conflict of interest. Some company managers may question whether the advice they receive is in their interest or their adviser's interest. Attorneys in the law firm may question a conflict of interest regarding outside parties involvement. The ability to remain objective when negotiating non-arm's-length transactions may also be questioned. These may seem extreme concerns, but they should not be ignored in a decision to offer stock for the services of legal counsel.

Double-Check the Cost. As mentioned earlier, the cost of doing business with a law firm is high under the best of circumstances. Therefore, it's just good common sense to make a practice of regularly reviewing counsel's billings. To err is forgivable. To not check the error is expensive. Time and again, good relationships between management and legal counsel have dissolved because it seemed that counsel was taking advantage regarding billings. This assumption, more often than not, turns out to be unfounded. That is why professional legal counsel is always ready to discuss, substantiate, and if necessary adjust billings. It's up to the company to keep the lines of communication open and frank. Establishing a good working relationship and then maintaining it is of benefit to both company and counsel.

The Multiple Counsel Approach

It's common practice to have more than one type of legal counsel working for a company. It frequently happens that entrepreneurs have used a general practitioner type of attorney for years to advise them on a variety of needs. Then when they get involved with a Seniorpreneurial company, this old legal counsel friend may not be able to fill the bill. Don't fear, the comfortable long-time relationship doesn't have to be abandoned. Attorneys are used to working together, and the good ones recognize the limitations of their legal expertise. So if you need more sophisticated corporate advice—say, for acquisition or merger, a contemplated public offering, or patents, trademarks, real estate, or other specialties—don't hesitate to obtain it, and use your long-time trusted counsel to coordinate. The two lawyers can complement each other and probably at a cost savings to you and the company.

Conclusion

Regardless of the entrepreneurial effort, management, management, management is the primary secret to success. For Seniorpreneurial enterprises, the ability to readily assemble a superior management team is one of the advantages of being a senior. This applies to both inside and outside team members.

After the team is selected, the initial task is to firmly establish goals. With goals defined, the challenge is to assemble a business plan that will serve as a guide to achieving the goals. Compiling the business plan is the subject of the next chapter.

8
Planning the Seniorpreneurial Venture

Business plans boil down to operating the company on paper. The aim is to validate an idea and challenge every aspect of the business. A business plan is a written presentation that carefully explains the business, its management team, its products or services, and its goals, together with strategies for reaching the goals. The entrepreneur or team members who write the plan will find it a painstaking process. But keep in mind, this is *the* selling tool, and it requires careful consideration of all the multiple facets of a start-up or business expansion. It cannot be written as an afterthought, and it should not be taken lightly. Check with any professional investor anywhere in the country, and you'll hear horror stories about ill-conceived, poorly written, or sloppily put together business plans. As great as the company's potential may be, it is essentially doomed to rejection, before it can even get a foot in the door, if it has a poorly conceived business plan.

Planning is even more important for Seniorpreneurial businesses. Because the management team is experienced, the plan is expected to be outstanding, and the benchmarks have to be results-oriented. Several more points differentiate the Seniorpreneurial plan from traditional business plans. These include a more clearly defined exit strategy which requires a closer look at company structure and the Seniorpreneurial business plan valuation approach. Prior to looking at some of the Seniorpreneurial business plan details, let's review some basics.

The Primary Purposes of Your Business Plan

There are two primary purposes to a business plan. The first has an outside objective—to obtain funding. There's no business without capital. The second serves an inside purpose—to provide a plan for early corporate development: to guide an organization toward meeting its objectives, to keep the Seniorpreneurial business itself and all its decision makers headed in a predetermined direction, to explain in an engaging way with interesting information how the company will be run for the next 3 to 5 years. The Seniorpreneur must put all the "hows" and "needs" together in one neat package. The human and physical resources must effectively interrelate with the marketing, operational, and financial strategies of the company. Unless a Seniorpreneur has magical powers of persuasion, this is not the time to try to fake it.

The business plan is considered a vital sales tool for approaching and capturing financial sources, be they investors or lenders. They want to know that the plan has been carefully thought-out by the Seniorpreneurial team. They want to be convinced that the team has the skills and expertise needed to actively manage the company and that it is prepared to seize opportunities and solve the problems that arise. That's why the business plan must be well prepared, professional in tone, and persuasive in conveying the company's potential.

It cannot be stressed too strongly that *a good business plan is the cornerstone of successful financing.* If you want investors' money, you've got to give them good reasons to buy in. The business plan is where you lay out the reasons. It doesn't have to be unduly lengthy or complicated, but it must be informative and relevant. It needs to maintain logic and order, and show the company as effectively positioned as a good investment.

More important, the business plan should be specifically directed to the funding source and satisfy its particular concerns. For example, you would orient and write the plan differently for presentation to a banker than you would for a venture capitalist, an underwriter, or a private investor. The venture capitalist would want to know what risks are involved, whereas the banker wants more information about how good the security is. These concerns must be individually addressed. There are no hard-and-fast rules for preparing a business plan—no established, formal format. The key word is *ingenuity*. Strive for inventiveness; strive to be interesting and captivating.

Incorporate the Nine Guiding Principles into Your Plan

Here are some general guidelines covering the basic elements of a business plan. These should be helpful in writing any business plan, no matter to whom it is directed.

Make It Easy to Read

There is so much competition for investment dollars today that if you want to get the jump on the next person, your plan will have to be well formatted and easily understood. Your introductory statement summarizing your operation is one of the most important sections; it must capture readers' attention and motivate them to read the balance of your plan. Caution: If they need a dictionary at their side in order to read, they'll stop. Construct a glossary if you have to use a lot of technical words.

Be Sure Your Approach Is Market-Driven

Not product-driven. If you want to obtain money, you must understand that investors are primarily interested in how the product or service will react and be received in the market. Before they buy into your plan, they want to see your research demonstrating and substantiating how the customer will benefit and be motivated to purchase.

Qualify the Competition

Start by qualifying your product according to cost or time savings and revenue generation. Also show your projections for sales growth, how your product or service is superior to others, and how you intend to exploit the competitive advantage.

Present Your Distribution Plan

Be specific as to how the company will sell and distribute its product or service. Clearly describe the methods and what it will cost to get the product or service into the ultimate customer's hands.

Exploit Your Company's Uniqueness

Explain what will give your company a competitive edge in the marketplace—special attributes like a patent, trade secrets, or copyrights.

Emphasize Management Strength

Show proof that the company is comprised of highly qualified people who can cover all the bases. Indicate the incentives that will keep them together, and how they, the directors, and the advisers possess the necessary credibility.

Present Attractive Projections

Paint a realistic picture—substantiated by assumptions—of where your company is going with funding. Be detailed and keep it credible. Good validated projections and forecasts are impressive.

Zero In on Possible Funding Sources

As mentioned earlier, it's different strokes for different folks. Design versions of the plan to fit the idiosyncrasies of each source you plan to approach. A banker's interest lies in stability, security, cashflow coverage, and sound returns, whereas a venture capitalist is more interested in high leverage resulting in outrageous returns. Both want to know how the proceeds are going to be spent.

Close with a Bang

Drive home the point that you're offering a good deal. Be definite about how investors will get their money back and when. Specify the return rates; state how the risk investor will receive a 30 percent or 50 percent compound annual return, or whatever you're offering. For lenders, show that their funds are adequately secured and that your cashflow more than covers their interest and principal payments.

The Next Step: Obtain Critical Reviews

You're not finished yet. One of the big differences between ordinary plans and Seniorpreneurial plans is that they have been critiqued to work. After you have drafted your business plan, solicit feedback on it. Ask a cross section of people whose judgment you respect to review it. Don't fall in love with your wordsmithing. Make any revisions that are necessary, and then prepare a good oral presentation. In fact, you should have both a 2-minute and a 5-minute oral attention grabber. Follow up with a detailed 15- to 30-minute presentation. All should be modeled on your written business plan.

A word of caution: When preparing your financial projections, avoid the shortcut of relying on packaged computerized information—those preset formats in which you plug in figures and percentages. Individualize your financial projections. Think them out carefully. No two businesses are alike. Show when you bring on additional personnel, and remember that each new hire adds other costs beyond salary—items like benefits, desks, supplies, maybe even another computer or additional travel expenses. These items need to be tracked for each expense period. Don't just show advertising costs as a percentage of sales. Most advertising expenditures are made some months before sales result. A lot of them have to be prepaid before they are run. It's just not justifiable to show "plugged" computer figures for most expense items. Individualize them. And keep in mind that a start-up company will not fit the standard industry norms.

Your projections should include the financial obligations of bringing your product or service to the marketplace: enlisting new management people as well as workers; taking on more physical space or manufacturing capacity; purchasing support materials and services; and monitoring buildups in inventory and accounts receivable.

Outline for a Business Plan

There are many specifics that should be included in a successful business plan. The following general outline contains many suggestions which may seem obvious, but it is often easy to overlook the basics. Again, this outline should be used as a preliminary planning guide. It's up to the reader to add lots of detail, meticulously gathered and presented in succinct Seniorpreneurial form. (For a complete guide to writing a business plan, see my 1994 book *The McGraw-Hill Guide to Writing a High-Impact Business Plan*. This book includes an offer to receive a free disk with a complete business plan and financial spreadsheets.)

Cover Sheet

Indicate full formal name of company
  ABC Company/ABC Corporation/ABC Inc.
  (If you have a logo, use it.)

Indicate ownership status
   A sole proprietorship/A New York corporation
List full street address
   555 West Fifth, Suite 55, Anytown, State, ZIP USA
List mail address if different
   Mail address P.O. Box 55, Anytown, State, ZIP USA
List phone and fax/telecopier number
List principal contact name and title
   E. E. Seniorpreneur, President
   Home phone number optional
Date the plan
   Month and year

Table of Contents

Categorize the contents. Use section names and page numbers. You have a choice of only main category headings (History, Management, Product, etc.) or detailed categories (History—date founded, founding members, place founded, etc.). Make note of any charts, tables, or graphs.

Executive Summary

A very important part, the executive summary briefly sets forth the contents, taking key sentences from each section of the plan to overview the project for the reader. Limit the summary to two or three pages: more is too many. Consider using your mission statement or a brief visionary type of paragraph. It should be concise and to the point. This section is the first thing that investors read, and they may not read further if you haven't captured their interest.

History

The first several paragraphs should briefly describe the product or service, to whom it is sold, the current status of your industry, and where your new company fits in. This is your second chance to give the reader an overview to establish a basis for detailed understanding. After this brief introduction, include a description of how, when, and by whom the company was started, its achievements and acceptance setbacks. Then bring these experiences to current-day status.

Product or Service

To succeed with a Seniorpreneuring company, you must know your product or service; to succeed in obtaining capital, you have to be able to clearly describe your product or service. After giving a simple, straightforward description, outline the need for the product or service in today's marketplace, how it will make a difference, the benefits derived from using it (or what will make the customer buy it), and its advantages. Explain any special training needed to sell or use it. Include all relevant regulations that may affect its sale or use. Expound on any exclusivity or technological uniqueness. Unless your plan is going only to specialists in your industry area, assume you are writing for the layperson. Forget industry jargon and replace it with words that the nonspecialist can understand. If you tend to write overly technical descriptions, engage a professional writer.

Market Description and Analysis

This section profiles three key areas: customers, industry, and competition.

Prepare a Customer Profile. Describe what customers form your market, where they can be found, why they purchase your product or service rather than another, and whether it appeals to a single individual or to groups. Document quality, warranty, service, and price significance: pinpoint the buyer and user. Point out political influences, if any. Describe market coverage, whether local, regional, national, or international.

Prepare an Industry Profile. Discuss pertinent trends—past, present, and future. Offer available statistical data on sales and units. Use charts, graphs, and tables if they can make the presentation clearer and more impressive. Refer to trade associations if helpful.

Prepare a Competitive Profile. Stress advantages of price, quality, warranties, service, and distribution. Include the operational strengths and weaknesses. Project potential market share trends in sales and profitability.

Don't guess in this section. Check all your facts and note all your sources. You can be sure that these will be checked with a fine-tooth comb during an investor's due diligence process. If you're citing voluminous reports or statistical information, note that you have them available for further review.

Marketing Strategy

This is a critical section that should clearly specify the company's marketing goals, how they are to be achieved, and who will have the responsibility for achieving them. Qualify all distribution methods (representatives, dealers, and so forth) and describe any planned advertising or public relations activities. Include references to sales aids, foreign licensing, and training plans as appropriate. Simply, detail how you are going to sell the product or service.

Operations Plan

This section is primarily oriented toward facilities, manufacturing capability, and equipment. Disclose all present capabilities as to equipment and facilities, as well as further projections for offices, branches, manufacturing, and distribution. It often helps if you include current floor plans as well as expected future space plans for production or manufacturing companies. For all fast-growth companies, task/time charts can be especially useful in this section. They help impress on the reader that the Seniorpreneur has a real handle on the operational challenge.

Research and Development

The length of this section depends on whether you're a service or product company and—if you're a product company—on how technical your product is. The object is to explain all past research and development efforts and accomplishments as well as future expectations. Here is your opportunity to justify past time and dollar expenditures. Substantiate the patentability of inventions, proprietary processes, or other advantages that your company will have over the competition and the resultant, anticipated market impact.

Schedule

Describe the timing and sequential steps that will be taken to bring the company up to full speed. Graphs or charts help indicate the timing and interrelationships of the major events in the company. Take it month by month for the first year. Thereafter, indicate the progress expected quarterly. Areas that may be important include completion of prototypes, starts of beta tests, early significant sales, when key people are to be hired, physical expansions or moves, opening of branches, trade show or convention dates, major equipment purchases, and the like.

Management

In the eyes of the investors, the *quality of the management team* often determines the potential success of the company. Consequently, this section should cover career highlights, accomplishments, and positions held, with an emphasis on good performance records. Describe how the team has worked together in the past. List all directors, consultants, advisers, and other key professionals who will be involved in company operations and point out how they add value. Detailed résumés of key management should be appended with bios of others as appropriate.

Risks and Problems

Risks could be a red flag. There are diverse opinions about the inclusion of this category. Some investors object to the obvious and prefer to discover their own negatives. Others prefer that the company openly acknowledge risks and potential problems. It's a toss-up; however, high-profile, success-threatening risks should be brought out.

Use of Proceeds

Judiciously present a timetable indicating how much money will be needed, when it will be needed, and how it will be used. Most companies require multiple stages of financing, including both debt and equity. Show the proposed capital structure, including who is going to own what part or percentage of the company at what stage. Start-up plans need to detail start-up use of proceeds and then generalize on the additional stages.

Finances

Present the company's current equity capital structure as well as future plans. Itemize the equity payments made with dates paid. List all outstanding stock options. Include both historical and current profit and loss statements and balance sheets. Present current and proposed salary structure for those who are already on board and those who will come on board at a later date. Show projections, including balance sheets, profit and loss statements, and cashflow studies. These should be month by month for the first year, quarterly for the second and third years, and yearly thereafter. It is mandatory that detailed assumptions accompany all projections. It is also very helpful if the very first part of this section summarizes the details. In fact, in many cases, details can be appended or supplied separately.

Appendix

Include a glossary (if pertinent) and all essential pieces of evidence, such as résumés, product brochures, customer listings, testimonials, and news articles.

Your Plan Is a Lot of Work

It's suggested that you seek out available books on writing a business plan. They can be found in many bookstores and all libraries. Read two or three to give you the essence of a good background for specifically outlining your plan. Each company is different, and your plan must be tailormade to your particular situation. The ideal business plan just doesn't exist, and generic plans just don't cut the mustard for Seniorpreneurial companies. Expect to spend a minimum of 2 or 3 months and 200 to 300 hours writing your plan. It's not unheard of that a Seniorpreneur spends up to a year putting together a detailed plan. Additionally, you'll have to spend some time preparing and rehearsing your oral pitch. Remember, your words and story not only have to paint a pretty picture; they must be persuasive as well.

It's of little use to approach the writing of a business plan as a necessary evil. Rather, look at it as a helpful tool that can be used to exploit the advantages of your product or service.

Some companies may question the necessity of a business plan, citing successful firms that never had one. Times are changing. When the goal is to raise money, it's not only the entrepreneur's money that is at stake. Advisers, team members, directors, investors, and bankers need to be thoroughly convinced. They want to know that they won't be wasting their time and money. They want to know that the Seniorpreneurial management team has a clear sense of direction and is prepared to move toward its established goals.

A good business plan is the answer. What's more, much of the same information would have to be gathered anyway to be made available to potential shareholders before they place their money in the company.

The Seniorpreneurial Difference

As was mentioned earlier, the Seniorpreneurial plan has some peculiarities of its own. The primary difference is in the fact that the operation is headed by a senior or a group of seniors. It means that seniors have to carefully and consciously address the point of company continuity. While the senior-led company has a 20- or 30-year experience and knowledge advantage, prospective investors have a natural concern about the age of management. Consequently, a senior-led company should take steps to provide for stability in operations regardless of concerns for health or disability. This is addressed in several ways.

Groom a Management Team

Seniorpreneurs know they have to cover the bases—the management bases, that is. Every attempt should be made to retain key officers that are multidisciplined. Attempt to identify an accounting type who also has some production experience. Hire a sales manager who understands marketing. Retain a vice president of operations who has worked with accounting and budgeting. When multidiscipline choices are made part of the initial job descriptions, everyone understands up front that a key part of the company's philosophy is a shared work approach. This approach doesn't end with hiring; it continues in actual company operations. It means that the various individuals share the important parts of their ongoing operations and management strategy with their cross-disciplined partners.

Purchase "Key Person" Insurance

Purchasing "key person" life and work disability insurance on the key members of an operating company is just plain smart business. It's a necessity in senior-managed companies. These simple basic term policies are paid for by the company and designate the company as beneficiary. In the unfortunate event that a senior team member has a debilitating health problem or dies, the company receives some monetary compensation to assist it in recovering from the loss and hopefully to ensure its ongoing operations. Investors will require such insurance and allowances for the expense should be noted in the use of proceeds of the business plan.

Consider the Effects of Change

Another seniorpreneurial business planning point considers that constant change is inevitable. These changes—some caused by leaps forward, others caused by setbacks—require that the business plan be almost constantly updated and that flexibility be acknowledged. Quarterly reviews may not be enough. Updates may have to be done every 6 weeks. Seniorpreneurs are always making progress or subtle changes of direction in their companies. It may be a new contract, it may be approval for a new product, it may be a successful beta test. It could easily be a new member of the management team. Regardless, you will fast discover that a business plan often goes stale as the first copies go out the door. Don't hesitate to do simple update sheets as supplements to a plan. Further, it's not the least bit unusual that continuing revised versions are made in the plan itself. That's why it's so important that the key members of the Seniorpreneurial team be intimately involved in business plan writing and revisions. This ongoing revision process brings home the strategic value that both the management team and the plan play in ensuring that everyone is singing from the same songbook.

When a Seniorpreneurial team is established, many problems are confronted on an ongoing basis. The solving of these problems—some that are small and faced on a daily basis, others that may be faced only once in the lifetime of the company—are all important in their time. Many of these problems can be identified in the process of constructing, implementing, or revising business plans. It's a Seniorpreneurial difference: seeking out potential difficult areas, addressing them up front, and determining solutions before they become problems.

Seniorpreneurial Structuring and Valuations

Another important Seniorpreneurial difference regards the initial company structure, ratios, and valuation strategies. While these are points to be considered in any business, they are very important to the Seniorpreneur. They have to be tested right up front. You have to be sure that the end goals are feasible, that enough monetary gain can be had, and that the risks and work effort to be made can be justified. While these topics are books unto themselves, we'll briefly address each point sufficiently to make the Seniorpreneur aware of what points come into play and the primary fact that both legal and accounting counsel should be sought pertaining to these key areas.

Choosing the Right Structure: Legal and Tax Advantages

By structure, I'm referring primarily to the legal entity of the company—sole proprietorship, partnership, corporation, or otherwise. Commonly, a corporate entity is the vehicle that is chosen. It offers the best liability protection for the principals and is the easiest to financially structure and comprehend.

The sole proprietorship, in which one individual owns the company lock, stock, and barrel, isn't conducive to growing a senior-managed company, which requires that multiple members of a management team receive equity consideration. The same is true of the partnership, except in the very early stages prior to the injection of any significant amounts of financing. Incorporation is the way to go, and even here there are several choices to consider. This is why the Seniorpreneur should involve corporate legal counsel from the beginning. Typically, a start-up is formed as a *Subchapter S corporation*, which allows the initial shareholders to treat the expected early losses with favorable personal tax considerations. As the company's capital needs grow, the corporate legal structure can be changed to what is termed a straight *C corporation*. As the most common corporate vehicle, it's preferred by most professional investors because it is treated as a legal entity distinct from individuals or other legal entities. C corps offer the maximum liability protection of any legal business structure.

Several Points of Caution

It is imperative that experienced legal counsel be retained to input these decisions. There are many pitfalls that can cause unneeded problems downstream. These can be addressed early on. For instance, a corporation should adopt a Section 1244 stock plan under the Internal Revenue Code right upon incorporation. This gives the initial investors an identified way to write off their equity investments up to $1 million should the company fail. Another caution is to be sure that legal counsel understands the Seniorpreneurial goal for exiting or providing for the company's continuity. Again, discuss these points with both legal and accounting counsel prior to adopting a formal structure.

Looking Forward to Limited-Liability Companies

A final structure point: As this book goes to press, a new type of corporate structure is being explored. It was initially conceived in Wyoming and is now being accepted by numerous other states across the country. It is called a *limited-liability company* (LLC). While some attorneys are counseling their clients to adopt the LLC as their business entity of choice, others are continuing to show caution pending clarification of a few sticky issues, primarily those oriented to taxation.

An LLC provides the opportunity to have your cake and eat it too. It is intended to provide the same opportunity for tax saving and flexible tax planning as do the sole proprietorship, the partnership in its various forms, and the S corporation, but it also affords all owners the shelter from personal liability characteristic of the traditional corporation.

All this is available without the restrictions on the number and nature of shareholders and other matters imposed by the S corporation.

So what's the problem? The problem is that the IRS has not yet issued a revenue ruling confirming that it will treat the LLC as a "partnership" for federal income tax purposes. Although such a ruling has been granted in connection with the Wyoming statutes, as well as those of many other states, Seniorpreneurs should ask legal counsel about the status in their particular state.

The legal structure of the Seniorpreneurial company can play an important role in successful Seniorpreneuring. The key is to obtain top-notch accounting and legal counsel at an early stage.

Previewing Valuations

Valuation, for our purposes, is the total dollar value of the company at any point in time. Obviously, at the beginning, this value is nothing, zero. Hopefully, as the company matures, it's multimillions. The challenge then, with the small exception of making it all happen, is how we determine these dollar values at various stages in the company's evolution. How do we know how much the company is worth so that when we are seeking new capital infusions, we don't underprice or overprice the percentages of the company we're selling? How do we project these values, especially in the early stages, and how do we keep these valuations consistent throughout the growth process?

These are tough questions with no easy answers. In truth, valuations are not simple science. They are a subtle combination of art with some science. Given the nature of this animal, we can readily see that there could be lots of room for continued disagreement; in fact, that is the one reality of valuation.

The Seniorpreneur's bottom-line challenge is to justify the valuations with a substantial, substantive, and convincing story—a story backed with realistic marketplace facts and sound comparative data. The first thing needed is a basic understanding of the fundamentals of valuations. What are the commonly accepted guidelines? Some of these guidelines are contained in what are called *ratios.*

Previewing Ratios

All financial planning relies on *ratio analysis.* This applies to both existing operations and future projections. Ratios become the science when projecting valuations or the anticipated worth of a company in the future. The Seniorpreneurial company's interest in these ratios is to use them, along with internally prepared projections, to assist in determining valuations and to self-qualify for financing sources. For example, a venture capital firm may have an internal policy that states that owing to past experience, it is not interested in investing in projects that carry less than a 20 percent return on sales. As another example, a conservative bank may feel that loaning to companies with less than a 1.8-to-1 current ratio is too risky.

These ratios, which relate to two or more categories of financial data, are used to forecast future needs as well as judge present and past performance. Past ratios are very useful, because they can be compared across time periods, against former projections, and against industry averages. They can be used to identify and track problems as well as to maintain management consistency. There are six basic financial ratios that are commonly computed from balance sheets and income statements (whether historical or projected).

Expense Ratios

Expense ratios show the company's various expense categories in relation to its revenues. They are used to compare the company's recent performance with past time periods, to project future results, and to compare against industry norms. These expense ratios are calculated for all major expense categories—cost of goods sold, various material costs, selling expenses, general and administrative expenses, and just about anything the company wants to track.

$$\text{Expense ratio} = \frac{\text{expense category}}{\text{annual sales}}$$

Profitability Ratios

Profitability ratios show a company's profitability in relation to either sales or investment. They are used to indicate the *operational efficiency* of the company. The most common are return on sales, return on assets, and return on equity.

$$\text{Return on sales} = \frac{\text{profits after tax}}{\text{total sales}}$$

$$\text{Return on assets} = \frac{\text{profits after tax}}{\text{total assets}}$$

$$\text{Return on equity} = \frac{\text{profits after tax}}{\text{total equity (assets} - \text{debt)}}$$

Utilization Ratios

Utilization ratios indicate a company's ability to manage short-term assets. They are used to show the *financial efficiency* of the company. The most commonly used utilization ratios are receivables in days, inventory in days, and payables in days.

$$\text{Receivables in days} = \frac{\text{accounts receivable}}{\text{annual sales} \div 360 \text{ days}}$$

$$\text{Inventory in days} = \frac{\text{total inventory}}{\text{annual cost of goods sold} \div 360 \text{ days}}$$

$$\text{Payables in days} = \frac{\text{accounts payable}}{\text{annual purchases} \div 360 \text{ days}}$$

Liquidity Ratios

Liquidity ratios show the company's ability to meet short-term debts. They are used to indicate *credit strength* or financial risk. The most common liquidity ratios are the current ratio and the acid-test ratio.

$$\text{Current ratio} = \frac{\text{current assets}}{\text{current liabilities}}$$

$$\text{Acid-test ratio} = \frac{\text{current assets} - \text{inventory}}{\text{current liabilities}}$$

Debt Ratios

Debt ratios indicate the proportion of debt in the company's capital structure. The ratios are used to indicate the *credit strength* or financial risk of the company. The most common ratios are debt to equity and the long-term debt percentage.

$$\text{Debt to equity} = \frac{\text{total debt (current liabilities + long-term debt)}}{\text{total equity (assets - debt)}}$$

$$\text{Long-term debt} = \frac{\text{long-term debt}}{\text{total capitalization (assets - current liabilities)}}$$

Coverage Ratios

Coverage ratios indicate the company's ability to meet fixed financial charges of long-term debt in the capital structure. They are also used to show the *credit strength* and financial risk of the company. The most common coverage ratios are the number of times debt interest is earned, and the number of times debt payments (both interest and principal) are earned.

$$\text{Debt interest} = \frac{\text{company profits before interest and taxes}}{\text{annual debt interest payments}}$$

$$\text{Debt payments} = \frac{\text{company profits before interest and taxes}}{\text{annual debt (interest and principal) payments}}$$

Assuming that Seniorpreneurs know these financial qualifiers, they can test their internal projections against them and, at minimum, have a sense if they can make a first-round cut when seeking financing. This can save a lot of time, not to mention frustration. For the Seniorpreneur, ratios are very valuable when contemplating or executing a senior business plan.

Investor Equity Valuation

The Seniorpreneurial question here is "How much of my company do I have to give away for the financing I'm seeking?" As with all valuation questions, there's no simple answer. Generally, the later the stage of development or the further advanced the company, the smaller the percentage of ownership the Seniorpreneur has to give up. Most Seniorpreneurial start-ups need to secure some amount of outside investment to support their ultragrowth. Consequently, the challenge is to give up the smallest amount of equity and still ensure that the ultimate goals can be achieved. Although there are some guidelines and some ranges, the final figures are the result of negotiations or a persuasive story.

If the Seniorpreneurial company is pure start-up, without prototype or much less sales, the investors are taking the vast majority of the financial risk. At this stage, it's not unusual for an investor to request 50 to 80 percent of the deal, maybe even more. However, if the Seniorpreneur or the team is investing at the same time, that money should buy equity stock on the same terms as the investor(s). Even for high-quality projects that are the dreams and prey of venture capital firms, venture capitalists like to see the Seniorpreneur retain a 20 to 25 percent stake. They feel that anything less reduces the incentive and commitment to make the deal work.

So if this could be considered the normal range for start-up investing, how can the Seniorpreneurial team increase its stake? Many factors come into play here, including:

- A complete management team with proven, above-average prior start-up experience, in-depth knowledge of the product or service, and substantial experience in marketing
- A proven beta test or market test that indicates the viability of the product or service
- A strong patent or proprietary position
- A generally acknowledged real need for the product or service

Strange as it may sound, if the company has a need for substantial second- or later-round financing, most sophisticated investors don't want the original team to get so diluted in the initial rounds that the incentive commitment is lost. If this seems to be a potential problem, one solution is to structure the company so that the Seniorpreneurial team has some performance incentives which allow it to regain equity percentages or exercise options that make the Seniorpreneuring efforts very worthwhile.

In more advanced-stage deals, the valuations are also always negotiable. However, reality plays a part; good common sense, tied into the realities of the financial marketplace, sets the guidelines.

Here is one important valuation reality check. If you are seeking, say, a $1 million investment for 50 percent of your company, what you're saying is that the value of your company before the investment is $1 million. Can you justify that figure? Can you show cause that your concept or idea, what you have put into the company so far, is worth $2 million? A lot of entrepreneurs cannot.

Here's a more complex, but very real-life, example of a venture capital valuation scenario. Assume your projections show $150,000 in after-tax profits in year 3. Also assume that the prospective investors feel comfortable with your projections and won't impose a discount factor. Finally, assume that similar companies in your industry are being valued at four to five times after-tax earnings. On the basis of these three assumptions, you can figure the value of your company as falling within this range:

$$\$150{,}000 \times 4 = \$600{,}000$$

$$\$150{,}000 \times 5 = \$750{,}000$$

Now we can carry this to the next step: It takes two more assumptions. First, you're seeking $200,000 from investors, and second, most investors would feel that a 30 percent annual growth (return) on their money would justify the risk of their investment in your deal. Thus, the $200,000 investment, if it grows at 30 percent a year, would be worth approximately $440,000 at the end of 3 years. If your company value is $600,000 to $750,000 at the end of year 3, and the investors' value must be worth $440,000 to meet their return objective, the $200,000 today must buy from 59 percent to 73 percent of your company, as follows:

$$\frac{\$440{,}000}{\$750{,}000} = 59 \text{ percent}$$

$$\frac{\$440{,}000}{\$600{,}000} = 73 \text{ percent}$$

Remember, this is a starting point for negotiations. You're confident that you will exceed your projections by leaps and bounds and the investor is very skeptical that you're capable of meeting the third-year projections until the fifth year. This type of valuation is very subjective. The more you can do to substantiate your case, to convince the investor that you have not only a good product or service but also a superb Seniorpreneurial team that can execute the plan flawlessly, the better your chances of receiving higher valuations and less dilution.

This type of valuation is commonly known as the *present value formula*. It is expressed as follows:

$$PV = \frac{FV}{(1 + i)^n}$$

where PV = present value
FV = future value
i = investment rate of return
n = number of years the investment is held

Thus,

$$\$200{,}000 = \frac{FV}{(1 + 0.30)^3} = \frac{FV}{2.197}$$

$$\$200{,}000\,(2.197) = FV$$

$$\$439{,}400 = FV$$

There are a number of additional valuation methods available. In fact, although most investors approach the science of valuation in the same manner, almost all investors have their individual approach to the art. The Seniorpreneur's challenge is first to build a convincing business plan that can withstand investor scrutiny and then to be prepared to negotiate aggressively.

Creating a Special Executive Summary

Another unique aspect of the Seniorpreneurial business plan is the putting together of a *special executive summary*. This summary is not the same as that in the business plan; it does, however, take advantage of the high points in the plan. It serves as an entering wedge to semi-interested parties as well as potential investors.

The business plan executive summary, discussed under the Business Plan Outline section, usually summarizes the business plan in two or three pages. The special executive summary expounds on the most enticing parts of the business plan for about six to eight pages. In essence, it's a condensed business plan that shows the company to best advantage. It's an entree, when initially seeking help, to locate and identify potential financial sources. It can also be used as an overview for those who do not need to know all that much about the company (like staff personnel or suppliers), or for those from whom management wants to keep proprietary information. It can be changed and adapted to any particular audience. It's kind of the bait before the hook, a plan used to capture one's initial interest and motivate one to request more information.

A special executive summary should not be taken lightly. It is indispensable, and should be kept updated. This is easier to do than revising a whole business plan if the Seniorpreneurial team simply wants to test some new plan ideas or gain some quick feedback. It may very well be the key to reaching the right source.

Making the Transition from Business Plan to Operating Plan

Once the company is up and running, senior management should convert the business plan to an *operating plan.* This process is simply retitling the plan as an operating plan and then religiously keeping it updated, using it as an operational guide on a continuing basis. The operating plan helps keep both management and staff focused on the tasks at hand. The parts that are pertinent to various departments can be pulled from the master plan and passed on to the appropriate staff individuals responsible. Continuous updates should be given top priority in all Seniorpreneurial companies. The basic plan should be reviewed quarterly—at minimum, semiannually. Remember, for investors, the business plan is what they buy into. It becomes the benchmark for accountability. They intend to hold management responsible for achieving the goals and objectives that are set out in the plan. It is inevitable that things will change as the company achieves full operation. In some cases, these changes will have only a small effect on operations. In others, they could result in a drastic shift in total company focus. Given the ultimate Seniorpreneurial goals, it's apparent that a continuing update of business plan strategy in the form of an operating plan helps keep everyone singing from the same songbook.

Seniorpreneurial Plans Take Your Best Effort

All companies should have a business plan. Preparing it may take months, but you won't get to first base without it. The outlines presented in this chapter may not fit every company's particular requirements, but they should contain enough general information and suggestions to provide a solid base for preparing your plan. More detailed materials and information on writing business plans can be found in many bookstores and libraries.

For Seniorpreneurs, there are some very important points that need to be given extra attention to set their plan apart from ordinary business plans. These include continually updating their plans, paying special attention to the corporate structure and valuation portions of the plan, creating a special executive summary, and finally, converting the Seniorpreneurial business plan to a Seniorpreneurial operating plan.

A company should give its plan its very best efforts. You will discover that a well-prepared Seniorpreneurial plan will serve as a solid sales tool for approaching any financing source—investor or lender—as well as provide management with a written game plan for guiding operations and maintaining a check on expectations.

A final note: *Failing to plan is planning to fail.*

PART 3
Getting Financed

9
Securing Seniorpreneurial Debt Financing

Entrepreneur-managed companies are constantly on the search for new capital, either through debt or equity, and it is seldom easy to come by. The Seniorpreneur understands that raising money is a way of life.

Only experienced entrepreneurs realize that the financing of companies is done in stages and that they have to be flexible in identifying the latest trends in financing. Many first-timers erroneously believe that they can successfully generate sufficient cashflow on a near-term basis, then bootstrap their way to financial success. This doesn't work in today's fast-moving business climate, especially in many medium- and high-tech areas. This chapter examines the potential problems of financing and offers many solutions.

There Are Several Types of Financing

Contrary to the dreams of many start-up entrepreneurs, initial financing can be the hardest part of launching a new business. There are many popular misconceptions that an idea, a start-up team, and a preliminary business plan will get them in the venture capitalist door. They expect to exit, happily, with the check in hand. They don't realize that traditional venture capital funds, which are supported by institutional investors, finance only a fraction of a percentage of the new companies started each year. Many entrepreneurs are not cognizant of the fact that over 90 percent of start-up money comes from private sources.

The first step is to put together a business plan to use as a fund-raising tool (see Chapter 8). The second step is the actual raising of the financing, or financial marketing. Each alternative to raising money requires a different approach to the business plan. Financing never happens quickly; it is never simple. In fact, it is usually quite painful and exasperating. Seniorpreneurs can find themselves chasing down blind alleys if they don't prepare properly.

There are a number of sources of financing and a variety of forms of capital. Some are used to finance seed or start-up companies, while others are used for expansion. Start-ups are usually limited in the types of financing they can get—typically personal savings used as equity or personally secured subordinated debt. On the other hand, companies with a proven track record have a much larger choice of financing alternatives—such as banks, venture capital firms, or public offerings. What all Seniorpreneurs soon discover is that there are several factors that they must constantly reckon with, in pursuit of the elusive dollar. These are the dilution of equity ownership, potential restrictions on daily operating flexibility, and debt-imposed constraints on future growth. These factors will be touched on time and time again throughout this chapter.

Your Two Basic Choices for Financing: Debt and Equity

For all intents and purposes, the Seniorpreneur has two basic choices when considering financing: debt (pledging a part of one's soul) or equity (giving away a piece of it). Commonly, one does both.

In simple terms, debt is borrowed money secured in some fashion with some type of asset for collateral. Equity, on the other hand, is contributed capital, usually hard dollars. Debt may be secured by a personal signature only, and equity can also be in the form of a contributed asset. But most often new businesses require long-term debt or permanent equity capital to support major expansion and anticipated rapid growth. The advantage of borrowing is that it is a relatively simple process to arrange. It does not take a great deal of time and does not dilute equity ownership. The disadvantages are that it is a high-risk strategy as far as company growth is concerned, in that incurring debt subjects the company to a firm obligation, usually including the principals as cosigners. A downturn in business or an increase in interest rates could result in the inability to service debt payments.

Likewise, there are two basic sources of financing: self-funding and external funding. Self-funding, although preferable, is seldom as practical as external financing.

Advantages of Self-Funding

Self-funding involves the investment of the Seniorpreneur's personal money. It has the following advantages:

1. It allows the Seniorpreneurial team to take its time on the business plan and initial product development.
2. It means that the only financing source team members have to answer to is themselves.
3. It saves them the time otherwise devoted to finding one or more financial partners.
4. It establishes a strong internal discipline regarding the spending of funds.
5. It frequently shortens the time needed to get the product to development stage.
6. It usually lessens overhead costs.

The biggest point in favor of self-funding is the fact that it is the best way to build additional value, and hence equity, into the company. A company with a prototype product or service that has been self-financed is worth much more than several individuals with just an idea.

External Funding Is More Complicated

External funding, while not as preferable as self-funding in the concept or seed stage, comes from a lot of different sources of both debt and equity. They can be divided into two groups: informal and formal investors. The informal are traditional family and friends. The formal include venture capital firms and the more formal types of investment groups usually brought together in a private placement. With all these possibilities, external funding can become quite complex.

There are pros and cons to debt, equity, self-funding, and external funding. We'll address all these areas as we proceed through the chapters on Seniorpreneurial financing.

Seniorpreneurs Use Combinations

Unlike oil and water, debt, equity, self-funding, and external funding do mix well. In fact, it's a Seniorpreneurial secret. Senior-managed companies must mix their financing sources and choices.

Which source to use, and when, becomes a matter of individual option, although there are some pretty well-established precedents. Founders' personal investments, including both personal assets and family and friends' equity and loans, are usually what finances companies in the concept or seed stage.

Development-stage companies commonly seek funding from private placements, early-stage venture capital firms, and various grants from both foundations and government sources.

Early-stage production companies may receive financing from bank loans, leasing companies, and research and development partnerships (for incremental product development). Strategic partnerships are often entered into at this stage with potential customers, suppliers, and manufacturers.

Companies at the next stage of ramping up, which is full-scale production and expanded marketing, often receive additional dollar injections. These come from second and larger rounds of traditional venture capital, larger companies that are looking for product distribution opportunities, institutional investors, more venture leasing companies (for manufacturing equipment), and additional strategic partners (often seeking secondary manufacturing and distribution rights both domestically and internationally).

After this stage, the Seniorpreneuring company has some heavy choices to consider. The harvest point is a natural here if the plan has been to build a company and then sell out. The venture still needs more money (what's new), but the choices are now a lot broader: more venture capital, bridge or mezzanine financing while going public, being acquired (perhaps by one of the earlier-stage strategic partners), or selling out to a cash-rich company.

So Debt or Equity?

If we're saying that Seniorpreneurs use combinations, how do we distinguish which and when? The use of debt almost always requires that some equity come in first. A rough rule of thumb is that a dollar of early-stage equity can support a dollar of debt, if there is some additional security to back the debt. Lenders feel that a start-up has little ability to generate sales or profits. Consequently, lenders want to have their debt secured, and even then, they feel that the asset value will be decreasing with time. Also, there's always the possibility that management will not be up to the company-building challenge at hand.

This secured debt will most likely be short-term financing (1 year or less), to be paid back from sales. Short-term debt is traditionally used for working capital and small equipment purchases. Long-term borrowing (from 1 year to 5 years) can be used for some working capital needs, but usually is assigned to finance property or equipment that serves as collateral for the debt.

While commercial banks are the most common source of short-term debt, there are more choices for long-term financing. Equipment manufacturers provide some, as does the Small Business Administration (SBA), various state agencies, and leasing companies. These are discussed in more detail in the following sections.

It's true, Seniorpreneurs can finance start-ups with more debt than equity, but there are some distinct disadvantages. For example, if they negotiate extended credit terms with several suppliers, they restrict their flexibility to negotiate prices. Heavily leveraged (i.e., debt-financed) companies are constantly undercapitalized and will experience continuing cashflow problems as they grow. Paying close attention to strained cashflow requires that a lot of management time be diverted from company operations. It also affects the balance sheet, making it difficult to obtain additional equity or debt.

On the other hand, there is one big positive in using debt. Debt doesn't decrease or dilute the Seniorpreneur's equity position and it provides nice returns on invested capital. However, if credit costs go up, or sales don't meet projections, cashflows really get pinched and bankruptcy can become reality.

Seniorpreneurial companies use varying combinations of debt and equity. They determine which is the most advantageous for the particular stage of growth they're financing. Their aim is to create increasingly higher valuations or profit structures.

Understanding the Stages of Seniorpreneurial Development

Before we delve into the details of Seniorpreneurial debt, let's review the tasks and financing requirements of the traditional stages of entrepreneurial development, as described briefly above. These stages are seed or concept, start-up, first, second, third, and harvest.

Seed or Concept Stage

At the wild-eyed, perhaps incurable, seed or inventor stage, there is an idea, a concept, no management team, and no prototype—and patentability has not been determined. No business plan, timetable, or market research has been assembled. Founder(s) may be technicians.

Tasks. To begin development of a prototype, assemble some key management, develop a business plan, assess market potential, structure the company, and assess patentability or proprietary standing.

Financing. Traditional venture capital firms have little interest in funding a company at this stage. The risk level is just too high, and the time for achieving a payout or harvest is not determinable. Personal savings or money from friends and family funds this stage. It ends with the completion of a seed-stage business plan and the formation of the company.

Start-up Stage

At least one principal founder of the company is pursuing the project on a full-time basis. The prototype is being developed, the business plan is being refined, a management team is being identified, market analysis is being undertaking, and beta tests are being set up or initial customers are identified. More formal funding is being accomplished.

Tasks. Complete and test the prototype and obtain evidence of commercial interest. Assemble and identify an initial management team, finish the business and marketing plans, establish manufacturing, and initiate sales.

Financing. Traditional venture capital firms may show an interest at this stage, assuming that a top-rated management team is assembled, patentability or proprietorship is proven, and marketability is demonstrated. Fund raising is a major effort at this stage, and it may take from several months to a year or more.

First Stage

The company is now a going concern. The product has proved to be manufacturable and is selling. If it's a service company, some customers have tried the service. The management team is in place, the company has experienced some setbacks, customers can confirm product usage, marketing is being refined, adjustments are being made in the business plan, and the money-raising efforts continue.

Tasks. Achieve market penetration and initial sales goals, reach close to breakeven, increase productivity, reduce unit costs, build the sales organization and distribution system.

Financing. At this stage, traditional venture capital firms are interested in investment—in fact, it's the stage they prefer. Financing is needed to get the production bugs worked out and to support initial marketing efforts.

Second Stage

Significant sales are developing, as are assets and liabilities. The company is sporadically achieving breakeven, and cashflow management becomes critical. Second-level management is being identified and hired. Export marketing is being explored, and more sophisticated management systems are being put into place.

Tasks. Obtain consistent profitability, add significant sales and back orders, expand sales from regional to national, identify international marketing plans, and obtain working capital to expand marketing, accounts receivable, and inventory.

Financing. More sophisticated and second-round venture capital financing comes into play at this stage. The founders and investors are forming plans for the harvest.

Third Stage (Also Mezzanine Stage)

All systems are really go, and the potential for a major success is beginning to be apparent. Snags are being worked out in all areas from design and development of second-generation products to marketing and distribution and on to management and all its applied systems.

Tasks. Increase market reliability, begin export marketing, put second-level management in place, and begin to "dress up" the company for harvest.

Financing. At this stage, the company may need to obtain bridge or mezzanine financing to carry increased accounts receivable and inventory prior to harvest. There is a great amount of pressure to prove second- and third-generation products, increase profitability records, improve the balance sheet, and firmly establish market share and penetration.

Harvest Stage

The end may be near for Seniorpreneurial companies. The company is sifting and sorting out its options—going public, being acquired, selling out, or merging. What started out as a dream has become a Seniorpreneurial reality. The next challenge is to start all over again, but this time with a pocketful of dollars.

With an understanding of the stages of development of Seniorpreneurial companies, we can delve into the various types of debt used in Seniorpreneurial financing.

Identifying Debt Financing: Forms and Sources

Pure debt (loan/borrowing) financing can take several forms. It is available from various sources such as banks, finance companies, factors (see the discussion below), and leasing companies, not to mention individuals. Another important, but often overlooked source is trade payables. Debt financing is considered increased risk for the company, since borrowed funds require repayment. However, loans do increase the borrower's return on equity (leverage). Costs to be considered in using debt financing are not only interest, which can be high, but also indirect costs that can be associated with some forms of debt. These include *compensating checking-account balances,* in which the borrower is required by the lender (bank) to maintain a stated minimum balance in a non-interest-bearing checking account.

This means that if the borrower received, say, a $100,000 bank loan, the bank could insist that the borrower keep a minimum of $10,000 in a checking account; if the account fell below the $10,000, the full amount of the loan would be automatically callable for repayment. The borrower is required to pay interest on that $10,000, even though it can't be touched. Additionally, the lender may impose strict loan covenants in the form of company performance ratios that must be maintained. For example:

- The company's net worth versus assets cannot fall below a certain level.
- The company's inventory must be maintained at a certain level.
- The receivables cannot go over a specific level.
- The payables cannot exceed a predetermined ratio.

If any of these covenants are broken while the loan is in effect, the total loan or portions of it can be called due and payable.

Understanding the Forms of Debt Financing

Before the sources of debt financing are examined in detail, it is helpful to have an understanding of the principal forms of debt financing that these sources can provide.

Accounts Receivable Financing. For this form of short-term debt financing, the company pledges its receivables as collateral for a loan. Commercial banks are the most common provider of accounts receivable financing; other sources include commercial finance companies and factors (see the discussion below; banks seldom factor).

The bank will discount the face value of a company's invoice (commonly 10 to 25 percent) and immediately remit the balance to the company. As receivables increase, accounts receivable loan lines can be increased (discounted as to the value of the receivables pledged). Receivables usually will not be accepted if they are over 90 days old, and the bank will reject invoices for companies that they do not feel meet their credit standards. The invoice may be payable as a notification receivable (the company notifies the customer that the receivable has been sold to the bank) or as a nonnotification receivable (the invoice is paid directly to the company, and the company then remits the monies to the bank). A nonnotification is preferable, since some customers deem that a company using receivable financing is in financial difficulty.

Conditional Sales Contracts. When a company knows that by purchasing a new piece of machinery or equipment it can increase its productivity and profitability, it should consider making that purchase through a conditional sales contract. Under this contract, the company agrees to the equipment purchase with a nominal downpayment plus installments payable over 1 to 5 years. The bank holds the title to the equipment and usually has full recourse against the original equipment supplier for the balance on the loan should the company default. When the contract is completed, the bank turns over the title to the company, since the "conditional sale" has been satisfied.

Equipment Loans. Equipment loans, also called *chattel mortgages,* are made to secure loans on machinery, equipment, and business property that collateralize the loan, much like a mortgage on real estate. They are commonly executed through the security agreement forms of the Uniform Commercial Code (UCC). The title (chattel) remains with the company unless there is a default, in which case it reverts back to the bank. These loans are used mainly for new equipment and extend for periods of 1 to 5 years.

Lines of Credit. A bank will make a line-of-credit agreement with a company on either a formal or an informal basis. It will agree to extend a maximum loan balance for a 1-year period. Often, the bank charges an extra 0.5 to 1 percent line-of-credit fee for making this commitment. The loan funds are commonly used for seasonal financing to build inventory or carry receivables. They are generally paid back as the inventory or receivables are liquidated.

Banks usually collateralize lines of credit by pledges of inventory, receivables, equipment, or any other assets they can get their hands on. If the loan is unsecured, the bank will require that all debt to the company's principals or shareholders be subordinated. Often, line-of-credit loans take the form of renewable 90-day notes. The bank will insist that the complete line be paid off once a year and that it remain at a zero balance for 1 to 2 months (called "resting the line"). A compensating balance is also common, with the bank insisting that the company keep a checking account that maintains 10 to 20 percent of the outstanding line of credit. Some banks may "discount" the loan by deducting the interest in advance. Clearly, line-of-credit loans can be very costly—charging extra fees, discounting the loan, requiring compensating balances, and resting the line all add up to a higher effective interest rate.

Plant or Property Improvement Loans. Improvement loans are uncommon among start-up entrepreneurial companies, since they seldom own their plants or property. Start-ups are simply too risky for long-term (10- to 20-year) mortgage commitments. However, the senior-owned and -managed company is very likely to have a hard assetlike property. Should the company make significant plant or property improvements, the loan will be mid- to long-term, secured by a first mortgage on the improvements and a second mortgage on the underlying plant or property.

Time-Sales Finance. Time-sales financing, also called *floor planning*, is used when the company offers to arrange the financing of its products to its dealers and then on to the ultimate customer. The most common suppliers of this type of financing are commercial finance companies, although some commercial banks also offer this service. The company sells its products to a dealer via an installment or conditional sales contract and then sells the contract to a finance company. Some larger companies have subsidiary divisions which do nothing but finance the company's product sales. Many times this same type of contract is then used to sell and finance the product to the ultimate user.

From the company's point of view, floor planning is another way to obtain long-term financing using short-term methods. The bank, which frequently discounts the contract, obtains double or even triple security. The bank takes the contract on a full-recourse basis, first from the company for the dealer's obligation, and then from the dealer for the ultimate customer's installment obligation. The installments may be collected directly by the bank or indirectly through the dealer or manufacturer. Time-sales financing can be a key to Seniorpreneurial growth. The company is making sales by helping its dealers make sales by helping its customers buy financing and the product.

Securing Seniorpreneurial Debt Financing

Unsecured Term Loans. The key words here are *unsecured* and *term*. Unsecured is pretty simple. No underlying collateral is pledged to liquidate the loan in the event of default by the borrower (company). Term, on the other hand, has three key features:

1. The bank loan is extended for a period of up to 5 years.
2. Periodic repayment is required.
3. The loan agreement is tailored to fit the special needs of the borrower. For example, small interest-covering payments may be made with a balloon (large) payment at the end of the term.

Banks watch term loans with a special cautionary eye. This is because the loans are for relatively long periods and a lot of changes can take place in a company over 3 to 5 years. The loans frequently include covenants which prohibit additional borrowing, merger or sale of the company, or payment of dividends, as well as other special restrictive clauses.

You May Have to Sweeten the Deal

The last several decades have seen wide fluctuations in the costs of borrowing money. Interest costs have been as high as 25 percent. What's more, long-term loans often carry *equity kickers* in the form of stock warrants or rights to purchase stock. (This is common practice with venture leasing companies and many sources that provide side or "off balance sheet" financing.) An equity kicker is a deal made by the lenders with the company. The gist of it is that because the company is new and considered high-risk, the lenders are betting that the company will become successful. To offset that high risk for the lenders and to entice them to make loans, the company issues a warrant that allows them to buy X number of shares of the company's stock at today's prices sometime in the future.

It may not sound fair, but savvy Seniorpreneurs know that equity kickers are often the costs of borrowing money for early-stage companies.

Subordinated Debt: An Alternative

An alternative to bank borrowing is the placement of subordinated and sometimes convertible debt debentures with private lenders, venture capital firms, or organizations such as small business investment companies

(SBICs, discussed later in this chapter). Most subordinated debt is unsecured, semisecured, or secured by a specific type of collateral; it is always junior (secondary) to senior or common bank loans. For example, the company has a bank loan for $500,000 that is secured by inventory, receivables, and equipment. The company wants to buy some new equipment to open a new production line. With a small downpayment, the equipment will be enough to secure the new loan. However, if the company should go bankrupt, the bank has first claim against its assets, and the new equipment lender would have to take a secondary position against the assets after the bank. That's what makes the new lender subordinated.

But let's assume that the new loan helped the company reach its goals. The loan agreement may contain a convertibility clause that allows the new lender to convert its subordinated debt (or debentures) to common stock at an agreed-upon date at prices most likely determined at the time of the loan. In essence, the loan is a *subordinated convertible debenture*—that is, debt that can be convertible to equity as stock.

Putting together subordinated and/or convertible debt placements takes experienced legal and accounting advice. Additionally, careful consideration must be given to the long-term effect of equity dilution, since the subordinated convertible debenture holders could conceivably team up with other minority shareholders and, by their conversion rights, gain effective control of the company.

Understanding the Sources of Debt Financing

Now that we've examined the forms of debt financing, let's look at some sources for debt financing. The following section describes a number of them. Descriptions include general characteristics as well as estimated costs for the debt, typical lengths of maturities, how the use of proceeds can be spent, and advantages and disadvantages of using the particular debt source.

Commercial Banks

Banks are traditional lenders for secured short- or medium-term loans. They are "no risk" lenders in that they insist on some form of collateral and are likely to require the personal guarantees of the company's officers. Term loans are usually revolving lines of credit to finance built-up inventory or receivables and are quite often seasonal or loaned against a particular contract. Systematic payments are required over the life of the loan. Banks will also make mortgage loans on a longer-term basis against buildings, real property, and equipment.

Commercial banks do not ordinarily provide unsecured loans or lend to start-up companies. The overall banking crises of the late 1980s and early 1990s made traditional bank financing difficult—and in many areas of the country, almost impossible—to obtain. Today, however, many banks are back in the lending business again.

Costs	Floating rates to 5 points above prime
Maturity	30–90-day notes; credit lines to 3 years; long-term mortgages to 7 years
Proceeds	Working capital; inventory; receivables; machinery
Collateral	Unsecured; secured against specific assets or personal guarantees
Advantages	Usually lower costs than other lending organizations; many branches
Disadvantages	Prefer established businesses; require personal guarantees and/or collateral; restrictive covenants

Commercial Finance Companies

Commercial finance companies provide asset-based lending, most commonly against receivables and occasionally against inventory. Their rates are usually higher than those of banks, and they usually require regular monthly reconciliation of their collateral (receivables or inventory). They are more aggressive lenders than banks, but seek highly liquid collateral, which they are apt to discount highly. If they make equipment loans, which must be backed by appraisals, the maximum period is 5 years, and they insist on stiff prepayment penalties. They most likely will insist on receiving monthly financial reports on the company.

Cost	Floating rates to 7 points above prime
Maturity	Depends on loan size, usually 1 to 8 years
Proceeds	Working capital; acquisitions; machinery; equipment; real estate
Collateral	First liens on assets; personal guarantees
Advantages	Fairly quick processing
Disadvantages	Higher costs, monthly tracking

Factors

Firms whose primary business is *factoring* are called factors. Simply put, factoring is accounts receivable financing. In other words, the company sells its accounts receivables, at deep discounts, to a factoring company. A standard practice is for the factor to buy the company's receivables outright, without recourse, immediately upon proof of shipment of the goods. This applies only to preapproved customers of the company, and the company is still responsible for returns or defective merchandise. Factoring is common in such industries as clothing and furniture manufacturing, plastics, shoes, textiles, and toys. In recent years, some factors have entered into some high-tech areas. However, their terms are stiff because of the high rate of technological change. Factoring is high-cost financing, but it saves some clerical costs (credit checking, cost of bad debt collection, and write-offs) and turns receivables into cash quickly.

Costs	Floating rates 5 to 10 points above prime
Maturity	90-day to 1-year agreements
Proceeds	Unrestricted
Collateral	Often personal signatures
Advantages	Quick cash
Disadvantages	Requires top-credited customers; high costs

Leasing Companies

Leasing companies (which include some banks and most commercial finance companies) tend to offer the entrepreneur more flexibility than commercial banks. The company may lease an asset (equipment, office equipment, trucks, autos) or buy or sell it to the leasing company, and then lease it back (lease-back). Leases can often be made for longer time periods than commercial loans and can be set up with varying payment plans.

Payments can be scheduled monthly, quarterly, semiannually, or in some cases annually. Depending on the tax advantages, the lease contract may also contain balloon payments. Most equipment lessors encourage and offer easy upgrade plans (without major penalties) for fast-growing companies that continually need to move up to next-generation equipment. In recent years, a new type of leasing company has made major inroads in the leasing area. Spawned by venture capital types of financing, these new lessors are know as *venture leasing companies* because one of their primary requirements is that the company has received considerable venture capital financing. This adds a higher level of creditability to the new company; however, it's not uncommon that the company may have to issue warrants or options for its stock to obtain the most favorable leasing terms. Sometimes, lease-backs can also be arranged with private individuals.

Costs	Prime plus 6–8 points
Maturity	Negotiable; operating leases as short as 6 months; financing leases for useful life of asset
Proceeds	Machinery; equipment; real estate; acquisitions
Advantages	Easy deals; 100 percent financing; lessor carries risk
Disadvantages	High costs; no ownership benefits

Savings and Loan Associations

Savings and loan associations (S&Ls) in general have been experiencing major upheavals, changes of ownership, and a lot of financial setbacks. But many are still operating. The entrepreneur should not overlook the fact that with all their problems, S&Ls are still viable financing sources. The distinction between S&Ls and banks continues to lessen, except that S&Ls are still more inclined to finance against real property.

Costs	Competitive with banks; fixed or variable rates tied to the prime rate
Maturity	Long-term to 15 years; occasionally lines of credit
Proceeds	Real estate; some working capital; equipment
Collateral	Always secured; personal guarantees
Advantages	Attractive rates; experienced real estate lenders
Disadvantages	High minimum loan amounts; restrictive covenants

Small Business Administration

The SBA has always been considered a lender of last resort. In the past, a company had to be turned down by two other traditional lenders to qualify for an SBA loan. However, in recent years, the SBA has initiated a variety of new programs that are in place with varying degrees across the country. One major improvement is what is termed an *SBA bank*. The primary business of these banks is originating, placing, and servicing SBA loans. You can find information about the SBA banks in your area by contacting your local or regional SBA office.

Basically, the SBA has a number of different loan programs with various qualifiers. The rates are reasonable, but subject to government funding availability and guarantees. All SBA loans have a lot of restrictive covenants and require a lot of paper processing. The entrepreneur who is successful in obtaining SBA assistance is one who acknowledges and adapts to the paperwork system.

Costs	Floating and fixed rates tied to prime
Maturity	5 to 25 years
Proceeds	Working capital; machinery; equipment; real estate
Collateral	Secured by liens; personal guarantees
Advantages	Low-cost considering risk; do not finance some types of assets
Disadvantages	Liens; personal guarantees; paperwork

Small Business Investment Companies (SBICs)

The SBA licenses and provides leveraged financing to SBICs, which in turn provide various forms of venture capital to entrepreneurial enterprises, usually in the form of convertible or subordinated debt.

Amount available	$100,000 to $1 million
Structure	Convertible debt; debt with warrants
Cost	Reasonable interest; dividends; equity
Proceeds	Working capital; acquisitions; leveraged buyouts
Advantages	Subordinated capital; 5-year debt; fixed interest
Disadvantages	Equity dilution; must prove fast growth

Minority Enterprise Small Business Investment Companies (MESBICs)

MESBICs are identical to SBICs except for the fact that they are designed for, and available only to, minority-owned businesses.

Industrial Revenue Bonds

Industrial revenue bonds are not for start-up or early-stage companies, with the exception of those companies that have substantial equity financing. They are issued mainly to finance companies with large real estate needs or companies with large equipment needs. Also, in most cases, the issuing agency holds title to the property and leases it back to the company.

Costs	Floating or fixed rates at 70 to 85 percent of prime at tax-exempt status
Maturity	Usually 5 to 15 years or more
Proceeds	Real estate; large equipment
Collateral	Secured by fixed assets
Advantages	Low rates; good maturities

Disadvantages	Depends on market availability; strict government rules; high closing costs, especially legal

Life Insurance Companies and Pension Funds

Debt financing through life insurance and pension funds is specifically for established companies with substantial equity financing. Additionally, it is obtainable for large investment projects that frequently run into the millions.

Costs	Fixed rates tied to long-term markets
Maturity	5 to 25 or 30 years
Proceeds	Real estate; machinery; equipment
Collateral	Real estate; machinery; equipment
Advantages	Reasonable interest rates, long-term maturity
Disadvantages	High minimum amounts; restrictive loan agreements

Government Sources

SBA banks, SBICs, and MESBICs are just some of the better-known government sources for debt financing. However, since both federal and state governments seem to have frequent policy changes, it is difficult to include a comprehensive listing. The Seniorpreneur would do well to leave no rock unturned when exploring debt financing. Federal, state, and local government programs can be uncovered that apply to specific types of industries or financing applications.

The best starting place is to inquire with your state's economic development commission. However, don't take no for an answer when you ask about new business development programs. Keep inquiring—ask friends, business associates, chambers of commerce, and larger city economic development commissions (they take on all kinds of bureaucratic names and titles). Some very innovative financing deals have been put together by Seniorpreneurs who dug deeper and used a lot of creative thinking to combine several different government assistance programs that saved them lots of tough-to-find financing dollars.

Small Business Innovation Research Grants (SBIRs)

Several grant programs are funded and administered by various federal agencies. SBIR grants (first stage up to $50,000, second stage to $500,000) are primarily available for new product research and development. The products that result, if successfully developed, belong to the company. But the stipulations are that the government has an option to purchase or use the technology. These grants are offered to individuals as well as companies.

Amount available	First stage to $50,000; second stage to $500,000
Structure	Grant by federal agency
Cost	Documented proposal must be submitted
Proceeds	Seed capital for R&D of a product
Advantages	Low cost; no equity giveaway; no debt
Disadvantages	Limited capital commitment

Other Grants

Numerous grants are available from the federal government, state governments, foundations, and private sources. These are not exclusively for research and development. It is estimated that the total grants from all sources amount to $100 billion annually. A directory listing most of the grants available in the United States is published by the federal Office of Management and Budget.

Leveraged Buyouts (LBOs)

Leveraged buyouts (LBOs) represent a form of financing that has been around for decades, but became glamorized in the 1980s. Basically an LBO amounts to borrowing against the assets of a company and then using the cashflow realized from the operations of the company to service the debt. Buyers, after purchasing a company, frequently sell off some of the assets to reduce the debt load and, as part of their operating procedure, drastically cut operating costs to increase cashflow. Obviously, LBOs are not applicable for pure start-ups because there are no assets. However, if the Seniorpreneur is buying out an existing company to then exploit a particular technology, or purchasing a group of companies for the purpose of expansion, LBOs may apply. Sources of financing for LBOs are commercial banks, asset-based lenders, industrial bonds, venture capital firms, and private investment pools. LBOs usually get their funding assembled from and through investment bankers.

Credit Enhancement

Debt financing through credit enhancement is not used too often because it's difficult to set up. However, it is worth some Seniorpreneurial think time to determine if you have the right connections or potential to pull it off. Often a company cannot borrow from a lending source without providing liquid or semiliquid assets as collateral. The challenge is to find a third party that has an interest and a belief in the company and is willing to provide the needed liquid collateral to secure the debt. The collateral is usually in the form of marketable securities, certificates of deposit, or letters of credit. In exchange for "enhancing" the company's credit, the third party usually receives a fee, payable at the time the loan is provided, along with warrants to buy stock in the company at some future date.

Trade Credit

One of the best is saved till last. In small companies, trade credit—in the form of accounts payable to suppliers—can make up large percentages of a company's total balance sheet. If you can buy goods and services and be given 60 to 120 days to pay for them, it's the same as having a *no-interest* loan for 2 to 4 months. Suppliers offer such terms to induce new companies to buy from them. It takes careful attention on the part of management not to abuse these generous terms.

Seniorpreneurs need to be sure that they keep their word with these suppliers, lest they need additional help to fill a quick order and suddenly find themselves in the position of being put on a COD basis.

Two other forms of trade credit are worth mentioning. With seasonal or special dating terms, a supplier ships in advance knowing that payment will not be made until after some predetermined time. With consignment terms, the supplier ships and does not require payment until the item is sold. Again, be sure you honor these type of terms with prompt payment when the time period finally arrives.

There can be a big side benefit to warming up to suppliers for trade credit. Suppliers can also be used for inexpensive research and development as well as market research. They frequently have internal design departments to help customers and potential customers work up engineering. Don't hesitate to ask them to help you work up designs, patterns, or drawings, or to provide technical expertise. They may have a CAD system available that's just what the doctor ordered. They frequently are a vast depository of marketing data and information. Don't hesitate to ask; you just might get what you're looking for.

As mentioned earlier, debt financing is one of the primary choices for Seniorpreneurs in putting together a total financing package. In the next chapter, we'll take a look at the other primary choice: equity.

10
Securing Seniorpreneurial Equity Financing

Seed-Stage Financing

Obtaining money for a Seniorpreneurial company is really pretty simple—it's just another sale. Your customers have something you want—their money. You have something they want—equity or a piece of the action of the potential growth of your enterprise. The key, as in all sales, is to determine the right price and close the sale. To do that, you have to develop a *financial marketing mindset.* Just as you would prepare a marketing program to sell your product or service, you need to prepare a financial marketing program. That means you prepare a business plan and plan a verbal pitch, develop a marketing scheme, present the package, and close the sale. It takes intimate knowledge, unbounded enthusiasm, and a scuff-resistant ego.

Your business plan is going to show you how much money you will need, whether it should be debt or equity, and at what stage or time period the money is needed to accomplish what tasks. By consulting with your peers, legal counsel, and accountants, you will have determined the most proper legal structure for your company as well as the proposed valuations. From this, you can then develop your financial marketing program, which in turn will help you narrow in on the type of investor you will be seeking.

For seed and concept companies financing invariably means that the Seniorpreneur starts with money from family and friends and then proceeds to obtain informal investor financing prior to attracting the interest of the more formal investors such as venture capital firms.

You're Looking for Angels

Part of the contingent of private financing sources, or informal investors, are people affectionately referred to as *angels*. Along with family and friends, they are the largest providers of early-stage financing, both from a dollar standpoint and from their sheer numbers. They are a heterogeneous group that is very difficult to identify and capture. They may be your next-door neighbors or relatives of your friends. They may be *affiliated* in that they have some contact with you or your business, or they may be *nonaffiliated* in that they currently have no idea you even exist. Obviously, it's easier to start with someone who is already familiar with you and has a vested interest in the relationship. Even though there is no typical angel, just as there is no typical Seniorpreneur, it's still helpful to establish an overall profile.

What's an Angel Look Like?

Various surveys and research reports have yielded some interesting characteristics for identifying angels. Although the exceptions probably override the rule, the profiles lend some interesting food for thought:

- 90-plus percent are male
- Typical ages are 40 to 60 years old
- Hold master or multiple advanced degrees
- Have prior start-up experience
- Personal income between $250,000 and $1,000,000 per year
- Invest minimally once a year; average is $2\frac{1}{2}$ times
- Invest $25,000 to $50,000 per deal, totaling $130,000 per year
- Seldom take more than 10 percent of a deal
- Seek a minimum 20 percent compound per annum return
- Expect liquidation in 5 to 7 years
- Have a strong preference for manufacturing deals
- Like technology they're familiar with

Prefer start-ups, early-stage companies

Dislike moderate growth

Like consulting role: board of directors or advisers

Like to invest with other sophisticated investors

Invest close to home (50 to 300 miles)

Primary investment motivation is a high rate of return

Secondary motivation is capital appreciation

Learn of investment opportunities from associates and friends

Less than 30 percent of referrals come from attorneys or accountants

Would like to see more opportunities than they currently see

Refer investments they make to their investment network

Contrary to venture capitalists, angels don't put comprehensive business plans at the top of their criteria list. However, they rank management ability the highest, and seek a clear, demonstrated market need, plus a large market potential for the product or service.

How to Find Your Angel

The financial marketing mindset with angels is a little different from that with venture capitalists. Venture capitalists know what they want and how to go about getting it. Their primary focus is financial; they're investing other people's money and are getting paid to obtain outrageous returns. Angels, on the other hand, react to your proposal by determining in their mind if you're being fair. While they are also looking for a financial return, they frequently are seeking a psychic or intangible reward—such as helping minorities, creating jobs, revitalizing urban areas, or simply contributing back to society for their success. With senior-managed companies, angels may be looking to buy a job.

Your First Task Is to Locate Them. It's a tough task. Angels don't advertise; they network quietly. Start with your calling card file; it may contain some hidden angels but most likely will lead you to more angels. Spread the word that you're seeking financing, that you have prepared a business plan, that you're prepared to talk with anybody, any time, any place, and that you're prepared to pay a finder's fee. That's right—many times you will have to pay a fee to someone who puts you in touch with someone who writes the check. It's a financial marketing reality.

Professional service providers are always a good place to start. Attorneys and accountants are very good networkers with a potential vested interest. Suppliers or vendors can be helpful. Sometimes they invest; many times they simply furnish leads. Still, it's a good way to get into the subject of extended credit terms. Try customers and even employees (they may have some home equity to borrow against). Competitors, especially in other parts of the country, may reveal some strategic alliances as well as information that may lead to an angel. Dialing for dollars, also called *telemarketing*, works when you can obtain a list of wealthy individuals. Don't forget any already successful entrepreneurs, ex-entrepreneurs, or dentists and doctors. Not only can they bring in their money, but they can help attract other angels.

The Bottom Line Is Networking. Attend local venture capital groups; there are 80 to 100 of these located in almost every larger city in the country. Check the business events listing in local newspapers or regional business magazines. Venture capital groups meet specifically to network and exchange business opportunities. Many of them have a forum for presenting prospective business projects, and a lot of angels attend or are plugged into the networks surrounding these groups. They are prime hunting grounds for Seniorpreneurs. To obtain a directory, contact: International Venture Capital Institute, P.O. Box 1333, Stamford, CT 06904. The author is cofounder of The Rockies Venture Club, 190 East 9th Avenue, Suite 320, Denver, CO 80203.

Boutique Banking. A final source is boutique investment banking firms and some business brokers. They focus on financing start-ups and matching angels. As intermediaries, they charge fees which can vary considerably. It's suggested that you qualify them and their principals by soliciting advice from your accountant and attorney.

The Best Ways to Approach Angels

Once angels are identified, the common approach is to furnish them with a copy of your business plan. After they have reviewed it, try to get together with them face to face. I suggest you handle this a little bit differently than you would other financing opportunities. If you can't arrange to meet angels in person, give them a copy of your special executive summary. Better yet, if you have your company up and operating, invite them to come in for a firsthand look. Assuming your special executive summary captures their interest, arrange for an in-person meeting. This is your opportunity to sell them on what your company has to offer—that is, management and a product or service with a lot of potential. It's just like any other sales job—display the wares and convince people that you have something they need.

Initial contacts via phone or impersonal referrals don't cut it. They're just not enough. Angels have to understand your company and gain a feeling for the enthusiasm that backs it. Your challenge is to get them to become personally involved, to buy into your determined dedication. If all they have is your business plan, it's too easy for them to refuse. You want to get them emotionally committed.

Keep in mind that you know more about your business than they do. Be cautious about how you present your projections, remembering that you will be expected to achieve them. Be sure they're realistic and achievable. Although angels are a lot more flexible than venture capitalists (and consequently you can close the deal in half the time), you still need to be sure that you establish a relationship with a strong bond of good faith and that you earnestly attempt to keep all your commitments.

Preparing the Scene

Once you have passed the seed stage, your company will start to become attractive to a more sophisticated level of investors. These are typically venture capital firms. Although most venture capitalists are not interested in investing at the start-up stage—they prefer to stand by until a company has "proved itself" some more at the first stage—it's still a good time to make an initial contact. Remember, you're forming a financial marketing plan and, just as in advertising, "repetition brings it home." By instigating a first-level contact with venture capital firms at seed or start-up stage, you can come back at the next round of financing (while keeping them posted on your interim progress); the familiarity with both you and your project will be in place. You will have had the chance to prove that you can do what you told them you were going to accomplish.

Understanding Traditional Professional Venture Capital

Professional venture capital firms have traditionally thought of their job as the early-stage financing of relatively small, rapidly growing companies. Over the past 10 to 15 years, their internal job descriptions and responsibilities have vastly increased. Sure, their primary objective is still to make a sizable return on their investment, and they would like to do so on a passive basis. However, they have learned that they also have to take an active role alongside management. They have realized that venture capital investing requires a long-term investment discipline.

A Brief History

The industry of formally managed professional venture capital was started shortly after World War II when several wealthy families, including the Rockefellers, the Whitneys, and the Phippses, started to invest in the new technologies that came out of the war. They went on to seed-finance many now well-known companies—Itek, General Signal, Memorex, and Minute Maid, to name just a few. In 1946, the first formal investment partnership was put together in Boston under the name of American Research and Development (ARD). ARD made many early-stage investments—most notably, in Digital Equipment Corp. (DEC).

The most successful single individual in early professional venture capital was Alex Rock. His seed investments are legendary, including Fairchild Semiconductors, Teledyne, Scientific Data Systems, Intel, and Apple Computer.

Traditional venture capital received a big boost in 1958 when Congress passed the Small Business Investment Act, which created the small business investment companies (SBICS) program. Government came to the rescue again (so to speak) when in 1978 it reduced the capital-gains tax for long-term investment and clarified the 1974 Employee Retirement Income Security Act (ERISA) that then allowed pension funds to invest in professionally managed venture capital. Billions of dollars poured into these funds as the institutional investors (pension funds, insurance companies, major corporations, individuals and families, endowments and foundations, union and multiemployer plans, and foreign investors) sought the 20 to 30 percent per annum returns that the venture funds had traditionally made.

Today's professionally managed venture capital firms have proved their ability to evolve with the financial times. They have endured the big-time losses from their early-stage investments in computer hardware companies (over 500 initially, down to a handful today) and have entered the biotech era with a lot more trepidation. They have adjusted, readjusted, and continue to readjust their investment philosophies as they seek to improve their knowledge of the art and science of venture capital investment.

Venture Capital in General

Although the entire industry can be broken into many diverse categories, the formal venture capital community can generally be divided into two main groups: traditional private institutionally funded partnerships and corporate venture capital funds. Although they have different objectives for investing—private funds for a money return and corporate funds for gaining technology—they have some similar operating policies and modus operandi.

1. They can be very difficult to get an audience with.
2. They are very select in the deals they get involved in.
3. They are seeking large investment dollar projects.
4. They invest only in deals with significant upside potential.
5. They aren't too attracted to start-ups.
6. They seek very high growth rates.
7. They have very stringent investment criteria.
8. They may be very limited as to their industry focus.
9. They place a high premium on the quality of management.
10. They have a concern for bringing more than money to the deal.

Another item in common for both private and corporate funds is the minimum and maximum amounts they're willing to invest. On the minimum side, it's usually $100,000 to $500,000. While some may go as low as $50,000 for seed projects, others may not go below $500,000. Their line of reasoning regarding minimums is that it costs them just as much time and money for due diligence in making a $50,000 investment as it does for $500,000.

Regarding the maximum amounts, there really isn't any ceiling. Most funds are individually limited to X percent of their total funds. However, all funds are capable of putting together syndicates with other funds to provide almost unlimited financing for the right Seniorpreneurial project.

Traditional Venture Capital

The traditional venture capital firms manage funds that range in size from $10 million to $100 million and more. Funds that manage over $100 million are called *megafunds.* Besides coming in many different sizes, they also have a lot of different orientations. Some funds specialize in seed-stage investments, while others do only advanced or bridge financings. Others concentrate on leveraged buyouts. Still others invest only in a specialized area, such as medical services, retail sales, manufacturing, or computer software. Some large firms run what is termed a *balanced fund,* which invests over a broad spectrum of industries and company development stages.

For all funds, the primary criteria are (1) solid, experienced management teams who have identified a creditable market niche with a large growth potential and (2) the possibility of the firm's expanding to $100 million plus in annual revenues.

Very frequently, the partners in the fund will have prior experience and current knowledge in the areas in which the fund invests. Thus they are better equipped to take an active part in guiding a fledgling company in planning, marketing, developing supplier connections, finding new personnel, and bringing in additional financing sources.

Here Is Some More Insight. A little more insight into the formation and operations of all venture capital funds helps in understanding their investment motivation. Each fund typically has several general partners as well as analysts, researchers, and clerical personnel. The general partners have the responsibility to put the fund together and to solicit and obtain the actual limited-partner institutional investors. These limited-partner investors typically commit to a gross total dollar investment. The actual dollars will be invested in stages: commonly one-third of the money when the fund is started, one-third after the first year, and the balance during the second year. Limited partners are expecting that their investment will not be fully returned until the seventh through tenth year. They also expect to earn an annualized 30 percent compound interest on their money.

The general partners, on the other hand, receive an annual management fee to oversee the investment. They make all investment decisions without routine input or approval of the limited partners or passive investors. Additionally, although there are many different types of agreements, the general partners are entitled to receive a percentage of the profits (typically 20 percent) after the initial investments are repaid. It is clear that fund managers are under a large amount of pressure to perform, and those who do are justifiably rewarded.

There Are Three Categories to Consider

Although most traditional venture capital funds orient their investments toward products, some do seek out service-type companies. Computer software and medical services are examples. For product investments, and to some extent service investments, there are three categories to consider: revolutionary, evolutionary, and substitute.

Revolutionary. Examples of revolutionary products are cameras, televisions, and computers. Venture capital tends to shy away from the revolutionary deals. They take too much cash and they take too long to develop.

Evolutionary. Examples of evolutionary products are instant or autofocus cameras, color or portable televisions, and personal or laptop computers. These products are ideal for venture capital, which looks toward the next generation or cheaper versions. To really merit consideration, the next generation should be 30 percent cheaper or faster, or have a 30 percent improvement in quality. Better yet, all three.

Substitute. Substitute products are ones that can develop niche markets. Examples include fast-food chicken or hamburger and regional spinoffs on automobile fast or quick lubes. Venture capital firms have differing opinions about substitutes. Some really like them if the niche is well defined, has an easy market entry, and offers what seems to be broad appeal. Other firms beg off on substitutes, feeling that they need too much marketing and advertising—both of which are hard to quantify when tracking the expense outlays.

Regardless of the categories, the uppermost consideration for traditional venture capital partnerships is the potential monetary return. This may not be the top criterion for corporate venture capital funds.

Corporate Venture Capital

Many corporations form venture capital subsidiaries for a variety of reasons, one of which is *not* to make a large return on their initial investment. This doesn't mean that they don't want to make money or that the Seniorpreneur should avoid exploring corporate venture capital as a source of financing. In fact, in many cases, corporate venture capital can be a better deal for the Seniorpreneur than the traditional firms. The corporate firms tend to overfund their portfolio companies in an attempt to drive the realization of the project to a faster conclusion. Because large corporations typically don't have an entrepreneurial mindset, they tend to overstaff and overequip all areas of operations. Consequently, where the Seniorpreneur is striving hard to produce results over a shortened time period, corporate venture capital makes a great fit.

What Corporate Venture Capital Seeks. If corporations aren't seeking large returns, what are they after? A good start is strategic alliances in one form or another. It could be from a basic or applied research basis, one in which the corporations can support a patent or invention. It could also be a marketing alliance in which they can obtain exclusive marketing rights. Or it could be a manufacturing agreement in which the Seniorpreneuring company manufactures private-label products for the corporation. Ofttimes corporations are trying to find new talent or teach practical entrepreneuring to existing personnel. At other times they may be doing some public relations posturing or supporting a philanthropic mission.

Corporate venture capital funds look for start-ups that will require large capital contributions. As a start-up grows and expands, they are prepared to invest sums of $5 million or more—often up into the tens of millions. They seek projects that can utilize multiple plant sites or locations, including foreign locations. With an investment of this size, it's obvious that corporations are looking for projects that have very large market potential. Their long-term vision means that they expect the company to have revenues in excess of half a billion dollars in 10 years or so. Given this approach, it's obvious that one-product companies won't do. Candidate companies need to have multiple-product spinoffs that allow for secondary products and licenses for international exploitation.

Why They Need Big Projects. The reason corporations need such big projects is that they are hunting for alliances to incubate future acquisitions, ventures that they can grow and support to become whole new corporate divisions. They are seeking to provide work for any plants they may own that will have unused manufacturing capacity. They need projects in which they can invest excess cashflow and teach entrepreneurial thinking to their middle-management layers. They realize that many new technologies come from smaller companies. Consequently, if they can establish a strategic partnership during the early stages of a company's development, they can gain an insight into the windows of these new technologies and markets.

Large companies like IBM and Exxon spend in excess of $3 billion annually just for research and development—a sum equal to the whole traditional venture capital industry. It seems clear that initial returns on their venture capital investments are not the prime motivator. Traditional venture capital firms seek to turn or liquefy their investments in 3 to 7 years, whereas corporate venture capital firms have time frames of 10 to 20 years to grow new ideas into mature industries.

The Negatives of Dealing with Corporate Venture Capital. With all these positive points for corporate venture capital, assuming the Seniorpreneur's project is large enough, what could be negative? The biggest negative is the unstable nature of the corporate approach. This type of fund has a history of being the "in" thing to do and just as suddenly falling out of favor. Large corporations are ruled by the economic times of Wall Street and its obsession with quarterly profits. This means that when the corporate venture capital firm is plush with excess cashflow, it has a keen interest in making venture-type investments. When things get tight, when pressure is put on budgets, invariably corporate venture capital gets slashed, since expenditures of hard cash get sliced first.

Additionally, some corporate venture fund managements are restricted as to the final decisions to invest. They may have to obtain approval from the corporate hierarchy to exceed predetermined investment levels or to invest in what may be considered fringe product areas. Since many new Seniorpreneurial ideas cross common product lines, or even combine technologies from different industries, corporate venture capital is typically not appropriate in the earliest stages. Even though venture capital is supposed to be entrepreneurial in style, corporate bureaucracies don't necessarily end at the door of corporate venture funds. It can take an excruciatingly long time to get upper-level approval for the Seniorpreneur who is depending on staying on a fast development track. Be sure you clear this point prior to getting too far downstream with corporate funds. Be sure the fund management has the authority not only to approve your project, but also to write the check.

Watch Out for Management Changes. Another negative is the fact that the upper-level managers of corporate venture funds don't stay around long. The good ones leave for higher personal payouts with the private funds, making "portfolio orphans" of their former employers. These frequent personnel changes add to the confusion for the Seniorpreneur, since one of the many side benefits of making a venture capital connection is that the venture capital management itself has the ability to bring other players into the game. The fund manager who inherits the portfolio orphan may not have the enthusiasm, knowledge, or additional contacts possessed by the original manager who pushed the Seniorpreneur's deal through to begin with. The result is an abandoned company, running low on money and time, lacking valuable industry contacts, and left without a dedicated lead venture fund.

Finally, corporate venture funds want to establish the maximum values of a deal at the time of original investment. This tends to "cap" the harvest potential for the Seniorpreneurial team. Bad blood can develop if the team loses its high profit incentive, especially if the project runs into some snags. Loss of incentive is bound to happen when the Seniorpreneurial team is in a bad renegotiation position and becomes susceptible to diluting its total package to compensate for the addition of more dollars or time.

The prime motivation of corporate venture capital firms is to grow their own acquisition candidates. They tend to arrange initial investments in such a way that they can acquire the Seniorpreneur's equity at some future time. They are ideal capital partners for Seniorpreneurs who require large sums of investment, who need longer time periods for development, and who can benefit from teaming up with a large corporate partner in research, development, manufacturing, and market distribution.

How to Find a Venture Capital Firm

Identifying venture capital firms is a fairly simple process. There are numerous directories available. *Pratt's Guide to Venture Capital Sources* is the bible for the industry. *Pratt's* and other guides (including state and regionally sponsored directories) are available in any good city library. These guides furnish name, address, and contact information as well as the preferred investment size and in many cases the particular industries in which the firm prefers to invest.

How to Qualify a Venture Capitalist

Qualifying a venture capital firm is a little more difficult than finding one. It requires that the Seniorpreneur use some common sense and recognize some of the ground rules. For example, if you're a biotech development company, do not approach a firm that clearly states it does not invest in biotech. It's surprising how many companies spend a lot of dollars sending plans by overnight delivery to venture funds which plainly state in their published information that they refuse to invest in a particular industry. Most funds have a list that shows their areas of interest as well as areas in which they do not invest.

While many funds invest in companies located all over the United States, some prefer only projects located within 200 or 300 miles or 2 or 3 hours of their headquarters. If you identify a firm that likes your industry, but you're located outside its preferred geographical investment area, call the company and inquire about other firms in your area. Many funds will participate in investments with other firms if there is a "lead" investor who agrees to monitor a portfolio company. These lead investors are usually geographically located close to the investment. When a fund indicates that it has a preference for a particular industry, it usually means that one or more of the general partners has some background in that industry. This can be especially helpful to the Seniorpreneurial team, because it doesn't have to spend a lot of time getting the venture capitalists up to speed on industry knowledge. It's also helpful because the venture capitalist can pick up the phone and get quick answers to due diligence questions. After making an investment, the venture capital firm is usually able to bring a lot of its industry contacts into the deal to help the portfolio company grow and sometimes even provide staff.

How to Get in the Door

All venture capital firms will tell you that their best deals come from the companies in which they have already invested. The second best way to get in the door is to have someone who has already established creditability with the fund make an introduction. If you can't find such a person, your legal counsel, accounting firm, or banker can make an initial contact on your behalf. If these sources are unable or unwilling to do so, don't hesitate to make initial contact yourself. The best approach is to place a phone call to the fund managers listed in the guides. When they finally return your call, simply outline your project and ask if you could send them your special executive summary. If your summary generates an interest, they will request your complete business plan. It is very difficult, not to mention a waste of valuable time and money, to send numerous plans out blindly to numerous funds.

Every venture capital firm in the country receives two or three plans per day; some get 30 or 40. It may take 2 or 3 months for the firm to get around to scanning the reports. Even then, so many plans are so poorly written that they don't even deserve a reply.

With so many plans coming in the venture capitalist's door, you can also see that sending your plan by overnight delivery, or faxing your summary, simply is a waste of dollars. It's suggested that you ask, and if the firm requests fast delivery, by all means do so. Typically, however, your plan will sit around for a week or two, so save the bucks.

Again, the best avenue is finding someone who can front you in the door. Once the initial contact has been made, simply send your plan with a brief cover letter and keep your fingers crossed. If you don't receive a reply in 2 or 3 weeks, a progress call is appropriate. Calling every few days will only alienate the initial screener of your project and guarantee that your plan will fall deeper into the pile.

However, don't get discouraged by this discussion about how hard it is to get a receptive ear. Remember, venture capital firms need product too; it's just the realization of the old axiom that "entrepreneurs run and money walks."

How to Present to Venture Capitalists

Assume that a venture capitalist, after what seems an eternity, expresses a further interest in your project. What is likely to happen next? A phone conversation with a request for more information will most likely occur, with discussion of a possible face-to-face meeting. There's always the chance that the meeting will be held at your facilities, but the most likely scenario is that you will be requested to visit the venture capitalist's office.

This initial meeting is a get-acquainted session and the venture capital firm's first "size up the management" opportunity. First impressions count; be prompt, have clean fingernails, wear a suit and tie, be relaxed, smile, and come well rehearsed. Your presentation should last 15 to 30 minutes and should be modeled after your business plan. The venture capitalists simply want to hear your business story in your own words. They will have read your plan thoroughly, a couple of times, and will have prepared numerous questions. But first off, they want to size you up.

Don't Bring Your Attorney Along. Don't—I repeat, do not—bring your attorney or accountant along. Professionals talk too much about the wrong things. No intermediaries at all is preferable; remember, the venture capitalists want to become intimately familiar with the management team. If there is going to be a wedding, they are going to marry the bride, not the bride's father or mother.

At the meeting, your goal is to impart your basic philosophy and display the capabilities and skills of your management team. You can do this by making a straightforward, clear-cut presentation that has simplified the technical aspects of your project. Venture capitalists need to understand the nature of technology and the current and future stages of Seniorpreneurial development. Discuss practical applications and substantiate the size of your markets. You must indicate an in-depth knowledge of your competitors by discussing their strengths and weaknesses, followed by why you can replace them and how you are going to do so.

When talking about your management team, describe specific experience that makes each member uniquely qualified, especially as to what is applicable over the last 5 years. Note where and how your team has been assembled, how members have worked together in the past, and how you see individual skills complementing one another on your project. If you have a missing management link, discuss it frankly and suggest that you're open for recommendations. All venture capital firms have a vast knowledge and network to identify and obtain key management players.

Be Realistic About Your Financials. In presenting the financial aspects of your project, use truthfulness and reality as your guides. If your operations are existing, discuss the good and bad points. Talk about where you made mistakes and blew some time and dollars and where you're really proud of belt tightening; give some examples of the ingenious methods you used to economize. Be realistic in your projections. Keep in mind that the venture capitalists probably have some practical experience in your industry area. If not, they definitely have seen countless optimistic projections that resulted in bad start-ups. Worst, best, and most likely scenarios aren't bad, but every projection has got to be backed by detailed assumptions. Assumptions can make or break the creditability of any projections. Be sure yours are well grounded.

In summary, the venture capitalist has the following objectives:

- To meet you and your key team members face to face
- To obtain more information on the business and how it is going to make money for all parties
- To determine if it's possible to "cut a deal."

What to Ask a Venture Capitalist

It takes two to tango, and the mating dance with venture capitalists is no exception. If they invest in your company, you're assured of a long-term arrangement. You need their money, but you will also want to take advantage of their many other services. This means you will want to qualify your get-along ability in the early stages of your contact. Venture capitalists understand this. In fact, they respect such an approach and are most willing to help create a relationship that is compatible in personalities and style.

Ask about their investment philosophies. This is very important so you can make sure that all goals match. If the venture fund's strategy is to harvest only by public offering, and you feel your most likely early harvest will come from being acquired, you need to reach an acceptable understanding right from the start. Just because they don't agree with you doesn't mean they can't help. There is a good chance they can give you a very good referral to a fund that subscribes to your way of thinking.

Also talk with venture capitalists about how they feel they can help you. What resources can they bring to the table to complement and enhance your plan? Get a feel for participation on an ongoing basis. Will they be active or passive investors? Do they want a seat on your board of directors? How often will they require what type of reporting?

Inquire about their investors. Are there some who are in the same industrial area as your operations? Are there any strategic partnering possibilities with their investors, portfolio companies, or other deals they are involved with?

Think of it this way. You have a right to a prenuptial agreement just as venture capitalists have the right to a marriage license. It behooves both parties to gain a deep insight into the boundaries of the relationship, and the first meeting is the best way to start the process.

What to Expect from the Meeting

Toward the end of the meeting, don't expect immediate decisions or even a lot of indications of where your potential backers are at. If you have to know today, their answer is no. Typically, they will have asked you to bring additional documentation to the meeting. If their first impression is favorable, they will ask you to send in some more data as a result of the meeting. Their most common response to the question "What do you think?" is "We'll be in touch."

What Will Happen Next?

Proceeding on the premise that the venture capital firm is positively disposed toward funding your project, you will next have to conduct preliminary negotiations on the deal. This means that the venture capital firm will have completed some additional information gathering and is at least comfortable enough to determine whether some basic agreement can be reached on the valuation and structure of the potential investment.

Venture capitalists are not necessarily cavalier at this point. However, because of their experience, they have a pretty good determination as to what it will take before they agree to invest. A very important point for the Seniorpreneur to understand is that venture capitalists are not inclined to "beat" the Seniorpreneur into a submissive equity position which the Seniorpreneur does not want or will be uncomfortable with over the lifetime of the project. Venture capitalists attempt to create a win-win deal. They are fully aware that the Seniorpreneur can get back at them while operating the company. They simply have investment parameters and return goals to obtain, and they are keenly interested in exceeding these goals with all investments they make.

Be reasonable in your expectations; listen to their side, their judgments, and then negotiate. Negotiate means give and take. There will be a lot of points to review and a lot of areas for open discussion. The venture capitalists will provide the basic format in the form of a letter of commitment. Follow their lead. Discussions don't mean conclusions, and often you'll find ways to enhance your position that turn out far better than you originally thought.

The Commitment Letter:
Its Five Sections

Commitment letters come in many forms, from one-pagers to terribly long and complex documents. The subject is too vast to detail in this book, and there are just too many variables. Suffice it to say that the

Seniorpreneur must have legal counsel involved prior to the final signing. Again, I suggest that you let the venture capitalists take the lead. They have their preferred format, and your chore is to respond. There are five basic sections to any commitment letter.

Terms. This section states the terms on which the investment will be made, including loan and equity options. The intent is to state what the venture capital firm intends to do and what it intends to receive for doing it.

Collateral and Security. This section declares how the investment, loan, and/or equity option will be collateralized. In most cases, collateral will originally be all assets with some contingencies.

Conditions of the Investment. This section sets forth the conditions which surround the investment—including financial and management reporting requirements as well as ratio and default requirements.

Representations. This section includes many different representations that you or the company makes—corporate standing, lawsuits, tax positions, investment to date, use of proceeds, criminal convictions, and more. Do not sign any representations that are not truthful or that you cannot fulfill.

Conditions of Commitment. This section describes conditions that, if not met, will void the venture capital firm's commitment to fund your project. For example, you are required to pay the venture capitalists a fee or reimburse certain expenses; all legal documents must be acceptable to them; their due diligence must meet with their approval.

This letter of commitment, also referred to as a *term sheet,* will be the basis of what is called an *investment memorandum.* The investment memorandum is the final document signed after the completion of additional due diligence. For now, your concern should be to negotiate every item in the commitment letter, but don't get bent out of shape about every detail. The venture capital firm will be reasonable about all the items being discussed.

Due Diligence:
A Complete Checkup

To the uninitiated, few things are more mysterious than the investment or due diligence process. What goes on? What is it comprised of? How long does it take? In fact, what is it?

Due diligence is simply the process of conducting background checks and representations made by the company. It's verifying employment and education, as well as the general reputation of the management team. It's studying and reviewing the industry, complete with market analysis. It's verifying facts and statements made in the business plan. It's a detailed review of the proposed project that seeks out misrepresentations, mistakes, and an independent appraisal of potential.

This is a process that can't be rushed. Every venture capital firm has its own format and schedule. After considering a lot of variables, the firm will require additional visits with the management team, visit office or plant sites if they exist, ask questions about management's intentions, and ask further questions about the business proposal.

They Will Check Everything. Venture capitalists will investigate the individuals; check credit records; and talk with references, past employers and employees, fellow workers, acquaintances, suppliers, customers, and maybe even neighbors. In some cases, they may even request personality or psychological testing. They are seeking to verify experience, leadership qualities, team-building abilities, honesty, reliability, guts, and vision.

They will conduct industry studies by talking with competitors, suppliers, and potential customers. They will query any industry-relevant associations or membership groups. Venture capitalists are looking to verify the uniqueness of the product. (Is it truly unique or is it old hat in the industry?) They are trying to determine if your approach is unique or just a variation on an existing theme. They will most likely bring in several consultants, maybe even question government sources, attorneys, accountants, bankers, and other venture capital firms.

Recognize that all this sleuthing will have a positive result. Ofttimes, venture capitalists will uncover information you weren't aware of, and most times their due diligence enables them to better assist and work with you.

How Long Will the Process Take? Surprisingly, 4 to 8 weeks is the average. The more you can cooperate, the faster and easier the process will be. If the venture capitalists request information or data sources, reply quickly. They're just as anxious as you are to get the project off dead center and on the way to providing everyone with outrageous rewards.

The Marriage

After the due diligence process is completed, the next step is the *close*. As mentioned earlier, this step is orchestrated by the investment memorandum. This is a more detailed document than the letter of intent but will cover all the items in the letter of intent. Just more *t*'s and *i*'s. Obviously, you'll need an attorney, preferably one who is experienced in this type of transaction. Be sure you're comfortable with the terms; you'll have plenty of opportunity to raise questions, make changes, and clear up any misunderstandings during the draft stages and prior to the actual close. A final note: Keep your harvest goals in mind.

The Ongoing Relationship

Trust is the biggie. Make sure you establish it from the start and work hard to maintain it. Keep lines of communication open at all times. This doesn't mean there won't be disagreements, even of the heart-stopping form, but don't let these disintegrate to silence. Use the venture capitalist member of your board of directors as you intend to use all members—working. If you have questions, ask. If you have problems, discuss them. Venture capitalists have lots of experience in assisting companies and appreciate management that will listen to their advice. Their single underlying objective is growth. They want to liquefy their investment worse than you do. Be open, honest, and Seniorpreneuring.

Traditional Venture Capital Funds

Traditional venture capital funds are professionally managed companies with high-risk investment portfolios. Their capital is supplied by institutions such as insurance companies, pension funds, and limited partnerships.

Amount available	Usually $500,000 and up; occasionally for start-ups
Structure	Convertible preferred stock
Cost	Generally a minimum 30 percent per annum compounded interest
Proceeds	For very high growth to sales of $50 million
Advantages	Large amount of capital available; easy second- and third-round sources
Disadvantages	Must have high growth potential; require high equity give-up

The Preferred Investment Vehicles

Regardless of the source of your financing—family and friends, angels, or venture capital—you will need some formal vehicle to make it all nice and legal. On the surface, it would seem that if you're going to sell stock, you could take your investors' checks and issue stock certificates. Or if you're obtaining a loan, just take the check and sign a note. Unfortunately, it's not quite that simple. And in fact, you don't want it to be.

Today's "sue the buzzards" mentality causes some real problems for Seniorpreneurs when it comes to raising money. The main problem is the Seniorpreneurs themselves. Considering their natural propensity and rightful enthusiasm for their project, they tend to oversell. This is okay if everything works out the way it is planned. But we all know that Murphy's Law will enter the program and that not always what is well ends well. In the worst case, your company may not survive.

The problem then becomes that the friendly original investors are not the least bit happy about the fact that *you* did not perform up to expectations or lost all their money. Their fee-happy lawyer is more than pleased to take on the case of suing you because you said that there wasn't any significant competition, that your engineer was a genius and couldn't miss on inventing the black box, that you had umpteen customers lined up—the endless list goes on. What it comes down to is your word against theirs, and most likely they have more money (which is why you went to them in the first place) and so can afford the up-front legal fees that will be repaid when they sell your "house."

There is a solution to this dilemma. Look into the various documents and regulations that have been blessed by our government bodies, protective measures that serve as an insurance policy for Seniorpreneurs against disgruntled investors—be they friends, family, angels, or venture capitalists. These are discussed below.

The Selling of Securities

Simply stated, it's against the law to sell stock unless you are licensed to do so or can qualify for an exemption from the Securities and Exchange Commission (SEC) and the various state securities commissions. The very worst that can happen is that you will have to pay penalties or you can be put in jail. The least that can happen is that you will be required to refund any monies you raised. Reimbursement can be very difficult if you've already spent a sizable portion before the legal problem arises.

Regulation D

For some entrepreneurs, the best vehicle to accomplish initial equity financing is Regulation D, which is a limited offer and sale of a company's stock, or securities, without registration under the Federal Securities Act of 1933 (1933 Act).

Some risks continue under Reg D, but compliance is significantly easier than before Reg D. A major, major point is that *by complying with Reg D, the company, its officers, and its directors take out an insurance policy of sorts regarding disclosure.*

There Are Six Basic Rules

Reg D consists of six basic rules. The first three are concerned with definitions, conditions, and notification. Rule 501 covers the definitions of the various terms used in the rules. Rule 502 sets forth the conditions, limitations, and information requirements for the exemptions in Rules 504, 505, and 506. Rule 503 contains the SEC notification requirements. The last three rules deal with the specifics of raising money under Reg D. Rule 504 generally pertains to securities sales up to $1 million. Rule 505 applies to offerings from $1 million to $5 million. Rule 506 is for securities offerings exceeding $5 million. A primary goal of this book is to gain an overview of the methods of raising capital; consequently, we will concentrate here on Rule 504. For a complete review of all aspects of Reg D, see my book *The Entrepreneur's Guide to Going Public* (Upstart Publishing, 1994).

Rule 504

This rule is considered by many as the perfect answer for start-up companies that need to raise less than $1 million but can't afford to go through the whole SEC registration process. Until they grow to a point where they can afford it, Rule 504 offers such companies several outs:

- An exemption to raise up to $1 million
- No disclosure criteria
- Few general solicitation and resale restrictions
- No limit as to the number of investors

Actually, Congress' original intent for Rule 504 was to "set aside a clear and workable exemption for small issuers to be regulated by state blue-sky requirements, but by the same token, to be subjected to federal antifraud provisions and civil liability provisions." The Rule 504 exemption applies to almost any type of organization—corporations, partnerships, trusts, and other entities. However, it is not applicable to investment companies or companies already reporting to the SEC (subject to the 1934 Act).

The total offering amount under Rule 504 can be up to $1 million in a 12-month period, less the aggregate offering of all securities sold within 12 months before the start of a Rule 504 offering. So, if a company has raised $100,000 in private money in the previous 12 months, it can still raise up to $900,000 without being accused of breaking the rules through *integration*. Generally speaking, Rule 504 carries no specific requirements for *disclosure* (disclosing what the company is about, what it intends to do, or who is connected with it). This means that, theoretically, an issuer can have a purchaser sign a subscription agreement and purchase stock without any information about the company being disclosed. However, the rule is dependent on the *blue-sky laws** of each state in which the securities are offered. This means that if a state's blue-sky rules require disclosure, it must be provided regardless of Rule 504.

Rule 504 also provides that at least $500,000 of securities must be sold pursuant to a registration under a state's securities law. Consequently, an offer must comply with the blue-sky laws of each state in which it is offered. In many states, this negates the effective simplicity of Rule 504 and the federal government's intent, because many states' blue-sky laws are more restrictive than Reg D.

A word of caution to the Seniorpreneur. Regardless of the amount of disclosure the issuer is willing to provide, Rule 504 does not dismiss the issuer from the federal requirements. Nor does it provide an exemption from the provisions against fraud, including material omissions or misstatements. The penalties for noncompliance are severe: monetary fines and mandatory jail sentences.

The main area in which Rule 504 has helped is in allowing the issuer to generally *solicit*, or advertise, for subscribers to an offering. Some states have been quite lenient in allowing solicitation. Surprisingly, however, very few issuers have chosen to advertise their offerings in newspapers or other media.

With its limited disclosure requirements, Rule 504 also allows an issuer to sell securities to an unlimited number of investors. Theoretically, a company could raise $1 million by selling its stock at a penny a share to 100 million different investors. Obviously, the economics are not too attractive, but there's no rule that stops an issuer from selling $500 blocks of stock to 2000 investors. Rule 504 is the only rule under Reg D that permits an unlimited number of investors.

A final note on Rule 504 is that the exemption provides for sales of securities of either debt or equity. This opens the door for issuing *convertible debentures* to create debt-equity combinations. A convertible debenture is a debt issue (debenture) that is convertible to preferred

---

*Laws that protect gullible investors from promoters offering them the sky, the stars, and the rest of the firmament.

or, more commonly, common stock at some future date, usually at a predetermined price.

Alternate Exemptions

The enactment of Regulation D in 1982 (revised in 1993) simplified and facilitated the registration process for selling securities. That's a good reason for entrepreneurs to strongly consider Reg D, or state equivalents, for fund-raising efforts.

There are several other rules and exemptions that are worth looking into for the same reason. They are found under the headings of Regulation A and the Small Corporate Offering Registration (SCOR).

As pointed out in the last section, the principal advantage of an exemption from registration is that buy-and-sell transactions can take place as soon as the parties decide to proceed. It eliminates the necessity of preparing and filing a prospectus with the SEC, and it saves legal costs plus accounting and registration fees.

Exemptions under the Securities Act of 1933 are listed as exempted securities and exempted transactions. They can save both time and money. The only drawback is it takes a legal genius to interpret them. They're full of loopholes, and the courts have had no qualms about ruling against the entrepreneur in their interpretations. Even so, the end results should make exemptions worth pursuing. But since the whole area of exemptions is so complex, the Seniorpreneur should not proceed without first seeking the advice of qualified legal counsel to determine the best form of exemption to apply for.

Regulation A Offerings

Regulation A has a long history as an exemption for raising capital. It has been revised quite often, most recently in 1992. Reg A allows a company to offer its securities publicly without registering under the 1933 Act. Instead, an offering statement (Form 1-A) is filed and "qualified" with the SEC. A principal attraction of Reg A is that only 2 years of financial statements are required, and they may be unaudited if audited information is not readily available. Additionally, the completion of a Reg A offering does not automatically subject the issuer to reporting under the 1934 Act.

The dollar limit of a Reg A offering in any 12-month period has been raised to $5 million (of which $1.5 million can be sales by existing shareholders). Also, Form 1-A has been revised to allow the optional use of a "friendly" question-and-answer form (see SCOR below).

The new rules allow an issuer to "test the waters" before filing the offering statement. This means you can solicit indications of interest through the distribution or publication of preliminary materials. The materials are limited to factual information and must include a brief description of the company's business, a summary of the chief executive officer's experience, and a statement that no money is being solicited or accepted. These solicitations of interest must be filed with the SEC on the date they are first used. Oral indications can be solicited, but the solicitation materials must be discontinued when an offering statement is filed. Also, 20 days must expire between the use of the solicitation statement and the first sale of any securities.

Small Company Offering Registration (SCOR)

Form U-7, which is the basic registration and information form used in SCOR (in some states, this is called Uniform Limited Offering Registration, or ULOR), was adopted by the Securities and Exchange Commission in 1992. It allows a company to raise up to $1 million by selling securities. Form U-7 is a considerably less complicated disclosure statement than the standard form for other offerings, and it is constructed in a question-and-answer format. Some states even offer it on a computer disk.

SCOR has been touted as the simplest ever paperwork process for completing an exempted offering. Still, it's an area that calls for sound legal and accounting advice, although not to the extent of the other offering processes. Consequently, the issuing company can save some money in expensive professional fees.

A Final Exemption Note

Please note that many state securities commissions are rejecting federal rules and are choosing to adopt blue-sky laws that are more restrictive than the federal rules and regulations. Seniorpreneurs are strongly advised to check with qualified legal counsel on the fine points and the most recent rules and regulations as they pertain to their particular project. Still, Seniorpreneurs can feel assured that some form of exempted investment vehicle is available for their money-raising efforts.

Seniorpreneurs Use Both

Entrepreneurs often become shortsighted in their search for financing. Seniorpreneurs, on the other hand, recognize that the secret is to consider all available resources. They recognize that there are two basic choices—debt and equity—and that most successful financings are completed by using both of them. Many of the available resources have been reviewed in these chapters, from the various *forms* of debt financing (including subordinated debt) to the many different *sources* of debt financing. Equity sources have also been covered, with discussions of angels, venture capital, and the various exemption alternatives. Seniorpreneurs recognize that the financing of their companies, if not a full-time occupation, is at minimum a full-time preoccupation.

PART 4
Operations to Exit

11
Making It Happen Seniorpreneurial Style

Financing obtained, the Seniorpreneur now faces the challenge of making it happen—simply, executing the business plan—flawlessly.

"Simply" is obviously an understatement, as is "flawlessly." For me, another challenge is trying to write about making it happen. How does one go about explaining an extremely complicated process in terms that can apply to the variety of readers of this book? Many books are devoted to this one subject. However, there are some points that are of particular importance to the Seniorpreneur and they have been distilled in this chapter.

The Secrets Are Several

Planning is one. The Seniorpreneurial planning process needs to be taught and passed on to become a part of the culture of the senior-managed company. It's one of the critical steps in Seniorpreneurial success. Studies have shown that most people don't plan, set goals (even personal ones), or establish objectives.

Seniorpreneurs can't afford to have nonplanners on their team. They need to uncover team members' planning abilities early on by getting them into the planning process. If they show a reluctance to making plans, they will also be unable to assist in carrying plans out. Seniorpreneurs insist that their team members plan, and they insist that planning be pushed all the way down until it permeates the whole organization.

The Seniorpreneurial planning process is characterized first and foremost by flexibility. The flexibility comes into play because the plan has to be executed with a lot of common sense to allow for constant change. However, the change has to remain within the parameters of the short- and longer-term goals of the Seniorpreneurial plan. More important, the established benchmarks still must be hit. It's called hitting target dates and performance objectives while maintaining flexibility.

Another secret to making it happen revolves around the law of physics that every action causes a reaction. These active and reactive forces steer the company toward either success or failure, toward completing objectives called for in benchmarks or missing them in timetables. The Seniorpreneurial challenge is to create success forces as opposed to failure activities—in other words, to develop empowering management techniques.

A team is established initially to create realistic targets for each management discipline and then track those targets religiously. They are moving targets, and there are many of them. In the beginning, they center on engineering, or systems for service companies. As production begins, a primary target may be suppliers and keeping them in line. Administratively, it may be assuring that the paperwork flow doesn't develop a bottleneck.

Some targets move slowly and need constant urging; others, which are often worth more, move fast, and are harder to hit. An example is a newly discovered prospective customer who is about to make a purchase decision. The engineering department has to determine if an existing product can be altered to fit the new customer's particular requirements. Further, manufacturing has to cost out the profitability, production has to determine if it can deliver, and marketing has to be sure the product design will fit the customer's needs. The fast-moving targets are obviously harder to hit. The challenge is constant change, and the Seniorpreneurial team has to be prepared to take on increasingly tougher tasks as it is racking up growth.

Breaking Out the Planning Process

The business plan created by the Seniorpreneurial team during the planning process is really a big-picture plan. It describes the objectives and how they will be achieved by each management discipline. But it doesn't show much detail. It doesn't break out specifics for each managed area. This information comes in detailed operating plans. These plans should be prepared by the individuals responsible—most likely vice presidents of such areas as marketing, administration, production, and research.

Planning is the way that corporate goals set at higher levels become activities further down. As the planning process is pushed further down the organizational chart, it's helpful that the individuals involved in originating these departmental plans have a basic understanding of the planning process, purpose, and criteria involved. It's up to them to make the planning process happen by education and delegation.

Getting Clear on the Difference between Administrative and Operational Planning

Setting objectives is actually the starting point of planning. The objectives are determined and set forth in the company's business plan. Business planning is divided into two principal phases: administrative and operative. Administrative planning is concerned with determining bases of action, over a period of time, for the company and its various elements. It has greater futurity than operative planning, since it deals with periods of a year or more. Since the accuracy of foresight tends to vary inversely with the time span covered, the administrative plan must be stated in general terms, and it must be capable of modification as business conditions change. In other words, the Seniorpreneurial administrative plan must be flexible.

Operative planning is concerned with determining bases of action to accomplish specific projects or undertakings. Operative plans have limited futurity and they are ordinarily programmed within the time period covered by related administrative plans. Detailed operative plans are developed to support administrative plans. The Seniorpreneur is concerned with getting good operational plans developed by the people involved in executing them. This is part of creating a management system, because the benchmarks contained in an operating plan automatically indicate timetables that require reporting and consequently imply accountability.

Operational Planning: Making Your Dreams Come True

Operational planning is a design for getting a person or a group from a particular point to some preestablished and clearly defined goal. It is the business of making desires and dreams come true. It involves deciding what goals are sought and then specifying the steps needed to reach them. Operational planning should be directly linked to control processes and feedback so that the accuracy of the premise and assumptions supporting the plan can be reevaluated. Planning boils down to sensing an opportunity and establishing the means to achieve it. It involves understanding the environment in which your business operates and establishing the best way to get where you want to be. If you don't know where you're going, any path will get you there. If you don't plan, others will plan for you, and their actions will determine your priorities.

The manager who wants to plan must first establish objectives and then specify the factors, forces, and efforts necessary for their accomplishment. Operational planning establishes the activities necessary to meet designated objectives.

The Advantages of Formal Operational Planning. Formal operational planning has several important advantages:

1. It creates a formal network of printed information that would not otherwise be available.
2. It periodically forces operating managers to extend their time horizons and see the larger framework.
3. It requires people to communicate about goals, strategic issues, and resource allocations.
4. It systematically teaches managers about the future so they can better calibrate their short-term decisions.
5. It creates an attitude about and a comfort factor concerning the future.
6. It stimulates longer-term special studies that can have high impact on strategic decision making.
7. It establishes a formal reporting system.

It's Demanding Mental Work

Planning involves a lot of mental work. The planner must choose from alternative courses of action designed to achieve an objective. The raw material for mental work is managerial, technical, human, and company knowledge. Planning is essentially the intelligent synthesis of present knowledge and previous experience.

The Seniorpreneurial planner must possess knowledge, know-how, and facts to plan effectively. Knowledge refers to some basic body of principles, points of view, and other background information. Know-how refers to the body of facts and skills gained from practical experience. Know-how cannot usually be acquired from books. The third ingredient, facts, are known conditions, and assumptions about unknown conditions. Some of these conditions are controllable; others are uncontrollable. The operational planning principle becomes that the management team must get the facts, face the facts, and act as the facts dictate—not as they used to act, not as others are acting, but as the facts now dictate.

The Seven Criteria of a Good Operational Plan

Once the knowledge, know-how, and facts are assembled, an effective operational plan can be developed which will meet the following criteria:

1. The plan should state clearly the nature of the mission and its objectives. This helps those who are involved in executing the plan to understand, believe, accept, and support it.
2. The plan should provide measures of accomplishment in terms of quantity, quality, time, and expense. This assists in delegating responsibility and measuring results.
3. The plan should state the policies which should guide people in accomplishing the mission.
4. The plan should spell out which people or departments will be involved in accomplishing the mission.
5. The plan should indicate the time allowed for each phase of the activities.
6. The plan should specify the kinds and amount of resources (money, people, items) allowable.
7. The plan should designate the leaders who will be held accountable for accomplishments.

Why People Fail to Plan

Seniorpreneurs recognize that people who are unwilling or unable to plan cannot fulfill their functions satisfactorily. Adopting a plan means establishing goals, determining priorities, making choices, and then making commitments. Some people just aren't capable of making commitments in their lives or in the lives of others. Consequently, they just refuse to plan; they let others plan for them, and then they react. In business, this is called management by crisis.

For other people, planning simply takes the fun and surprise out of life. They prefer the challenge of playing catch-up. In today's competitive world, they feel that they perform best when under pressure. This type of player may win a game or two, but loses the season.

Another group of people resist planning because it makes them nervous, creates tension, and induces a fear of failure. Having to work under planned conditions causes mental and sometimes physical stress. For these people, the anxiety-inducing conditions created by planning just aren't worth it.

Why Plans Fail

Along with avoiding nonplanners, seniors making it happen need to have an understanding of why plans fail and what can be done to lessen the possibility of failure. What pitfalls contribute to failed plans? How can people work smarter in planning? Here are some basic reasons that plans fail.

Lack of Realistic Goals. Plans fail when goals are vague or completely unreachable.

- Seniorpreneurial goals must be specific, with detailed objectives.
- Goals must be measurable, with benchmarks everyone can understand.
- Goals must have built-in time frames to force accountability.
- The participants in achieving a goal must agree that although it's a stretch, the goal is obtainable.

Lack of Commitment. Commitment provides motivation; the people who are charged with implementing the goal must be committed to the plan used to achieve it. The best way to ensure commitment is to get participants involved in the plan. Guide them, but let them originate and substantiate the efforts needed to successfully execute the plan.

Failure to Anticipate Obstacles. Every plan has to allow for changes, leave some room for contingencies. This is especially true for Seniorpreneurial companies. No matter how carefully a plan is prepared, Murphy's Law is going to affect it in some way. Look for and discuss possible obstacles during the planning process. The discussion creates an atmosphere of flexibility as the plan is carried out so that the obstacles, when confronted, seem less devastating. They simply become hurdles to overcome with continuing enthusiasm.

Lack of Benchmarks and Reviews. Plans that fail don't have concrete benchmarks and predetermined review points. As a result, achievement begins to slip, and those involved in implementing the plan become demoralized because they feel no one cares until it's too late. This can't be allowed to happen in Seniorpreneurial companies. Benchmarks and continuing reviews are used to make sure that objectives are reached. They charge both the implementers and the overseers with responsibility. It's part of making it happen.

Failure to Be Flexible. No plan is going to be obtained 100 percent. Just as in allowing for obstacles, some flexibility must be maintained. Stubbornness in forcing adherence to all aspects of the plan will only ensure that it won't be attained. Failing to revise goals when it is appropriate is ignoring reality; effective planning provides some resiliency to change both details and direction without scrapping the whole plan.

Planning is used to reduce uncertainty and to manage risk. Working hard is inherent in Seniorpreneurial companies, and planning helps people work smarter. It's why Seniorpreneurial plans are goal-oriented rather than activity-oriented; that's a secret of making it happen.

Seniorpreneurial Street Smarts in Action

When a Seniorpreneurial company is up and running, top management must shift its focus toward some more obscure areas. At first blush, these areas don't seem to have much pertinence to the daily operations of a company. However, the shift of focus indeed makes the difference between entrepreneurs and Seniorpreneurs. These higher-level management issues and philosophies are what create value-added companies and contribute to off-balance-sheet assets. They can become the difference between succeeding and becoming an also-ran. Following are a number of success philosophies that Seniorpreneurs recognize and cultivate in the process of operating their enterprises.

Management by Objective

It's simple: You focus on an end result and try to make it happen. You determine what you're after and set out to get it. That's why Seniorpreneurs need to have a continuing stream of objectives. They must learn to focus all available resources on accomplishing several specific goals or operational objectives, within stated time periods. There is a terrible tendency on the part of entrepreneurs to scatter resources, to take on too many tasks. Line up your objectives and manage your operations to achieve them.

Alternatives

There are several alternatives to management by objective. Generally, they don't work for the Seniorpreneur because they focus on day-to-day objectives instead of longer-term goals, with the idea that everything will work out all right. However, in some cases or areas, they may prove to be the right choice in making it happen.

Managing by Hope. Hope operates on the premise that certainties are hard to find, that the best path to pursue is all paths. This is a form of reacting as opposed to being proactive. It works for some broad-based initial research or early investigation of methods for distribution. The caution is to watch for "paralysis by analysis," in which all the overwhelming variables lead to total indecision.

Managing by Crisis. Crisis has long typified the entrepreneurial effort. It's especially typical when the team is composed primarily of engineering types. They are usually good problem solvers, and when confronted by a crisis, they bring a lot of energy and innovative solution-forming abilities to the cause. Think about how much time, creative effort, and dollar saving can be gained if attention is focused on identifying potential problems and establishing alternatives instead of reacting to yet another crisis.

Managing by Subjectives. This is the mystery approach to where the company is headed. It's presumed that the boss knows, but nothing is shared with the rest of the staff. Subjective managing works for very simple enterprises but is a definite "no-no" for senior-managed companies. High-quality people aren't attracted to this type of organization; nor, if by chance they join, will they stay very long. People by nature want to know where they are going and enjoy contributing to how to get there.

Management by Extrapolation. The extrapolation approach works on the premise that today is, and tomorrow will be, about how it was yesterday. All that really needs to be done today is to figure out how to do the same thing tomorrow with a little more efficiency. This is a common approach among mature companies even today, but it no longer works for anything beyond routine tasks. It is better to shift attention to strategic planning for tomorrow.

Expand Carefully from a Profit Mindset

Optimism is an inherent characteristic of the Seniorpreneur. However, it can be detrimental as well as positive. It takes a careful balance of thinking to feel confident that all things can be accomplished while understanding that all things can't be done simultaneously. The tendency is to embark on an all-encompassing mission, to try to create a product or service that answers many needs, and develop them all at the same time. Successful Seniorpreneurs recognize that they have to focus on a particular area, get it properly developed and marketed, and—bottom line—do it profitably. Once the project is well on its way, they can move forward into other areas or market applications. Each step must be grounded on profitability, on being able to ultimately stand on its own—the sooner in the cycle, the better. Profits don't just happen. Like sales, they have to be made to happen.

The Seniorpreneur's job in making it happen is to move from the old to the new, to do a single thing exceptionally well, and to learn to do it consistently and profitably.

Gain Eyes, Arms, Ears, and Legs

And you do so by delegating. For Seniorpreneurs, delegation can be the biggest single growth challenge. Letting go of responsibility and authority as the company grows is very difficult. You have to learn that delegating is not a skill but an attitude. When you push responsibility outward and downward, you give up something. But you can count on the fact that two more responsibilities will replace each one you give up. And they will prove more challenging. One way to ease into the delegating attitude is to expand the parameters of job descriptions to make change occur. The only way your people can grow is if you let them take risks. The only way the senior company can grow is to practice delegating, to achieve results through others. This attitude needs to be bred into the company culture right from the start so that there is an ever-growing core of talent available to respond to the increasing challenges of making it happen.

Lead People; Manage Things

Seniorpreneurs recognize that people live up or down to the expectations that their leaders set for them as well as by the examples of the leaders themselves. Just as what we see in others is a reflection of ourselves (mirroring), what others see in us is what they emulate.

An interesting and sometimes revealing hiring exercise asks the following questions:

1. *If you could create the perfect job for yourself, what would it be?* The answer tells you if people have any idea of what they want and, just as important, if you can give it to them.

2. *If you had all the money you needed, what is the biggest thing you would buy?* The answer tells you about the size of a person's financial dreams. If the potential of your opportunity is only $50,000 per year and this person's dreams require $300,000 per year, you may not have a match.
3. *What 21 things are you committed to?* Ask people to write their answers down in front of you. First of all, if they are not committed to other things, they're not going to be committed to you or their new job. Another point brought out by this question involves the old adage "If you want something done, find someone who is busy." For the Seniorpreneur, the saying should be "find someone who is busy and committed."

Seniorpreneurs lead by stretching people, by giving them responsibility for things that they think they want to do, but are unsure that they are ready to do. Unless the Seniorpreneur's team grows, the Seniorpreneur will not. Being able to grow yourself assumes that you have learned enough to let people make mistakes without your getting angry and resentful. It's tough to do many times, and those tough times don't last long, but tough people do. To make it happen, be a leader of people and have them manage the things.

Leadership

Leadership is the heart and soul of management. What you lead is people. Leadership is the ability to inspire other people to work together as a team, following your lead, in order to attain a common goal. Seniorpreneurs believe in one-team management leadership, in which all team members are committed to a single, agreed-upon set of objectives. Senior leadership is exercised as the ability to lead and inspire others and is more instinctual that premeditated. It is acquired through the experiences of everyday life.

You Can't Fight Reality

Seniorpreneurs don't fight realities; they innovate and determine ways to capitalize on them in building successful enterprises.

After World War II, America emerged as the wealthiest and only unscathed industrial power in the world. Since then, we have lived off the fat of the land, paying the highest wages in the world, while cutting the demands of productivity from our work force. Additionally, we allowed our basic industrial facilities to become technologically obsolete. As a people, we became slack, complacent, self-centered, and self-indulgent compared with citizens of other countries.

The economies that grew the fastest between 1965 and 1990 were in the Pacific Rim. These countries have been moving into high-tech manufacturing with unbounded enthusiasm. Japan's progress is well documented. Hong Kong produces textiles and lots of clothes which are not only less expensive than ours but equal if not better in quality. Korea builds oceangoing ships that we are still unable to match in price or quality. Europe too has been moving forward. Western European nations have surpassed the United States in a lot of basic smokestack-type manufacturing and has proved time and time again that they are no slouches in research in many areas. Now they are gaining a whole new Eastern Europe work force, albeit at great expense and investment, that is eager to make up for decades of suppression.

How do these realities affect Seniorpreneurs? By their very existence. Seniorpreneurs should carefully consider opportunities in which they may be competing with these countries head to head. They should also look to the efficiencies of these countries and seek to enter into strategic partnerships in some way to take advantage of combined strengths.

What You Got When You Got What You Didn't Expect

It's experience! This is the process of discovering, with the result that you learn something new. It should grow, if properly cultivated, into cumulative capability. You have to venture forth and seek it, reach for it. You have to search your environment, stretch your mind, come up with something better, try a new approach, create a different way of doing things. That's called creative experience. Even failures count as long as they're added in a positive way to your storehouse of knowledge. Experience is what you get when you don't get what you expect. It's also called Seniorpreneuring.

Management Must Manage

Must is the operative word, the active word in the credo. Management is a living force, the force that gets things done to acceptable standards, high standards. But it must manage. That doesn't mean solving every problem, reaching every goal, being an outstanding success every time. No sports team wins all its games, but it has to be good enough to win most of them. In business, you have to be better than your competitors; how much better depends on the standards you set. But you must manage to achieve results. If you can't get those results all the time, that's acceptable too. Then you change your environment. Sell the business and get into something else. You change. That is management. What you don't do is go on accepting inadequate results and explaining them away. You must manage to make it happen.

Monitor and Respond

Many entrepreneurs have gotten into deep trouble with the company because they ignored a very important point. Amid all the pressures of operating a company, they forgot about one of their most important assets, their customers. New technology, foreign competition, and new pricing strategies suddenly put a dent in their growth plans. Often, the surprise could have been avoided if they had stayed in touch with their customers, talked with them, questioned them, found out their needs, asked what's new. Top management needs to stay eyeball to eyeball with customers instead of pushing that contact farther downstream. The Seniorpreneur must commit some time, all the time, to interrelating with the company's customers. Superb customer service is built around the idea of long-term partnerships with people. These partnerships are enhanced if the Seniorpreneur cultivates customer relationships. By monitoring the customer's needs, the Seniorpreneur is in a much better position to respond in making it happen.

Success and Unsuccess

A review of the many published reports, documents, surveys, and obituaries of successful and unsuccessful businesses reveals some interesting and thought-provoking points. A list of causes of failure is as effective as a success list in guiding entrepreneurs. It can point out many areas they should avoid as well as highlight areas to concentrate on when making it happen.

Causes of Failure

One-person management

Lack of internal communication

Lack of technical know-how by management

Squabbles within top management

Absentee management

Uncertainty of objectives

Lack of diversification

Inadequate records

Elaborate but unusable records

Too much capital investment
Excessive payroll
Inadequate sales representation
Sales to insolvent customers
Poor sales records
Ineffective bidding
Poorly managed subcontracting
Poor market research
Neglected tax liability
Excessive expansion cost
Excessive borrowing

The Big Four. Four other items continually stand out.

1. Successful companies have good financial records and make full use of them. Unsuccessful companies don't have good records.
2. Successful companies emphasize sales with top executives participating. Unsuccessful companies regard selling as a nuisance.
3. Successful companies consciously work on research and development. Few unsuccessful ones do the same.
4. Successful companies actively work on administration, have clear lines of authority, and make decisions without a lot of fuss. Unsuccessful companies are inept at administration. This old making-it-happen adage sums it up: "Management, management, management."

Marketing Variables

It stands to reason that a Seniorpreneurial team needs to assess its proposed marketplace when initially determining a product or service around which to build a company. The initial planning must take into consideration many variables affecting the development, production, introduction, and maintenance of the product or service. The team needs to consider the five variables under its control—price, product, place, promotion, and people.

When the company is up and running—and many times even before that—another group of variables comes into play. Although these are not within the control of the management team, they need to be accounted for, on an ongoing basis in a well-defined marketing strategy. These uncontrollable marketing variables include the economy, values, climate, environment, politics, and cultural and social trends.

As times and these uncontrollable variables change and evolve, the scope of marketing activities also evolves to meet the new challenges of the marketplace. In recent years, U.S. markets have expanded not only internationally but also intranationally. The American cultural landscape has broadened to incorporate buyers, products, and service representatives of more and more ethnic groups, age groups, sexual orientation groups, and gender groups in ever-increasing numbers. A brief review of some of the products and services developed, introduced, and maintained in the marketplace helps us understand the need to strategically incorporate these new factions in Seniorpreneurial market planning.

As women have entered the work force in greater numbers, and so increased their buying power, there have been some notable changes: a major growth in the childcare industry, a renewed private-sector movement into education, an expansion of the toy industry into new markets as well as large standalone operations, and diversification of the female clothing industry into maternity and business segments.

Dual-career couples have created new markets for the expanding food industry: microwavable everything; packaged ready-to-eat desserts, salads, snacks; a burgeoning catering industry providing food from parties to breakfast in bed; and retail and wholesale outlets with dinners-to-go alongside trendy footwear, motor oil, greeting cards, and management books. Dry cleaners, home-cleaning services, lawn care, and home maintenance are also appealing to these homeowners occupied elsewhere, including at the new fitness and recreational centers.

It's impossible to list all the ways that cultural diversity—and its recognition by business—has expanded marketplaces. The point is that keeping track of market changes, and capturing and capitalizing on the ever-evolving trends, is part of making it happen.

Marketing is a planning- and strategy-based process that attempts to satisfy the needs and wants of a constituency through a competitive advantage at a profit. The key is to satisfy the needs and wants of a constituency. If someone doesn't want or need a product, all the marketing in the world will not make the company successful.

Define the problem as your potential users see it. What problem are you solving? Do people really need or want to know what this problem is? What do your users wish they could do—and how are they solving this problem now? What are they willing to pay to solve this problem? The old saying "Necessity is the mother of invention" is true. If you can find a large number of users with the same need, you have a market in which to make it happen.

Seniorpreneurial style can be summarized by addressing two primary pressures: those from outside and those from within the organization.

Outside Pressures

Outside pressures emanate mainly from the customer. They're natural pressures resulting from growth and from a company that is gaining more and more visibility.

The Seniorpreneur has to be responsive to the outside forces that affect the customer base. Sometimes they're subtle things like a decrease in foreign interest rates that allows a foreign competitor to be able to reduce its sales price. At other times they're not so subtle, like a major technological breakthrough that completely destroys the company's technology edge. Maintaining responsiveness means staying close to customers and pushing customer contact. In an ultragrowth situation, awareness of the customer's perspective comes from the top, by communication and by action on the part of key executives.

Awareness can't just come from outside sources like market research. Market research is not a substitute for knowing your market, for physically going out and looking for yourself. You need to validate (and invalidate) questions in order to be sure that you don't become a victim of your own prejudices. Remember, you can't research something that doesn't exist. Twenty years ago if someone asked you to invest $5000 in a machine to do your payroll, your reply would have been, "I don't have a problem doing payroll." But since the computer has come on the market, we all use it to compute payroll.

You cannot market something that doesn't exist. But your customers will tell you what their problems are if you ask them. Then you can respond to outside customer pressures with solutions.

Inside Pressures

Inside pressures come from a variety of sources that reflect the increasing size and complexity of organizations as they respond to various problems and crises.

Inside pressure can be reduced by building a culture: a culture built on flexibility, cooperation, and appropriate competitiveness. Establishing a company culture allows you to be adaptable to the ever-changing mix of customers, production, marketing, and distribution requirements. All organizations, small or large, military or civilian, reflect the personality and character of the people who lead them. These leaders establish an organization's culture. The culture is built by an ever-expanding circle that encompasses communication, participation, monitoring, and responding.

Building Communication Culture. The Seniorpreneurial team needs to guard against communication becoming a one-way street. In the heavy-duty rush of day-to-day events, it's easy to hear and see only what's comfortable. Subordinates naturally shy away from being harbingers of potent Seniorpreneurial bad news. You need to build internal lines of communication that ensure that information flows up as easily as it does down. You also need to encourage outside communication from members of your boards of directors and advisers. They can help pose hard questions and bring realities into focus.

Building Participation Culture. Participation in day-to-day activities is one of the attractions of small companies. But it gets harder to maintain that hands-on attention as the company grows and the distance expands between the decision makers and employees or customers. As people are promoted, and new hires are made, it's important that one of their job qualifications becomes their ability to communicate. People do respond to structure and formal organizational charts. A person's boss is a primary reference point in the world of work. If that leader is weak or vacillating, the signal gets through.

As a Seniorpreneur, you need to be informed and communicative about your company's objectives. You must be able to describe how each person fits into the scheme of the company's plans and how that person contributes to the whole. Participation is how you encourage adaptive, enthusiastic, and supportive work forces—employees who no longer say, "It's not in my job description," but instead say, "I want to do this." You reply, "Go for it." Participation is how you gain a culture of trust and loyalty.

Building Monitoring Culture. Monitoring is a Seniorpreneuring skill that can be learned, taught, and refined. It is based on an understanding of relationships and events which is essential to executing strategies, plans, and programs. It should be built into the growth culture to increase productivity improvement through people—to encourage the operational autonomy that results in stimulating entrepreneurship.

As with all culture-building activities, proper monitoring begins at the top with the Seniorpreneur. You need to establish superior reporting systems that allow you to track and examine key operational data. You need to ensure that monitoring habits get instilled at all levels of the company's operations. This is how the culture is instituted, encouraged, and confirmed. Proper monitoring creates a bias toward action.

Building Responding Culture. A Seniorpreneur's single biggest challenge is letting go of responsibility and authority as the company grows. *Delegation* is the operational word. Delegating is not so much a skill as an attitude. You need to give up authority and responsibility by pushing it downward and outward. You gain eyes, ears, arms, legs, and ideas by doing so. Your people grow stronger, more responsive, and sharper with time and encouragement.

By delegating properly, you achieve responsiveness and get a communication return—a response in transmitting and sharing ideas, opinions, and critiques on the work being done, and the progress being made toward established goals. This is a lifeline process for the company. Interchanges about tasks at hand promote an understanding of the company culture.

Cashflow: It's Your Lifeblood

Cash is king for Seniorpreneurs. And cashflow is the bedrock of the kingdom. It's the lifeblood of any growing company. A company without cash is no company. During the start-up or concept stage, the founders usually trade off their time for cash. However, once the company is up and running, once full-time employees are hired, the Seniorpreneur must have cash not only to continue but also to fuel growth.

During the concept stage, it's usually the founders' personal cash or savings that enable them to write the business plan that will bring in seed-stage financing. Assuming they can then obtain the cash to execute the seed-stage plan, their concern becomes conserving enough cash to meet objectives and benchmarks while going on to pursue financing for the product development stage. The latter is a critical stage for almost all companies. This development stage of financing, almost without exception, takes longer than anticipated; as many Seniorpreneurs learn, having a commitment is not the same as having the cash in hand. Several months may transpire between signing an agreement and receiving the actual funds.

Rapid expansion brings on additional cashflow needs, and in each of these there are cashflow traps. The most prominent, and the ones that can be systematically tracked, semi-influenced, and controlled, are inventory and receivables.

Inventory: You Have to Control It

Uncontrolled inventory can really hurt rapid-growth companies. Scores of them have been bitten big time by it. Inventory overload can arise in three different ways. The first is high growth rates on complicated products. The company has to carry large levels of various parts—all bought in large quantities so as to get discounted price breaks—in order to meet increasing customer demand. The second is a sudden dive in sales. The company ends up with large amounts of finished product on hand, no sales, and all its cash tied up in the ballooned inventory. The third factor is a marketing program that calls for the company to be a significant credit supplier to its customers—by "floor planning" product, offering consignment, or allowing extended credit terms. More than one company has found itself in the position of having to let key people go because its money was tied up in inventory and it couldn't meet payroll. You can't eat or pay people with inventory. Losing valued employees is a high price to pay for failing to protect cash reserves for temporary glitches in sales.

Accounts Receivable: Control Them Also

A second great cash consumer is accounts receivable. A lot of Seniorpreneurial ventures start out as manufacturing or service companies and end up, much to their dismay, as banks. The stories are many; the tales of woe may vary in detail, but the substance is the same. The product or service is hot, everyone wants to buy, the Seniorpreneur wants to sell. Things go along smoothly for the first couple of months; dealers buy and pay on time. The company is shipping increasing amounts of product or proving burgeoning amounts of service. All of a sudden, dealers' or customers' payments slow down. For the first month or two, the company doesn't notice. It's too caught up in the euphoria of success, and too busy producing, shipping, or delivering.

At the first sign of trouble, it's very hard to say no to customers who tell you how much they like your product—how, if they just had the next shipment in, they could turn it over immediately and send you your receivable payment. First thing you know, 6 months have gone by and the Seniorpreneur is blindsided by no cashflow. People have to be laid off, payables get extended, and rampant rumors spread through the industry about how the entrepreneurial star is having money problems. The rumors compound the company's problems, in that formerly valued customers now determine to drag out their payments even longer on the chance that the company may not make it. Guess what? The Seniorpreneur doesn't make it. All because of cashflow.

Here Are Some Cashflow Pointers

Entrepreneurs tend to ignore cashflow, whereas Seniorpreneurs prepare for it. They prepare by having a top accounting person on their team who puts state-of-the-art inventory, receivable, and cashflow management systems in place. The systems are backed up by the knowledge that growth companies always need more money than they can generate internally. Inventory and receivable money has to come from outside sources. And the time to line up these sources is before there is a screaming need for them.

The Seniorpreneuring business plan should forecast this need. It should take into account when and how much extra debt cash is needed between probable equity financings. The financial management team should start romancing these sources early on by supplying a continual stream of updated information which keeps these sources in the know. This way there's no surprises. There's a prebuilt familiarity with management and the company's operations, and no delays in obtaining the financing to continue to support the company's growth. These sources are familiar:

Professional venture capital (for subordinated interim debt)

Debtors (banks, SBA, individuals)

Credit companies (commercial banks)

Suppliers (for extended payment terms)

Customers (payments in advance)

Factors (high-cost loan programs)

Fixed-asset-based lenders (to free up operating cash)

Here's a cashflow tip that can be applied to almost any type of debt financing. It's called a *skipped-payment loan,* and it's especially useful for Seniorpreneurs who operate seasonal businesses. If you find you have difficulty making fixed loan payments 12 months of the year, many financing institutions will permit you to skip predesignated payments. In effect, this allows you to customize your payment schedule to cashflows.

The skipped-payment plan is especially useful in construction and similar industries. The company makes 8 or 9 monthly payments, skipping 3 or 4 months in the normally slow winter season. The company ends up paying more interest over an extended loan period, but its cashflow problems are alleviated. An alternative is to double up on some monthly payments when cashflow is highest. The point is, don't just accept traditional lending practices. Be Seniorpreneurally innovative. You'll be surprised at the results.

Cashflow management is not just a key to successful Seniorpreneuring; it's a *must.* It's not just another part of the financial program; it's *critical.* It's not just a few more pages of financial projections; it's *integral* to the plan. It's not just a problem for the controller; it's solution planning by the Chief Financial Seniorpreneurial Officer. The Seniorpreneur has to control and preserve the cashflow lifeline.

The Strategy for Now

The mid-1990s may prove to be a slow- or no-growth period. If that is the case, Seniorpreneurs know that their company strategy needs to be flexible.

Three Approaches

Seniorpreneurs recognize that maintaining market share is the name of the game. In high-growth times, markets are naturally expanding, but in low- or no-growth periods, markets stay steady and the challenge is to maintain existing percentages of market share. Seniorpreneurs maintain market share by emphasizing product or service differentiation. They ask: "What makes our product or service different from and better than our competitors'?" Or they speed up new product or service introductions. They decrease the time periods they have been used to and seek out ways to shorten the time frames of introductions.

Second, Seniorpreneurs recognize that in slow- or no-growth periods, competition in pricing increases. They accept this as a business fact of life. They switch their emphasis from the external market scene to internal operations in order to maintain or improve profit margins. They match competitive pricing if they must, but most find better ways internally to hold profit levels.

Finally, Seniorpreneurs focus on financial management. They seek out better ways to operate their enterprises by keeping a close eye on working-capital-intensive items such as inventories and outstanding receivables. They hold inventories to acceptable levels, adopt just-in-time inventory methods whenever practicable, and take more frequent inventory counts so as to adjust the stock of merchandise on hand and eliminate large levels of slow-moving items. Additionally, they instigate tighter control over their customer receivables, make quicker calls on late payers, scrutinize new accounts for their ability to pay, and offer incentives for early payment.

This type of management helps senior-operated companies become leaner, meaner, and more profitable. It also helps them rebound faster and with higher profits when the situation turns around.

Street Smarts in Action

Seniorpreneurs use a team approach, one with team members who are most likely also seniors. That's an awful lot of street smarts gathered in one company! This access to a wealth of experience needs to be continually employed in the operation of the business. Many street-smart pointers have been presented in this chapter. Your challenge as a Seniorpreneur is to choose the ones that will work best in your particular situation. With the proper mix, you count on being successful in selling out your interests or providing for successful succession.

12
Selling Out or Succession

For some Seniorpreneurs, the reward comes from the fact that they have succeeded in putting together a company that earns a substantial, continuing return for them and their investors. They take entrepreneurial pride in the fact that they and their team have built a company—and most likely a lifestyle—their way. They enjoy the daily individual challenges they face, recognizing that each decision has a direct impact on their future and that the rewards for meeting these challenges, head on, go directly into their pockets.

For other senior company builders—and ultimately for all entrepreneurs—the reward comes in getting out of their enterprise. This chapter details the various alternatives for exiting or selling out. The primary exit strategies are absentee ownership, management buyouts, outright sales, employee stock option plans (ESOPs), mergers and acquisitions, and going public.

The toughest part of exiting is getting all the exit players to agree on the deal and the timing. Windows are rarely open for long and most require a preset determination as to the method, pricing, and timing. Even when agreement is unanimous, there are a lot of pitfalls.

Pricing and Terms

When Seniorpreneurs seek to harvest their company, two big factors come into play: pricing and terms. *Pricing* is the actual total amount of the deal, most often based on a valuation of the company and what's it worth. *Terms* are the amounts, methods, and timing of the payout.

Whenever they get into discussions on pricing and terms, Seniorpreneurs rely on the adage "You name the price and I'll set the terms." Stated in the reverse, "You name the terms and I'll set the price." Seniorpreneurs understand pricing and terms. Using them creatively is another area in which Seniorpreneurs excel. Many of the harvesting strategies described in this chapter pertain to buying and selling businesses in general. In other words, they are good exercises in Seniorpreneurial creative financial thinking. Seniorpreneurs may acquire additional companies to add to or enhance their primary company as they grow to the harvest stage. Acquisitions add value, and Seniorpreneurs are ever-conscious about increasing the true and perceived value of their enterprise. Ofttimes, acquisitions are made just prior to or even simultaneous with a harvest.

Pricing

Determining the price is seldom simple and is often complex. Above all, it is never easy. Whether you are buyer or seller, the most outstanding point to remember is that there are a lot of ways to determine price. You should always use a combination of methods in making a final determination. (A number of pricing and valuation "ratios" are provided in Chapter 5.)

Karl H. Vesper, in his book *New Venture Strategies* (Prentice-Hall, 1980), points out 17 pricing methods, which he breaks into six categories.

Net Worth Methods

1. Book value
2. Adjusted book value (goodwill added)

Asset Methods

3. Liquidation value (auctioneer estimates)
4. Fair market value (professional appraisal)
5. Replacement value (go shopping)

Income Methods

6. Historic earnings (maybe weighted) times a multiple
7. Future earnings, present owner, times a multiple
8. Future earnings, new owner, times a multiple

Cashflow Methods (New Owner)

9. Payment-servicing capacity (for payback on cash deal)
10. Discounted cashflow (assume eventual resale)
11. Adjusted cashflow (include salaries, perks, fringes)

Market Methods

12. Last trading price (if there was one)
13. Current competitive bids (or what they are likely to be)
14. Comparable company prices (whatever they may be)
15. Special formulas in some industries

Heuristic Methods

16. Intuitive value to buyer (including a job, independence, other personal perks, satisfactions)
17. Seller's preconception of price (buyer can yield on this and recover on terms)

Why look at all these methods? Usually the best way to cut a deal is to accept the seller's price and work out a successful negotiation by designing acceptable terms. However, the buyer needs to be satisfied with the price of the deal, as well as determine if the asking price is reasonable. It's common for the buyer to use several pricing methods as ammunition in negotiating either price or terms. This is why it's best, for both seller and buyer, to combine methods in determining a final price.

Seniorpreneurs need to be familiar with pricing *before* they even begin their project. Part of the planning process is determining the harvest point and price. The various guides provided throughout this book will assist you in successfully starting and operating your company. Now is the time to review pricing so that you have a good grasp on the key negotiating points and the various pricing methods that will come into play during harvest negotiations. Not all the methods described below will be used with or even be applicable to every project. However, you should find that at least six or eight will apply to your specific deal. The following descriptions should assist you in determining which methods are right for you.

Net Worth Methods. *Book value* is the quickest way to determine a price. It simply involves reviewing a company's balance sheet and finding its listed net worth (assets minus liabilities). An advantage to the buyer is that many assets may have been depreciated to below market value (common for private companies); if a sale can be negotiated on the basis of book value, the buyer may be making an undervalued purchase.

In reality, the chances of making a book value purchase are slim. Much more commonly, *adjusted book value* will be used to establish net worth and price a deal more fairly. Adjusted book value is simply book value plus some mutually agreed-upon price for "goodwill." It may, in fact, include allowances for such intangible items as customer lists, long-term employee value, location, time in business, and certain proprietary processes used in the business. The rationale is that these items, which cost a lot of time and dollars to assemble, aren't reflected directly on the company's asset side of the balance sheet. A common method for determining adjusted book value is to add three times the company's annual earnings to the actual book value (after deducting normal owner/managers' salaries).

Asset Methods. Distressed companies are often sold at what is termed "fire sale" value. This in effect is the *liquidation value* of the assets. Under this method, price is determined by figuring out how much the business would be worth if every part of the company were sold off quickly. Accounts receivable might be sold to a factor. Inventory could be "quick sold" to customers, competitors, or scrap dealers. Plant and fixtures could go to auction, or private deals might be made with competitors.

A step up from liquidation value, and a method commonly used in smaller private transactions, is *fair market value.* Here professional appraisers are retained, or the parties mutually agree from published price information on the current value (fair market) of the company's hard assets. *Replacement value* is akin to fair market value with the buyer's underlying question being "Can I buy this somewhere else at lower cost?" Here some intangibles come into play such as the true value of patterns, custom tooling, research, and design.

Income Methods. Income methods are reviewed from the income statement as opposed to the balance sheet. A common income method is *historic earnings.* The premise is that a company's value can be based on its past earnings—say, over 3 to 5 years or more. A second method is *future earnings under the present owner.* This idealized method assumes that an existing owner is capable of containing or reducing expenses, thus increasing profit margins. A third method is *future earnings under a new owner.* Here, rather than rely on the fact that the company has made X number of dollars each year over the last 5 years, the parties assume that a new owner will be able to increase earnings by bringing in new management techniques.

All three income methods are translated into price by means of a price/earnings (PE) ratio. PE ratios are listed publicly for all types of businesses. The most common sources are the daily newspaper quotations for companies listed on the New York Stock Exchange and the American Stock Exchange or, for over-the-counter companies, on NASDAQ (National Association of Securities Dealers Automated Quotations). Looking at both high and low PE ratios and comparing them with the prospective company's results is a good cross-check on pricing.

Cashflow Methods. Cashflow methods require factoring terms into the deal. The concern here is how much money the company can make to justify the price being paid. Three subfactors need to be considered:

1. How much money is being paid as a downpayment (to figure cost of funds or return on investment)?
2. How much money is needed to cover the debt service?
3. How much money is needed for operating capital (possibly affected by seasonal changes)?

A common cashflow method is *payment-servicing capacity*. The price must be such that the company's profits and cashflow can pay off interest and principal while also generating some reserves for unknowns.

If the potential new owner is planning on reselling the business at some time in the future, it's common to use a *discounted cashflow* method. Here, the current selling price is based on the future value of the company at its resale. The calculation is made with an interest-rate figure of choice—or better yet, with several different interest figures, depending on the buyer's prediction of which direction interest rates will take. This method requires the use of a calculator or discount table. The higher the risk of the deal (in the new owner's eyes), the higher the interest figure that should be used, and hence the lower the price.

A third cashflow method is *adjusted cashflow*. This method often appeals to Seniorpreneurs, since the prime considerations are the salaries and the perks (company car, travel, entertainment, and the like) included in the deal. These are tax deductions through the company which benefit the buyer, and the Seniorpreneur may have an interest in keeping the perks going through a continuing consulting agreement.

Market Methods. Market methods focus on what value others may place on the company or deal. One common method is *last trading price*. For a publicly traded company, this is the share price listed in its most recent stock quotation. For a private company, it may be the last price the company sold for, with adjustments for current conditions, or the price at which a comparable company was recently sold. If there are other bidders or interested parties, *current competitive bids* may be used. An alternative approach is *comparable company prices,* or simply what other, similar companies have sold for.

Finally, some industries, especially in the service sector, base price on *special formulas.* In these cases, there are numerous precedents for the particular industry. These types of companies turn over on a fairly routine basis and it's difficult to negotiate too far off the industry norms. The best source for these formulas is a reputable business broker or a banker. In all these market methods, remember that terms can have a lot of bearing on the total price paid or offered.

Heuristic Methods. The last group of methods deals with heuristics— or "It's anybody's guess what motivates the price." *Intuitive value,* is based on what feels right, but it may also have some justifiable grounds. For the buyer, it might be an intuitive feeling assigned to the risk involved. For the seller, it might be the desire to realize a dream that the company would be worth X dollars when it is sold. Again, this type of deal can be successfully concluded if the terms are worked out to everyone's satisfaction. In some cases, it is the *seller's preconception of price* that has to be dealt with—maybe X number of dollars or X dollars per month. It is impossible to know what personal factors enter into a seller's (or buyer's) conceptions. Again, the adage "You name the price and I'll set the terms" is the Seniorpreneur's way of dealing with this type of transaction.

The key to pricing is to use as many of the different methods as possible when analyzing a deal. The different methods will give you a solid range of prices from which to begin negotiating terms.

Terms

Whereas the study of pricing involves a determination of what is to be bought and at what price, the study of terms focuses on how the deal is actually structured. Among the many considerations that come into play when looking at terms, five in particular lend themselves to a high degree of Seniorpreneurial creativity. They are:

Cash downpayment

Installment payments

Guarantees of payment

Stock as payment

Options

Cash Downpayment. At first blush, it wouldn't seem that much creativity could be applied to a cash downpayment. You either pay or receive cash, or you don't. For a harvest, the Seniorpreneur isn't usually concerned with how a buyer gets cash. However, if the buyer is short on cash, the Seniorpreneur may wish to share a few cash-obtaining secrets to help the deal along. For Seniorpreneurs, the creativity comes from knowing how to generate cash.

In most Seniorpreneurial acquisitions, cash comes from company funds, personal funds, family or friends, borrowing, recruiting other partners, and the like. In a harvest acquisition, however, the Seniorpreneur might rely on what is commonly thought of as a leveraged buyout: simply using the assets of the proposed purchase as collateral for the downpayment borrowed from a lending source and then using cashflow to service the debt behind the balance of the transaction. Seniorpreneurs make acquisitions to enhance company value for their own harvest.

Assume that a Seniorpreneur has an opportunity to purchase a company which has undervalued assets (machinery, excess inventory, even real estate) that will not be needed in the ultimate company operations. The key is to find a buyer for the unused assets and arrange for a simultaneous transaction in which the unused-asset buyer pays cash on the day of the acquisition closing. Those monies are then used to fund the cash downpayment. As another example, the Seniorpreneur might arrange to sell a prospective company's receivables to a factor and then use that money for the cash downpayment. Seniorpreneurs are innovative both in obtaining cash for their acquisitions and in arranging harvests.

Installment Payments. Payment by installment is also pretty straightforward. The buyer arranges to pay the seller a fixed amount over a specified period of time. Seniorpreneurial flexibility can be written into this type of term agreement. For example, balloon payments might be added at the end of the time period to make up for lesser monthly payments. Or, the buyer might make monthly payments for the first year on the interest only, and then make interest and principal payments for the balance of the term. Payments can be scheduled to coincide with the seasonality of a business or with bonuses contingent on the successful completion of certain contracts. A common Seniorpreneurial form of time payment (which overlaps with the next category of guarantees of payment) is a consulting agreement with the Seniorpreneurial seller that has favorable tax consequences.

Guarantees of Payment. As mentioned above, the consulting agreement is one form of guarantee of payment. Another Seniorpreneurial approach is the payment of royalties. This also serves to "sweeten" the deal in that the Seniorpreneurial seller might be persuaded to take a lower initial price if the continuing royalty, over time, would result in a total higher payout. The Seniorpreneur who is in an acquisition mode has a bonus here in that royalty payments are made from future company earnings over the extended time period. Ofttimes, royalty payments can be structured to be paid only when the company reaches some predetermined sales goals, annually or collectively. They can also be constructed so that they apply only to a certain product and have no effect on later generations of the product line.

As a further type of guarantee, the Seniorpreneur can bring in a cosigner to an acquisition. This cosigner adds a level of comfort to the seller, and the Seniorpreneur can obtain the cosigner's cooperation by issuing a percentage of the acquired company's (or combined companies') stock. The cosigner gets some new, potentially profitable equity without much risk, and the Seniorpreneur gets the deal without scrambling for more cash or tying up valuable equity (which is saved for the next deal).

Stock as Payment. Stock used as payment is frequently referred to as "funny money," since the true value of the stock as a cash item may not be known until some time in the future. However, for the Seniorpreneur, it's a valuable "deal-doing tool." The buyer preserves hard cash or future cash flow by "paying" in stock which then promises, because of the new deal, to be worth even more in the future. The seller gets full payment on the basis of today's valuation, with the upside that the stock will be worth more in the future. Consequently, the seller receives a bonus price for the total transaction. This type of transaction is more prevalent when the buyer is a publicly traded company, but it can also be very attractive to the seller if the company's intention is to go public in the near future.

Options. The objective of an option is to give the buyer an opportunity to put the total deal together. The Seniorpreneur may need extra time to get some money in place, to close a companion deal, to identify additional equity sources, or to pretest the proposed company's product salability in the acquiring organization. Options are a highly versatile tool for Seniorpreneurs who are putting deals together. They can expand both the buyer's and the seller's choices.

Other Considerations

Price and terms are the primary negotiating points in buy, sell, or harvest transactions. However, a lot of other items need to be factored in to be sure that the deal works to everyone's best and lasting advantage.

Tax considerations should be prominent in all dealings. The laws change with such frequency that it's difficult to make any concrete, specific recommendations in a book. Best said, Seniorpreneurs never make strategic buy or harvest transactions without superior, current tax and accounting counsel.

Another primary consideration in all Seniorpreneurial deals is retaining highly capable legal counsel. Seniorpreneurs use attorneys to prevent trouble, as opposed to using them to get out of trouble. Generally, Seniorpreneurs are best served by negotiating their deals before legal counsel enters the scene. The basic price and terms should always be determined prior to engaging legal help. Attorneys prefer that the deal be struck before they are involved, because they realize it saves a lot of money and headaches in trying to continually revise agreements. In many cases, Seniorpreneurs may wish to "brief" their legal counsel before they start intensive negotiations—just to be sure their intended path is the right road. Briefings also help in keeping attorneys apprised as talks progress, so that they are up to speed when they're needed and keep the Seniorpreneur on the right path.

Senior Harvest Choices

Seniorpreneurs have a natural inclination to create real value added in their business. If the company they develop has no value to people other than themselves, the Seniorpreneurial mission hasn't been accomplished. The company has to make some major contributions in several areas:

- Technological advances
- Job creation
- Returns to investors
- Solid future-value creation
- Concrete benefits to society

Building a company that has ongoing value or one that has harvest value results in a proud senior management group.

With a basic understanding of pricing and terms, we can take a more in-depth look at the choices available when the Seniorpreneur seeks to sell out or exit in an ownership capacity. This is the *harvest plan*. As mentioned earlier, the choices include absentee ownership, management buyouts, outright sales, ESOPs, mergers and acquisitions, and going public.

Absentee Ownership

Many Seniorpreneurs wish to create "cash cow" companies. A cash cow is a company whose operating efficiencies, coupled with high profit margins, permit it to generate a high level of excess cash. The Seniorpreneur then uses the excess cash for several purposes, such as to repay original investor dollars, to buy out some investors, to increase cash compensation for the management team, or to develop additional enterprises. In some cases, these new enterprises may be independent of the original company; in others, they may be spinoffs or divisions. These spinoffs can be incubated in the original company until they are capable of standing alone.

Often the standalone point is reached after an alpha test on a product or service concept. The advantage, then, is that the product or service has built an underlying strength that enables the Seniorpreneur to obtain launch capital at more attractive terms than if capital had to be raised to complete the initial development. Initial development financing tends to take considerable equity and dilutes the Seniorpreneur's position. If this dilution can be prevented by accessing internally generated funds, the Seniorpreneur retains more control and gains an opportunity for even greater potential.

This type of situation is ideal when a product or service has cross-industry applications. If the product can be developed through alpha testing, the time is right to seek and negotiate a strategic partnership. The partnership may involve a much larger company that feels more secure in knowing that the technology really works and is proven in a different marketplace. The larger partner can provide beta tests, financial help, and marketing and distribution. The Seniorpreneur has created a very acceptable harvest for the spinoff company. What's more, this type of deal can move on a very fast track, since it simply involves a technology adaptation from the original enterprise (i.e., development time is minimized) and the largest chore is usually marketing. Spinoffs can be harvested in 2 years or less.

The Seniorpreneur who creates an absentee ownership company which has a lot of excess cashflow is positioned to then create multiple spinoff harvests. It's not a bad way to go and definitely leverages both dollars and talent—rather like having your cake and eating it too.

Management Buyouts

The harvest strategy of management buyouts can be looked at from two different perspectives: (1) The Seniorpreneur is the purchaser and is buying out other investor interests, and (2) the Seniorpreneur is bought out by several members of the management team. The financing mechanism used is similar in both cases.

During the 1980s, the common name for management buyouts was leveraged buyouts, or LBOs. In fact, they became one of the darlings of Wall Street as they were rolled into the junk bond dealings. Typically, the top level of management in a division of a larger company arranged to buy out the division with the financing provided by junk bonds.

In simple terms, a buyer group, usually representing some part of management, arranges a loan that is secured by the assets of the company to buy out the principal shareholders. In Seniorpreneurial cases, these shareholders could be the Seniorpreneur, the Seniorpreneurial team, a venture capital firm, or any other investor group that provided the primary financing to the company. Alternatively, the buyer group could be the Seniorpreneur buying out the primary investors. Or it could be the second level of management that buys out the Seniorpreneurial team, or part of the team, with the balance remaining with the ongoing company.

Here's How Financing Works. Regardless of who the buyers are, the financing arrangement is our chief concern. In smaller companies, the typical arrangement is that the buyers provide some amount of equity; the remaining purchase dollars are borrowed from a traditional lending source (commercial bank), which secures the loan by laying claim to all the company's assets. Frequently, the loan is additionally collateralized by the personal signature guarantees of the buyers. The rationale is that the ongoing profits of the company will be sufficient to service both the interest and the debt repayment.

In many LBOs of the 1980s, the equity portion of the buyout became minimal, frequently less than 5 percent of the total purchase price. Today, as was the case prior to junk bonds, 10 to 20 percent is a typical initial equity percentage.

The positive or Seniorpreneurial harvest in management buyouts is that the original investors recapture their initial investment with a large capital gain that is provided by the value added to the company during its development. The advantage to the buyers is that they can gain a substantial equity stake in the company, which in most cases they helped to grow. Eventually, they too will seek to harvest their interest, which (presumably) will further increase in value because of the leverage provided by debt in the buyout.

There Are Also Some Negatives. The negative side to a management buyout is the possibility that the buyout company will experience a major downturn in its markets or some other economic misfortune that prevents it from servicing the highly leveraged debt. The buyers could stand to lose not only the company, but also the equity they provided to accomplish the buyout. Generally, Seniorpreneurial sellers seek to receive full payment at the time of the buyout so they are removed from further risk. On some occasions, they may "carry back" some portion of the debt, usually as subordinated to the primary lender, which means that they too would lose should the replacement team be unable to continue running the company profitably.

Buyouts are an acceptable harvest for Seniorpreneurial endeavors. The Seniorpreneur and investor group get cashed out to pursue a life of leisure or other Seniorpreneurial interests. The buyers get to continue to manage a company they know well with an opportunity to gain their harvest rewards at a later date.

Outright Sales

Many Seniorpreneurs dream about the outright sale, especially if they're two-thirds of the way to their harvest objective and everything seems to be going against them—long hours, big problems, seemingly unobtainable solutions, just plain nightmares. But then early one morning they have the pleasant recurring dream of the big payday. Right there before their very eyes, some very intelligent soul is handing them a cashier's check with a whole lot of zeros on it and bidding them bon voyage as they set sail for a year's cruise around the world. Ah, such a dream.

Dreams do come true in the form of outright sales—but, unfortunately, not usually as depicted above. All cash up front and the Seniorpreneur's walking away seldom happens. However, as we have learned, there are a lot of ways to cut a deal.

Most successful Seniorpreneurial cash-out sales have some strings attached. Typically, they are sales to larger companies that are publicly traded. Consequently, a lot of sales are combinations of cash and publicly traded stock. Besides, no matter what the tax laws are at the time of a sale, it's almost prohibitive from a tax standpoint for a Seniorpreneur or the team to take all cash up front. Stock-for-stock exchanges can be structured so that the immediate tax consequences are lessened and the Seniorpreneur can sell the acquirer's stock at times that are more tax-convenient.

A problem with cash and stock sales is that the Seniorpreneur is subject to the unpredictability of the stock market itself, not to mention the ongoing performance whims of the larger company that did the acquiring.

Additionally, there are many, many sad stories of sales made in heaven that turned into pure hell when the Seniorpreneur agreed to stay on in an active or semiactive role. The Electronic Data Services (EDS) and General Motors (GM) story is world famous for the friction that resulted between EDS founder Ross Perot and GM chairman Roger Smith and the GM board of directors. Perot received financial comeuppance, but not before a lot of blood was spilled. Even then, Perot lost a dream of riding on the coattails of GM to create the world's leading computer services firm, one that would perhaps even outdistance IBM.

Continuing consulting agreements between the buyer and the Seniorpreneurial team need to be carefully constructed. Each executive who agrees to stay on needs to have a clear understanding of his or her new role. Many times, operations under a larger corporate structure vary considerably from the basic freewheeling style of a Seniorpreneurial enterprise. Fat management contracts lose a lot of appeal when the executive has to adjust to the day-to-day reality of big corporate quarterly operating pressures.

Outright sales can be an ideal harvest if they are tailored to fit the goals of all the parties involved. They take a lot of soul searching by the Seniorpreneurs and the team members but offer handsome rewards to all investors.

Employee Stock Option Plans (ESOPs)

Employee stock option plans (ESOPs), also known as employee stock ownership plans, are a way of selling the company. The process enables the employees to purchase equity interests in the form of company stock from the Seniorpreneur or founding investors. This can be a gradual process that enables the Seniorpreneur to gain liquidity. The employees frequently gain a higher level of ownership motivation. ESOPs gained a lot of favorable publicity in the 1980s and are expected to become even more prominent during this decade.

These types of plans are very complex and take a watchful management eye. They can be very burdensome to administer and require continuing legal and accounting input. However, for the Seniorpreneur who wishes to gain a continuing liquidity stream, is willing to give up predetermined continuing amounts of stock control, and feels comfortable with having employees knowledgeable about the company's financial status, ESOPs can have a fruitful harvest.

Mergers and Acquisitions

The names are almost synonymous, but the differences in a harvest situation can be great from a Seniorpreneurial point of view. In a *merger*, the Seniorpreneurial company is absorbed into another, usually larger firm, ofttimes to offset strengths and weaknesses. In an *acquisition*, the larger firm acquires the Seniorpreneurial company outright as a smaller division. The reasoning behind both approaches is that it's quicker and almost always less expensive to acquire an existing company than to start one from scratch. On a practical basis, the two blend into the same animal.

In either a merger or an acquisition, some common nonfinancial problems surface. In many cases, these problems come to the forefront only after the transaction is completed. They are oriented around the companies' culture mix and the integration of people, products, and pricing.

People Decisions Are Emotional. Employees in both the acquiring and acquired companies feel and express their feelings about M&A (merger and acquisition) transactions. Many times these feelings are negative: fears of job loss, uncertainty about small kingdom breakups, and trepidation about unknown management. Upper management and Seniorpreneurs can guide the emotional track for both the acquiring and target companies' employees.

As soon as practical in the transaction process, both sides should focus on reassuring employees and explaining the benefits of the transaction. They should discuss how the combined management and staff will be utilized, what (if any) downsizing will take place, the effects of any labor contracts, and the attempt to justify the educational and cultural differences of management style. They should place a clear emphasis on the opportunities that lie ahead for all parties concerned.

Product Integration Becomes Critical. Product integration decisions are determined by a multitude of factors. Included are R&D strengths, manufacturing methods, selling procedures, distribution channels, product or service pricing structure, product life cycles, and many more. People are involved in each of these functions, and consideration should be given to the interrelationships among these people. Again, will the two cultures mix to gain new levels of accomplishment? Should some employees be removed or transferred prior to the transaction because they will impede the success of the combination? If so, whose responsibility is it to talk with the affected employees and perhaps work out transition or placement costs?

Transaction Pricing Affects People. Pricing of an M&A transaction involves a number of valuations, assessments, structuring of terms, and negotiation. All these issues are tied directly into people and the products or services the combined companies will offer. Can economies of scale be realized that will allow greater R&D expenditures, which in turn may require increases in marketing budgets? Can the same selling and distribution channels be utilized for both companies and for new products? What happens to the management teams, both upper and middle? In short, will the price paid for the deal economically and emotionally factor into a compatible structure for the transaction?

Mergers and acquisitions don't automatically lead to higher growth or better combined entities. It takes careful strategic planning to accomplish the merging of people, products, and pricing. Seniorpreneurs give just as much consideration to these people, product, and pricing factors as they do the valuations and pricing of the deal. They recognize that feelings and emotions are involved, and they're sensitive to the people issues in mergers and acquisitions.

Going Public

When it comes to the subject of going public as a harvest strategy for Seniorpreneurs, I have to admit to a strong bias. I've been involved in taking companies public since 1970, when I was an officer and director of a company that I was instrumental in taking public. Since that time, I have been involved in over 50 public offerings. I have an intimate knowledge of the OTC market as a player, broker, trader, corporate finance officer, and syndicator. Additionally, I've been a public company founder (on more than several occasions), as well as an officer, director, and president (even Chairman of the Board), and I have invested in hundreds of companies, both as a private and a public investor. Finally, I was the author of the book, *Cashing Out: The Entrepreneur's Guide to Going Public*, and the revised edition *The Entrepreneur's Guide to Going Public* (Upstart Publishing, 1994).

With over two decades of hands-on experience, I feel I have gained a thorough knowledge of the business cycles, government actions and reactions, and an understanding of the internal politics and how all the various players that are central to the process interrelate when going public. Considering these biases, I state: *I feel the going-public process is the ultimate harvest reward for the Seniorpreneur.*

What Is Going Public? Basically, going public is the process by which a business owned by one or several individuals is converted into a business owned by many. It involves the offering of part ownership of the company to the general public through the sale of equity or debt securities—commonly considered selling stock. It means that the company's stock can easily be bought or sold through a stock exchange or on the over-the-counter (OTC) market. For Seniorpreneurs and their team members and investors, it means liquidity of their investment, usually at very high multiples over their initial financial outlay. But that's what we've been considering since page one—the harvest.

Although the subject is too complex to cover in this chapter, there are some points that are of particular interest to the harvest-minded Seniorpreneur.

Advantages. There are two fundamental reasons for going public. One is for the sake of the company; the other is to the founder's advantage.

For the Sake of the Company. Capital is the "wealth used in trade." It is the money invested in a company that allows it to

Fund operations

Purchase equipment necessary for production

Increase inventories of both raw and finished goods

Support growing receivables

Expand ongoing operations

Support the company's administration

Further research

Develop the next generation of products or services

Retire prior debt

Increase market share

Contained within each and every one of these capital purposes is often the objective for going public, to support and sustain the growth of the company. The public owners hope their added investment will enhance the company's possibility for successful growth and thereby increase the value of their share of the company. Other intangible company advantages include added prestige among customers, suppliers and business associates; enhanced ability to finance because of improved debt-to-equity ratios; and less dilution as the stock price goes up at higher price-to-earnings multiples.

To the Founder's Advantage. Bottom line, the founder's advantage is dollars. Simply, there are very few methods that result in the leverage of investment dollars to the extreme that being a founder in an initial public offering (IPO) offers. Millionaires and multimillionaires have been created time and time again. The percentage return on a founding investment can be phenomenal. Typically, a publicly traded stock sells at 10 to 15 times its earnings. This is the price-to-earnings (P/E) ratio. In a small initial public offering, the ratio may be as high as 30 to 40 times the company's annual earnings!

Since it's common practice for Seniorpreneurs and their team members to have a significant portion of their personal wealth tied up in the company, the IPO allows them the opportunity to liquefy some of this investment. In many cases, they have made loans, postponed salaries, and consigned for financial obligations. These can be repaid and/or cleared up with an IPO. Finally, having marketable stock gives the founders the financial liquidity advantage of selling stock on a timely tax-advantaged basis.

Disadvantages. The disadvantages of going public can be grouped under three categories:

- Disclosure and accountability
- Control or loss of control
- Expenses

Disclosure and Accountability. From an operational standpoint, the company must disclose a lot of information that it would normally prefer to keep internal. This can include such items as marketing methods, amount of markup, supplier and distributor names, sales by area and specific product line, and more. From a founder personal basis, the company must disclose a lot of information that pertains to the people involved in the company, including the number of shares they own and how much money they make, both salaries and bonuses plus expense or perk reimbursements. From an accounting standpoint, the company must disclose detailed financial information via audited financial statements.

This is a form of confession by the company to the public. Disclosure must include common ownership between the company and any suppliers or sales agents, and any unusual transactions between the company and its employees, especially its officers and directors. All this disclosure continues every quarter for the life of the company—thus continuing accountability. The forms are many and varied, and they must be filed continually with various governmental bodies, thereby making them public information.

Control or Loss of Control. The emphasis is really on loss of control. The company, because of having gone public, now has many more shareholders. Management has to report to these shareholders. It has to be responsive to them in the form of individuals, brokers, and analysts. This takes a lot of time for the CEO and the CFO—time they can't control because it's a job that, like it or not, must be done. Being public causes management to think twice about the timing and effect on the stock price when considering acquisitions, mergers, and both short- and long-term internal planning. Control can also be affected by who owns how many shares of the company. In most cases, the financial founders will still hold voting control; however, there may be cases in which pure majority ownership has been diluted below 50 percent. Good communication between management and the shareholders should obliterate this voting control problem.

Expenses. Few people realize how expensive it is to take a company public or the continuing expense of operating a publicly held company. The costs are very high. It's not the least bit out of line that the initial costs exceed 15 percent of the total dollars raised, and 20 percent-plus is not unusual for small offerings. On an ongoing basis, the costs are considerably higher than those for a private company, primarily because of the SEC reporting requirements and the extra shareholder communications expense.

But It's Worth It. As our society continues its evolution from an industrial/manufacturing foundation to a service/information base, we will find that the decade of the 1990s will produce an increasing number of Seniorpreneurial stars. These enterprising company owners are going to become richer faster and take more people with them than ever before. Why? Because our society has become more global and consequently more complex, we have become more aware of the problems raised by this increasing diversity. The challenges we will be facing are great. Once again, the doors of opportunity will open to those industrious individuals ready to jump in with appropriate and timely solutions. The spark that brings these issues to flame is capital, and going public is the flint upon which these capital reserves are struck. Going public is the ultimate Seniorpreneurial harvest.

So What's a Senior to Do?

The focus in this book has been to make seniors aware of the numerous ways to assist them in living a fulfilled lifestyle through entrepreneuring. Many points to ponder have been presented, along with many ideas that should be a call for action and the checklists to track the action-achieving process. In this last chapter, we have looked at the alternatives for harvesting a senior-led project. Is that what it's all about? Identify an opportunity, marshal the forces, implement the plan, execute the strategy, and then successfully depart the playing field?

That's not for me to say. The decision lies within each of us separately. My intention has been to present you with some of my knowledge of the process, share some of my experience, pass along part of my thoughts. Your challenge, as a street-smart senior, is to determine your personal levels of desire, ability, and capability to become a Golden Entrepreneur. May God bless.

Epilogue

I believe that one of the biggest advantages for present-day Seniorpreneurs is that they have the baby boom generation right on their heels. Some 76 million people are about to join the ranks of 64 million seniors. But that's only part of the good news. These 76 million boomers are becoming seniors with more money in their possession than any previous group ever to pass over the hill at age 50—thanks to their frugal parents.

According to a study by Cornell University economics professors Robert Avery and Michael Rendall, these parents are leaving behind a startling $12.1 trillion to the boomers. These inheritances started in 1990 with over $39.4 billion being left to 900,000 heirs. In 1995 the figure is projected to double to $84.3 billion for 1.5 million heirs. The numbers keep rising to peak in 2015 at $335.9 billion annually to over 3 million heirs.

These boomers grew up amid the breakdown of the American family unit, and lots of them will be collecting from multiple mothers, fathers, in-laws, and assorted third long-term relationships. Couple this with the fact that boomers have accumulated sizable amounts in their own right, and you have a major amount of disposable income available at early ages. It's thought that as the boomers begin receiving their inheritances in their early and mid-fifties, when many of their homes will be nearly paid for and their children's college education finished, they will be saving and investing a majority of their money. It's true, they were known for free-spending in the 1980s, but it's felt that they learned some lessons and will be concerned about their own retirement.

It's also felt that they will be active as opposed to passive investors, at least from the standpoint of watching their money. They have experienced a lot of monetary volatility, ranging from the bull markets to the 1987 stock market crash, from weak real estate to outrageous housing prices and back to some normalcy again. They are sensitive to interest rate fluctuations, having witnessed prime rates from 5 percent to 20 percent and back down again.

They have become skeptical about some investment advice—witness the extreme from tax shelters to the boom in the mutual fund industry. This bodes well for Seniorpreneurs and then for the boomers who are following them. It means that the boomers will provide large markets for Seniorpreneur products and services. But still, they want to invest some funds in higher-risk investments. It also means that present-day seniors can entrepreneur companies that boomers will take over or buy out.

As the turn of this century draws to a close, the global nature of business will increase. We've discussed how the world keeps getting smaller with goods and services moving from country to country. When we look at Eastern Europe, Russia, South America, and China, it is easy to see that these areas will have an enormous appetite for products, services, and technology. It will be the low-cost, efficient, quality producer of goods and services that will be successful. Seniorpreneurs must strive for higher productivity with lean and highly efficient work forces so that they can compete for global markets as well as local dollars in their businesses. We'll see more partnering and strategic alliances as well as outsourcing. Both small and large companies will stick to their core competencies and outsource or contract out ancillary functions and administrative duties. So much the better for Seniorpreneurs. They can choose to become the outsource supplier to larger companies or provide their products and services on a local basis.

What a challenge, what an opportunity! I'm excited about the fact that I'm a senior and will be participating in the Golden Entrepreneuring age. My best Seniorpreneuring wishes to you.

Seniorpreneuring Contact

If you would like more information on the Senior Entrepreneur's Foundation or would like to discuss your Seniorpreneurial venture, you are welcome to contact the author at:

James B. Arkebauer
P.O. Box 24210
Denver, CO 80222

Index

AARP (American Association of Retired Persons), 3, 46–47
Absentee ownserhip, 224, 232, 233
Accountant, 81, 125–129, 146, 178, 189
Accounts receivable, 220
Accounts receivable financing, 164–165
Acquisition, 224, 232, 237–238
Administrative and general management, 106–107
Administrative plan, 205
Advisors, 121–122, 124–126
Aging population service opportunities, 22, 100
American Association of Retired Persons (AARP), 3, 46–47
American Bar Association, 117
American Research and Development (ARD), 181
American Stock Exchange, 228
Angels, 177–180
Apple Computer, 36, 181
ARD (American Research and Development), 181
Ash, Mary Kay, 25
Attorney, 81, 129–133, 146, 178, 189, 232
Audit, 125–129
Aurora Foundation, 39–40
Automotive industry opportunities, 21–22
Avery, Robert, 243

Baby boomers, 10–12, 36, 47, 243–244
Bandag, Inc., 38
Banks, 168–169, 221
Better Business Bureau (BBB), 96
Bloch, Henry, 25
Block Brothers, 25
Blue-sky laws, 197, 199
Board of advisors, 120
Board of directors, 115–120
Boutique investment banking, 179
Business, buying (*see* Buying a business)
Business, starting (*see* New ventures)
Business, sale of (*see* Sale of business)

Business plan, 4, 71, 134–154
 corporate change, 144–145
 corporate structure, 145–147
  C corporation, 146
  guidelines, 146
  limited-liability company, 146–147
  sole proprietorship, 145–146
  Subchapter S corporation, 146, 147
 critical review of, 137–138
 guidelines, 136–137
  closing statement, 137
  competition, 136
  corporate uniqueness, 137
  distribution plan, 136
  financing, 137, 138
  management team, 137
  market-driven emphasis, 136
  readability, 136
 key person life and work disability insurance, 144
 management team, 144
 operating plan transition, 154
 outline, 138–142
  appendix, 143
  corporate history, 139
  cover sheet, 138–139
  executive summary, 139, 153, 179, 188
  finances, 142
  management, 141–142
  market analysis, 140
   competitive profile, 140
   customer profile, 140
   industry profile, 140
   marketing strategy, 140–141
  operations plan, 141, 202–204
  proceeds distribution, 142
  product or service description, 139–140
  research and development, 141
  risks and problems, 142
  schedule, 141
  table of contents, 139
 purpose, 134, 135
  corporate development, 135

Business plan, purpose (*Cont.*):
  financing, 134, 135, 179, 188
  risk reduction, 63
  valuation, 147–153
    enhancement, 63
    investor equity, 150–153
      present value formula, 152–153
    ratio analysis, 147–148
      coverage ratios, 150
      debt ratios, 149–150
      expense ratios, 148
      liquidity ratios, 149
      profitability ratios, 148–149
      utilization ratios, 149
    writing guidelines, 143
Business Rates and Data (Standard Rate & Data Service), 78
Business valuations, 86–92, 147–153
Business Week, 79
Butcher, Florence, 42
Buying a business, 4, 74, 77–95
  advantages of, 77
  due diligence, 83–86, 94
    checklist, 83–85
    marketing checklist, 85–86
  guidelines, 77
  negotiation, 92–95
    art of compromise, 92–93
    buyer qualification, 93
    due diligence, 94
    price or terms discussions, 93–95
  search process, 77–83
    deal flow, 79–83
      accountants, 81
      attorneys, 81
      bankers, 81
      business brokers, 82
      business incubators, 82
      classified advertisements, 80
      cold calls, 82
      government sources, 82
      salespeople, 81
      Small Business Administration, 82
      venture capital, 82–83
    industry information, 78–79
  valuations, 86–92
    assets, 87–88
      actual book value, 87–88
      adjusted book value, 88
      liquidation value, 88
      replacement value, 88
    cash flow projections, 90
    comparable sales value, 90
    discounted cash flow, 91
    earnings, 88–89
      future earnings projections, 89

Buying a business, valuations (*Cont.*):
    excess earnings, 90
    fair market value, 91
    income capitalization, 90–91
    net worth plus, 91
    rules of thumb, 91

C corporation, 146
Carver, Roy, 38
Carver Pump Company, 38
Cash cow company, 233
Cashing Out: The Entrepreneur's Guide to Going Public (Arkebauer), 238
Celente, Gerald, 13
CFO (chief financial officer), 125, 126
Chattel mortgages, 165
Chief financial officer (CFO), 125, 126
Child care opportunities, 21, 100, 216
China, 244
Classified advertisements, 80
Clinton, Bill, 14
Commercial banks, 168–169, 221
Commercial finance companies, 169
Compensating checking-account balances, 164
Competition, 63, 71, 136, 140, 179
Conditional sales contracts, 165
Consultants, 99–100, 121–124
Convertible debentures, 197–198
Corporate Director's Guidebook (American Bar Association), 117
Corporate structure, 145–147
Credit enhancement, 174–175
Cuisinart, Inc., 40

Debt financing, 4, 157–175, 200
  development stages, 161–163
    first, 162
    harvest, 163
    second, 163
    seed (concept), 161–162
    start-up, 162
    third (mezzanine), 163
  versus equity, 160–161
  external funding, 158, 159
  forms, 164–167
    accounts receivable, 164–165
    compensating checking-account balances, 164
    conditional sales contracts, 165
    equipment loans, 165
    equity kickers, 167
    lines of credit, 165–166
      resting the line, 166

Index

Debt financing, forms (*Cont.*):
    plant or property improvement loans, 166
    times-sales (floor planning), 166
    unsecured term loans, 167
  mixed sources, 159–160, 197–198
  self-funding, 158–159
  sources, 168–175
    commercial banks, 168–169
    commercial finance companies, 169
    credit enhancement, 174–175
    factors, 169–170
    government, 173
    grants, 174
    industrial revenue bonds, 172–173
    leasing companies, 170–171
    leveraged buyout, 174
    life insurance companies, 173
    Minority Enterprise Small Business Investment Company, 172, 173
    pension funds, 173
    savings and loans associations, 171
    Small Business Administration, 161, 171–173
    Small Business Innovation Research Grant, 173–174
    Small Business Investment Company, 167–168, 172, 173
    trade credit, 175
  subordinate debt, 167–168
DEC (Digital Equipment Corp.), 181
Demestral, George, 41
Department of Commerce, 79
Department of Education, 16
Digital Equipment Corp. (DEC), 181
Disney world, trends from, 13–14
Downsizing, 10, 11, 58
Due diligence, 83–86, 129, 192–193

Economy, trends in, 17
EDS (Electronic Data Services), 236
Education, trends in, 16
Electronic Data Services (EDS), 236
Employee Retirement Income Security Act (ERISA), 181
Employee stock option plan (ESOP), 224, 232, 236
Employment service opportunities, 22
Engineering and R&D management, 108
Entrepreneur:
  characteristics of, 2–4, 20–21, 24–45
    achievement, 26
    action orientation, 26–27
    commitment, 26, 27
    communication patterns, 26–28

Entrepreneur, characteristics of, communication patterns (*Cont.*):
    feedback, 27
  energy, 26, 28, 36
  experience, 2
  goal achievers, 25, 26, 28
  growth orientation, 26, 28–29
  honesty (ethics), 26, 29
  innovation, 26, 29–30
  intelligence, 26, 30–31
  leadership, 26, 31
    depth perception, 31
    foresight, 31
    global view, 31
    hindsight, 31
    peripheral perception, 31
  passion, 37
  risk tolerance, 26, 32, 35–37
    in-betweeners, 35–36
    nuagers, 35, 36
    olagers, 35
    synthesizers, 35, 36
  self-confidence, 26, 32–33
  senior assets, 42–44
    commitment, 42
    confidence, 42, 43
    freedom, 42, 43
    insider's knowledge, 42, 43
    objectivity, 42, 43
    reputation, 42, 43
    resiliency, 42–44
    resourcefulness, 42, 44
  versus seniorpreneur, 34–35, 104
  success qualities, 33–34
    creativity, 33
    empathy, 34
    enthusiasm, 33
    flexibility, 34
    hard work, 33
    knowledge, 34
  examples, 37–42
  qualifications for, 44–45
Entrepreneur, Inc., 79
Entrepreneur's Guide to Going Public, The (Arkebauer), 196, 238
Entrepreneurship:
  advantages of, 45
  environment for, 3–4, 9–23, 45
    changes, 10–13
      baby boomers, 10–12
      workplace, 10, 11, 18–20, 24, 58
    trends, 13–18
      determining, 13–14
      economy, 17
      education, 16
      family, 15–16

Entrepreneurship, environment for, trends (*Cont.*):
  globalization, 17–18, 71
  health care, 16–17
  natural environment, 17
  political, 14–15
  information contact, 244
  (*See also* Opportunities)
Environment, natural, 17
Environmental service opportunities, 22
Equipment loans, 165
Equity financing, 4, 158, 176–200
  business plan, 179, 188
  versus debt, 160–161
  external funding, 158, 159
  informal investors (angels), 177–180
    characteristics of, 177–178
    identifying, 178–179
      boutique banking, 179
      networking, 178–179
    initial meeting, 179–180
    investment vehicles, 194–199
      exemptions, 198, 199
      Regulation A, 198–199
      Regulation D, 195–198
        Rule 501, 196
        Rule 502, 196
        Rule 503, 196
        Rule 504, 196–198
        Rule 505, 196
        Rule 506, 196
      securities, 195
      Small Corporate Offering Registration, 198, 199
  mixed sources, 159–160, 197–198
  seed stage, 176–177
  self-funding, 158–159
  venture capital, 82–83, 178–194
    close of deal, 193–194
    commitment letter, 191–192
      collateral and security, 192
      commitment conditions (term sheet/investment memorandum), 192
      investment conditions, 192
      representations, 192
      terms, 192
    corporate, 181–182, 184–187
      drawbacks, 185–186
      investment motivation, 184–185
      management fluctuations, 186–187
    due diligence, 192–193
    fund formation, 183
    history of, 181
    identifying, 187
    initial contact, 188

Equity financing, venture capital (*Cont.*):
    initial meeting, 188–190
      financial projections, 189–190
      outcome, 191
      legal counsel, 189
    initial negotiations, 191
    investment amounts, 182
    ongoing relationship with, 194
    qualifying, 187, 190
    traditional, 181–184
      balanced fund, 182
      for evolutionary products, 183, 184
      fund criteria, 182–183
      fund summary, 194
      megafunds, 182
      for revolutionary products, 183
      for substitute products, 183, 184
ERISA (Employee Retirement Income Security Act), 181
ESOP (employee stock option plan), 224, 232, 236
Europe, 213, 244
Experience Inc. (Fucini and Fucini), 42
Exxon, 185

Factors, 169–170, 221
Fairchild Semiconductors, 181
Family, trends in, 15–16
FCPA (Foreign Corrupt Practices Act), 118, 119
Federal Securities Act of 1933, 195, 196, 198
Finance companies, 169
Financial issues:
  business plan, 134, 135, 137, 138, 142
  investor equity valuation, 150–153
  management, 107
  operations, 219–222
  start-up funds, 157–158
  (*See also* Debt financing; Equity financing)
Fitness and health service opportunities, 22, 100
Fitzgerald, Jon, 109–110
Floor planning, 166, 220
Food industry opportunities, 22, 216
Forbes, 79
Foreign Corrupt Practices Act (FCPA), 118, 119
Fortune, 79
Fortune 500 companies, 57
Franchise, 4, 74, 96–100
  Better Business Bureau actions, 96
  characteristics, 98–100
  consultant, 99–100

Franchise (*Cont.*):
    federal trademark registration, 96–97
    guidelines, 97–98
    service concepts, 100
    state registration, 96
    uniform franchise offering circular, 96, 97
    watch points, 96
Fucini, Joseph and Suzy, 42
Funny money, 231

GAAP (generally accepted accounting principles), 128
General Motors (GM), 236
General Signal, 181
Generation X, 36, 50–51
Global Paradox (Naisbitt), 58
Globalization, 17–18, 71, 244
GM (General Motors), 236
Going public, 224, 232, 238–241
Goldblatt, Louis, 42
Gore, Al, 14
Gore, William, 40–41
Gore, William L., & Associates, 40
Gore-tex, 40–41
Guaranteed sales, 76

Hanson, John, 41
Health care, trends in, 16–17
Health Industry Consultants Inc., 109
Hersey, William, 41
High-tech industries, 63–65
Hiring practices, 109–115, 211–212
Holiday Inn, 38
Home Shopping Network (HSN), Inc., 39
Hong Kong, 213
HSN (Home Shopping Network), Inc., 39

IBM, 63, 185
Illiteracy, 16
Industrial revenue bonds, 172–173
Information, importance of, 59
Information highway, 59–61
Inheritance, 243
Initial public offering (IPO), 239–240
Inside management team (*see* Management team, inside)
Insurance, 144
Intel, 181
Internal Revenue Code, 146
Internal Revenue Service (IRS), 147
International Venture Capital Institute, 82–83, 179
Interview techniques, 111–115

Intraprenuers, 71
Inventory, 219–220, 222
IPO (initial public offering), 239–240
IRS (Internal Revenue Service), 147
Isbell, Marion, 38
Itek, 181

Japan, 213
Junior seniors, 19, 46
Junk bonds, 234

Kellogg's, 39
Kentucky Fried Chicken, 42
Kerr, Coralee, 42
Key person life and work disability insurance, 144
Korn/Ferry International, 117–118
Kroc, Ray, 27

LBO (leveraged buyout), 174, 234
Leasing companies, 170–171
Legal management, 108–109
Leveraged buyout (LBO), 174, 234
Life insurance companies, 173
Limited-liability company (LLC), 146–147
Lines of credit, 165–166
LLC (limited-liability company), 146–147

McDonald's, 27
McGraw-Hill Guide to Writing a High-Impact Business Plan, The (Arkebauer), 138
McJob (entry-level jobs), 50
Magazine, 79
Maid to Order, 42
Management (*see* Operations)
Management buyout, 224, 232–235
Management team, inside, 4, 103–120
    age requirements, 104
    board of directors, 115–120
        board of advisors, 120
        committees, 119–120
            audit, 119
            compensation, 120
            conflict-of-interest, 120
            executive, 120
            nominating, 120
        corporate information, 116–117
        functions, 116–119
            company performance, 117
            company strategy, 117
            corporate management, 117

Management team, inside, board of directors, functions (*Cont.*):
    litigation, 118
    meetings, 117–118
    member compensation, 118
    member qualifications, 117
    number of members, 119
    qualifications, 115–117
  business plan, 137, 141–142, 144
  functions, 109
  hiring practices, 109–115
    interview techniques, 111–115
      candidate introduction, 112
      guidelines, 112–114
      interviewer's attitude, 112
      job information, 112
      outcome, 113
      questions, 113
    search process, 109–111
      company review, 110
      interview cycle, 111
      job offer, 111
      planning, 110
      recruitment and evaluation, 110–111
      research, 110
      results documentation, 111
      search termination, 111
  managers, 105–106
  requirements, 106–109
    administrative and general management, 108–109
      communication, 106
      decision-making, 106
      negotiating, 106
      planning, 106
      problem solving, 107
      projects and tasks, 107
    engineering and R&D management, 108
    financial management, 107
      capital raising, 107
      money controls, 107
      ratios applications, 107
    legal management, 108–109
      contracts, 108
      corporate, 109
    marketing management, 107–108
      evaluation and research, 107
      planning, 107
      product distribution, 108
      production continuation, 108
      support, 108
    operations management, 107
      inventory and quality control, 107
      manufacturing and purchasing, 107
    personnel management, 108

Management team, inside, requirements, personnel management (*Cont.*):
      conflict, 108
      criticism, 108
      culture, 108
      development, 108
      help, 108
      listening, 108
    staff, 104–105
Management team, outside, 4, 121–133
  accountant, 125–129
    audit, 125–129
      business familiarity, 127
      inventory, 128–129
    bookkeeper/controller, 125, 126
    certified public accountant (CPA), 125–127
    chief financial officer, 125, 126
    compilations by, 125, 126
    ethics, 129
    GAAP, 128
    reviews by, 125, 126
  advisors, 121–122, 124–126
  attorney, 129–133
    corporate information, 130
    fees, 131–132
      billing review, 132
      stock options, 131–132
    hiring guidelines, 130–131
    large versus small firm, 129–130
    multiple counsel, 132–133
  consultants, 121–124
    fees, 124
    functions of, 122
    hiring practices, 123
    identifying, 122–124
    necessity for, 123–124
Marketing, 61–65
  business plan, 140–141
  due diligence checklist, 85–86
  management, 107–108, 215–217
Mary Kay Cosmetics, 25
Massey, Morris, 35–36
Media world, trends from, 13
Medical management and billing service opportunities, 22, 100
Memorex, 181
Merger, 224, 232, 237–238
MESBIC (Minority Enterprise Small Business Investment Company), 172, 173
Microsoft, 36
Milton, Tom, 13
Minority Enterprise Small Business Investment Company (MESBIC), 172, 173

Index **251**

Minute Maid, 181

Naisbitt, John, 58
NASDAQ (National Association of Securities Dealers Automated Quotations), 228
National Alliance of Businesses, 16
National Association of Securities Dealers Automated Quotations (NASDAQ), 228
Natural environment, 17
New Venture Strategies (Vesper), 69*n*., 225
New ventures, 4, 74–76
  diversity, 76
  guaranteed sales, 76
  guidelines, 76
  long-term opportunities, 75
  pioneering, 75
  product/service gap, 76
New York Stock Exchange, 228

Office of Management and Budget, 174
Operations, 5, 203–223
  business plan, 141, 202–204
  management issues, 107, 209–222
    accounts receivable, 220
    business failures, 214–215
    cashflow, 219
      financing sources, 221
      guidelines, 220–222
      skipped-payment loan, 221
    creative experience, 213
    customer monitoring, 214
    delegation, 211, 218–219
    economic realities, 212–213
    flexibility, 213–214
    inside pressures, 217–219
      communication culture, 218
      monitoring culture, 218
      participation culture, 218
      responding culture, 218–219
    inventory, 219–220, 222
    leadership, 211–212
    management by crisis, 210
    management by extrapolation, 210
    management by hope, 210
    management by objective, 209
    management by subjectives, 210
    marketing variables, 215–216
    outside pressures, 217
    paralysis by analysis, 210
    profits, 210–211
  operating plan, 154, 205–209
    versus administrative plan, 205

Operations, operating plan (*Cont.*):
    advantages of, 206
    criteria for, 207
    failure of, 208–209
      lack of benchmarks and reviews, 208–209
      lack of commitment, 208
      lack of contingency plan, 208
      non-flexibility, 209
      vague goals, 208
    information for, 206–207
    resistance to, 207–208
    during slow- or no-growth periods, 222
Opportunities, 4, 21–23, 56–73
  aging population services, 22, 100
  automotive industry, 21–22
  child care, 21, 100, 216
  decision-making checklist, 68–71
  enployment service, 22
  environmental services, 22
  fitness and health services, 22, 100
  food industry, 22, 216
  future, 71–72
  high-tech industries, 63–65
  marketing, 61–63
    guidelines, 62, 64–65
    competition, 63, 71
    marketing myopia, 63
    product development, 62
  medical management and billing services, 22, 100
  newspapers, 60
  partnerships, 65–68
    acquisitions, 66–68
    arbitration clause, 68
    strategic alliances, 66, 67
    qualifying, 68
  personal services, 22, 100, 216
  retraining, 23
  small businesses, 57–59
  technology, 59–61, 65, 72
  television, 60
  Yellow Pages, 57
  (*See also* Buying a business; Franchise; New ventures)
OTC (over-the-counter) market, 238, 239
Outside management team (*see* Management team, outside)
Over-the-counter (OTC) market, 238, 239

Parade, 47
Part-Time Parents, 42
Partnerships, 65–68
Paxson, Lowell, 39
Pension funds, 173

Perot, Ross, 236
Personal service opportunities, 22, 100, 216
Personnel management, 108
Phipps family, 181
Planning:
  administrative, 205
  (*See also* Business plan; Operations)
Plant improvement loans, 166
Political world, trends from, 13–15
Pratt's Guide to Venture Capital Sources, 187
Property improvement loans, 166
Public offering, 224, 232, 238–241

Quayle, Dan, 14

R&D (research and development), 108, 141
Ramada Inns, 38
Real world, trends from, 13, 14
Regulation A, 198–199
Regulation D, 195–198
Reis, Judy, 42
Rendall, Michael, 243
Research and development (R&D), 108, 141
Retraining opportunities, 23
Risks, 26, 32, 35–37, 142
Rittenhouse, Mary, 42
Rock, Alex, 181
Rockefeller family, 181
Rockies Venture Club, The, 83, 179
Rossi, Anthony, 39–40
Russia, 61, 244

Sale of business, 5, 224–242
  absentee ownership, 224, 232, 233
  employee stock option plan, 224, 232, 236
  harvest plan, 232
  management buyout, 224, 232–235
    disadvantages, 234–235
    financial arrangement, 234
  mergers and acquisitions, 224, 232, 237–238
    personnel issues, 237
    product integration, 237
    transition pricing, 238
  outright sale, 224, 232, 235–236
  pricing, 224–229
    asset methods, 225, 227
      fair market value, 225, 227
      liquidation value, 225, 227
      replacement value, 225, 227
    cashflow methods, 226, 228
      adjusted cashflow, 226, 228
      discounted cashflow, 226, 228

Sale of business, pricing, cashflow methods (*Cont.*):
      payment-servicing capacity, 226, 228
      heuristic methods, 226, 229
      intuitive value, 226, 229
      seller's preconception, 226, 229
    income methods, 225, 227–228
      future earnings with new owner, 225, 227, 228
      future earnings with present owner, 225, 227, 228
      historic earnings, 225, 227, 228
      price/earnings (PE) ratio, 228
    market methods, 226, 228–229
      comparable company prices, 226, 229
      current competitive bids, 226, 229
      last trading price, 226, 228–229
      special formulas, 226, 229
    net worth methods, 225–227
      adjusted book value, 225, 227
      book value, 225–227
    valuations, 86–92
  public offering, 224, 232, 238–241
    advantages, 239–241
    disadvantages, 240–241
      control issues, 240–241
      disclosure and accountability, 240
      expenses, 241
    process, 238–239
  terms, 224–225, 229–231
    cash downpayment, 229, 230
    guarantees of payment, 229–231
    installment payments, 229, 230
    legal counsel, 232
    options, 229, 231
    stock as payment, 229, 231
    taxation issues, 232
Sanders, Colonel Harlan, 42
Santmyer, Helen, 41
Savings and loans (S&L) associations, 171
SBA (Small Business Administration), 82, 124, 161, 171–172, 221
SBIC (Small Business Investment Company), 167–168, 172, 173, 181
SBIR (Small Business Innovation Research Grant), 173–174
Scientific Data Systems, 181
SCOR (Small Corporate Offering Registration), 198, 199
SCORE, 82
SEC (Securities and Exchange Commission), 118–119, 127, 130, 195, 196, 198, 199, 241
Section 1244 stock plan, 146
Securities, 146, 195

Index

Securities and Exchange Commission (SEC), 118–119, 127, 130, 195, 196, 198, 199, 241
Senior Entrepreneur's Foundation (SEF), 1, 110, 244
Seniors, 19, 46
　perceptions of, 4, 46–55
　　advantages of age, 52–55
　　　business contacts, 54
　　　customer service, 54
　　　delayed gratification, 53
　　　money management, 53–54
　　　patience and persistence, 53
　　　prudence, 52–53
　　　success wisdom, 54
　　　work ethic, 55
　　changes in, 47–48
　　myths, 48–52
　　　generation gap, 50–51
　　　inflexibility, 48–49
　　　opinionated, 49–50
　　　technology adaptation, 51–52
Skipped-payment loan, 221
Small Business Administration (SBA), 82, 124, 161, 171–173, 221
Small Business Innovation Research Grant (SBIR), 173–174
Small Business Investment Act, 181
Small Business Investment Company (SBIC), 167–168, 172, 173, 181
Small Corporate Offering Registration (SCOR), 198, 199
Smith, Roger, 236
Sole proprietorship, 145–146
Sontheimer, Carl, 40
South America, 61, 244
Speer, Roy, 39
Standard Rate & Data Service, 78
Starting a business (*see* New ventures)
Stock, 146, 195, 229, 231
　public offering, 224, 232, 238–241
　sale of business, 224, 232, 235, 236
Subchapter S corporation, 146, 147
Subordinate debt, 167–168
Success, 79
Succession (*see* Sale of business)

Teams (*see* Management team, inside; Management team, outside)
Teledyne, 181
Telemarketing, 179
Times-sales finance, 166
Trade credit, 175
Trend Tracking (Celente and Milton), 13
Tropicana Juice, 39–40

UCC (Uniform Commercial Code), 165
UFOC (uniform franchise offering circular), 96, 97
ULOR (Uniform Limited Offering Registration), 199
Ultrapreneuring: Taking a Venture from Start-up to Harvest in Three Years or Less (Arkebauer), 25
Uniform Commercial Code (UCC), 165
Uniform franchise offering circular (UFOC), 96, 97
Uniform Limited Offering Registration (ULOR), 199
Unsecured term loans, 167
U.S. Industrial Outlook (Department of Commerce), 79

Valuations, 86–92, 147–153
Velcro, 41
Venture, 118
Venture capital, 82–83, 178–194, 221
Vesper, Karl H., 69*n*., 225

Wall Street Journal, The, 79, 80
Walsh, Julia Montgomery, 41
Walsh, Julia, and Sons, 41
"What You Are Is Who You Were When" (Massey), 35–36
Whitney family, 181
Wilson, Charles Kemmons, 38
Winnebago Industries, 41

About the Author

James B. Arkebauer (Denver, Colorado) is the founder of Venture Associates Ltd., an investment banking and consulting firm. He has been an entrepreneur for more than 25 years and his experience in corporate finance includes all phases of this discipline. He has been involved in risk analysis and evaluation of many new technologies, assembled management teams, and structured and implemented equity and debt financing for both private and public companies. He is co-founder and Chairman of the Board of Directors of the Rockies Venture Club, and he has been involved with the Senior Entrepreneur's Foundation since its inception; these are two of the country's leading support groups for entrepreneurs. Mr. Arkebauer lectures frequently to professional and civic groups of all ages and is often quoted in the national business press. He is also the author of six other books, including *Ultrapreneuring: Taking a Venture from Start-up to Harvest in Three Years or Less, The McGraw-Hill Guide to Writing a High-Impact Business Plan* (both published by McGraw-Hill), and *The Entrepreneur's Guide to Going Public*.